Aging
and Old Age

Aging and Old Age

Sheila C. McKenzie

Western Kentucky University

Scott, Foresman and Company
Glenview, Illinois

Dallas, Tex. Oakland, N.J. Palo Alto, Cal. Tucker, Ga. London, England

The author and publisher of this book would like to thank all sources for use of their material. Credit lines for copyrighted materials are included in the Acknowledgments, p. 289—which is an extension of this copyright page.

Library of Congress Cataloging in Publication Data

McKenzie, Sheila C   1943–
    Aging and old age.

    Bibliography: p. 278
    Includes index.
    1. Aging. 2. Old age. I. Title.
QP86.M26   155.67   79-24598
ISBN 0-673-15250-2

Preface

Aging and Old Age is an introductory gerontology text providing students with a basic understanding of the last stage of the human life span. Since gerontology is a multidisciplinary study, contributions from various fields are included in this text but the primary focus of the book is psychological. The scientific study of behavior as it relates to aging and old age is given special consideration and emphasis. Consistent attention is also given to normative behaviors and individual differences and similarities in performance, response, and activity.

The text is organized into twelve chapters. Chapters 1 and 2 are general in approach: they discuss the myths about growing old in our society and present an overview about the processes involved in aging. The remaining chapters deal with major topics of psychological concern. Chapters 3 and 4 deal with the relationship between aging and cognitive factors, including intelligence, learning, and memory. Chapter 5 focuses on the sensory changes that accompany aging. Chapters 6 through 8 deal with the relationship between aging and personality, including the impact of stress and psychological disorders. Chapters 9 and 10 deal with the social aspects of aging, including sexual behavior and social relationships. Chapter 11 focuses on death and dying. Chapter 12, the final chapter, takes a pragmatic approach to the achievement of physical and psychological well-being in later life.

Aging and Old Age is directed at students who have some background in the subject as well as those who have relatively little. To meet the needs of both levels of sophistication, a number of strategies are employed throughout the text:

- First, basic background concepts necessary for understanding gerontology are carefully outlined. For example, when the subject of aging and intelligence is presented in Chapter 3, the concept of intelligence is delineated, a distinction is made between intelligence and performance, and variables affecting intellectual performance are discussed.

- Second, when theoretical information and abstract concepts are discussed, practical suggestions designed to promote application are frequently presented.

- Third, when specialized terms are used, they are carefully defined in context.

- Fourth, when concepts and theories are presented, they are supported with examples, illustrations, and anecdotes.

As a further help to the student, each chapter of *Aging and Old Age* follows the same organization and includes useful pedagogical features. A Preview at the beginning of each chapter alerts the student to the important issues and concepts that will be covered. A Summary at the end of each chapter provides a concise review of the major concepts discussed. Also at the end of the chapter are a Progress Check and Recommended Readings. In the Progress Check, students are given an opportunity to check their mastery of the material by responding to questions on important points. The Progress Check is accompanied by page notations indicating where answers can be found in the chapter. Thus, students can identify areas of strength and weakness, review the material, and reinforce their learning. The Recommended Readings provide a description of several current recommended books and articles that students can use to find more specific information on a topic.

Aging and Old Age also includes a glossary defining key terms, which is cross-referenced to pages where the terms are presented in the text, a list of references, and an index.

Throughout this book, students are encouraged to maintain a critical attitude toward age-related theories, inferences, and conclusions; to be informed consumers of gerontological research; and to view research findings with a skeptical eye. Students are reminded of the paucity of definitive conclusions or set answers in the study of aging and old age. In the face of contradictory evidence and conflicting opinions, students are encouraged to weigh the merits of available data and draw their own conclusions.

I would like to acknowledge the contributions of certain people who have been associated with the development of this book. My thanks go to Sharon Barton and Anita Portugal, who edited this book and provided expertise, guidance, and support. I would like to thank Annie McKenzie for her proofreading services and Phil McKenzie for his clerical help. Cremilda Pereira, who typed the manuscript, has my gratitude. Finally, thanks are extended to researchers and authors who have permitted their work to be used and quoted in *Aging and Old Age*.

Sheila C. McKenzie

Contents

7 Aging and Stress   141

8 Aging and Psychopathology   163

12 Well-Being in Old Age   251

1

Old Age and Ageism

Preview ∾ *In this chapter we will introduce the discipline of gerontology, differentiate between aging and development, and provide an objective definition of old age. We will also examine certain demographic characteristics of the population aged 65 and over. Various myths and stereotypes that are imposed upon the elderly by society will be presented, and readers will be encouraged to distinguish between stereotypic attitudes and valid information concerning old age. Finally, we will introduce the concept of ageism, suggest factors that may operate to create ageism, and suggest factors that may operate to eventually eliminate it from our society.*

Our subject is the systematic study of old age and the aging process—the science of gerontology. Our first goal is to clarify what we mean by gerontology.

What Is Gerontology?

Gerontology is a very broad investigatory discipline whose goal it is to find answers to questions such as: "What's it like to be old?" "What causes aging?" and "What happens to people as they grow older?" Derived from the root words *geronto* (old man or old age) and *logy* (the science or study of), **gerontology** can be simply defined as the systematic study of aging and old age.

A multidisciplinary study

Because growing old and old age are multifaceted phenomena that involve changes that are psychological, social, and biological, gerontology is a multi-disciplinary study. In an attempt to better understand what occurs as people age and what factors are significant variables in old age, it is essential that research be generated from a number of fields.

Investigators primarily concerned with the psychological aspects of old age may provide information relating to intellectual changes, patterns of adjustment, attitudes, emotions, motivation, and learning. Those interested in social issues may concentrate upon subjects such as family relationships, retirement, political and religious activities, and social norms and expectations. Finally, investigators drawn from biological fields may focus attention upon physiological and anatomical changes that accompany the aging process. In some instances, it is necessary for researchers to cross academic boundaries and concurrently probe the psychological, social, and biological aspects of a particular concern related to the study of old age.

In this book our orientation will be primarily psychological. But without input on social and biological issues, it would be impossible for us to acquire an adequate basic understanding of aging and old age. Our psychological self does not function in isolation from our social environment or physical body. As the social environment changes, certain psychological changes are likely to occur. For example, when people retire (social change), they may become depressed, anxious, or highly contented (psychological change). Likewise, physiological and anatomical changes that occur within each person as a function of aging are likely to be accompanied by mental or emotional modifications. If a person's ability to hear or see declines (physiological and anatomical change), a tendency toward withdrawal or apathy (psychological change) could develop. There is a constant interplay and interdependence among psychological, social, and biological factors in the lives of all human beings. Those of us concerned with the study of aging and old age cannot disregard the potential significance of each. Without information from multi-disciplinary sources, it would be impossible to attempt to answer such questions as, "What's it like to be old?" "What causes aging?" and "What happens to people as they grow older?"

A formal definition

The definition of gerontology formulated at the Gerontology Center of the Institute for the Study of Human Development at Penn State is broad enough to be generally applicable and precise enough to provide a definite reference for students of aging and old age.

> *Gerontology is the study of aging*, which may be seen as a lifelong process involving the complex interrelationships of the individual with his or her environment. It is also research, training, and service which have a direct relationship to and impact upon the life-styles of adults in our society. Gerontology as a field of study encompasses many disciplines in the social and biological sciences, which view aging as a process of change with time, and also with the aged persons within a societal setting.

We're All Growing Old; We're All Developing

Every human being constantly shares with all other human beings a common experience. Regardless of race, age, sex, or economic condition, we are each growing older with the passage of every second. (You're older now than when you began to read the previous statement and will be older at the end of this paragraph.) Some of us fear the reality of growing older and may deny it. Others may resist the aging process and attempt to cling to characteristics considered youthful. Still others may philosophically accept the inevitability of increased age with its accompanying changes. However, regardless of how we feel about it, the fact remains that time continues to pass and we each continue to age. Because we are each growing older and because nothing, at this time, can be done to alter this situation, it must follow that considerations of the aging process must, to some extent, focus upon the effects of time passage upon all human beings regardless of specific chronological age. Whether six or sixty, we are constantly aging. This process is initiated at the moment of conception and continues until death. It is a gradual, generally imperceptible process: We do not simply "age" suddenly nor do we become "old" overnight. For this reason, we frequently fail to notice age changes in those adults with whom we interact on a regular basis. Likewise, it is not unusual to be astonished to see how "old" a friend has grown in a five-year interim between visits.

The difference between aging and developing

It is important to point out that aging is not the same thing as developing. There is a basic distinction between the process of development and the process of **aging** or growing older. All things age, grow older, or accumulate physical time units as a function of their presence within a world that operates upon a temporal basis. A stone ages, as does a desk, a cup, and an automobile. However, unlike such inanimate objects, living organisms are unique in that they develop, grow, and change as they become older. Whereas development is a characteristic of living organisms, it is not a characteristic of inanimate objects. **Development** is an orderly sequence of changes in behavior and/or physical attributes. As living organisms develop, they progress through certain developmental stages. Such developmental stages represent changes in the living organism that result from subtle inter-actions between genetic or hereditary factors and experiential or environ-mental influences—nature and nurture.

Developmental stages

A number of labels have been used to denote the sequential developmen-tal stages through which human beings pass during the course of the life span. Likewise, some variations in specific age designations within these de-velopmental stages are common. However, the generally accepted labels and accompanying age designations commonly used to segregate various peri-ods of development are something like this: prenatal (conception to birth); infancy (birth to 18 months); early childhood (18 months to five years); mid-dle childhood (five years to 13 years); adolescence (13 years to 21 years); adulthood (21 years to 65 years); and old age (65 years to death).

These developmental stages represent a gross frame of reference from which human growth may be viewed and conceptualized. It is apparent that the diversities, subtleties, and innumerable nuances inherent in each human being cannot be conveyed by such an unrefined system of classification. Human beings are immensely complex organisms and differ enormously from each other in a multitude of ways. We recognize intuitively that all individuals do not become "adults" at age 21—the arbitrary nature of such a classification was demonstrated when the government made 18-year-old "children" 18-year-old "adults" with the stroke of a pen. By the same token, we recognize that adolescence is reached by many people before their thir-teenth year and that people do not become "old" when they blow out 65 candles on the birthday cake.

However, a system of classifying developmental stages does have its prac-tical uses. It permits us to view individuals as passing through certain age-related periods in which certain behaviors *tend* to be emitted, certain chal-lenges *tend* to be confronted, and certain demands and expectations *tend* to be imposed. It allows us to think in terms of behaviors more frequently manifested by human beings during various life periods and to concentrate upon common features and generally shared human experiences that are encountered as a function of growth and development. Finally, the classifica-tion and investigation of human beings in terms of developmental stages permits the making of some fairly accurate predictions regarding the *average* psychological, social and physical characteristics of large numbers of individ-uals as they approach, occupy, and leave different growth or chronological periods. However, it is important to remember that such predictions are based upon statistical probabilities (educated guesses) and, therefore, are subject to error. To adopt the attitude that human beings *must* do certain things or behave in some particular manner because they have reached a specific age or stage would be a serious mistake. For a number of reasons yet to be discussed, adoption of such a rigid attitude would constitute an extremely serious mistake when consideration is given to those individuals who are found within the developmental category labeled "old age."

When Will I Be Old?

"What is meant by old age?" "When is a person old?" Such questions are impossible to answer to the satisfaction of all or to answer using behaviorally based or observational information.

Chronological age

Most of us have known individuals who have behaved as though they were "old" at a relatively low chronological age. Likewise, it is not unusual for a person who is 70 or 80 years old to behave in a vibrant, youthful manner. We recognize that old age is a subjective concept or that relative age "is in the eye of the beholder."

If you are 20 years old, the probability is relatively high that you are "old" in someone's eyes. You may seem ancient to your small brother or sister, to a neighbor's child, or to your own son or daughter. To label an individual "old," either on the basis of relative age differences or absolute number of years accumulated since birth, has often proven to be subjectively unsatisfactory.

Physical appearance

As an acceptable and satisfactory indicator of old age, physical appearance likewise has fallen short of the mark. Many physical characteristics popularly associated with old age are exhibited by individuals who are relatively young chronologically. It is not unusual to meet a person in his thirties who is bald, wrinkled, and has experienced some loss of sensory acuity, such as wearing glasses. Gray hairs may begin to develop when people are in their twenties. Although such physical characteristics traditionally have been perceived as a correlate of old age, they may result from many causes unrelated to chronological age. Poor nutrition, too much exposure to the rays of the sun, smoking, consumption of alcohol and other drugs, disease, and, probably most importantly, heredity are all factors that may, at any age, result in physical changes associated with advanced age. Correspondingly, proper exercise, nutrition, cosmetics, and certain surgical techniques may function to retard age-related physical changes. It may prove very difficult to accurately ascertain people's ages solely on the basis of how they "look." Old age cannot be determined on the basis of physical appearance.

Establishing a common reference point

"What is meant by old age?" "When is a person old?" Returning to these questions, you may have decided that adequate or totally satisfactory answers to them do not exist. To some extent, you are quite correct in this assumption. Moreover, you have probably gained some insight into the dilemma faced by investigators (developmentalists) who attempt to segregate the continuum represented by each human being's life span into separate or discrete stages. "When is a person old?" The answer to this question depends upon whom you ask, how you personally perceive old age, specific factors under consideration, standards of comparison being used, and a variety of other variables.

If we accept the fact that "old age" means different things to different people and that no single factor may be employed in isolation to satisfactorily define "old age," we still need to establish a common reference point for purposes of research and discussion. D. B. Bromley (1966), a significant contributor to the study of aging and old age, has designated 70 years as the beginning of old age. To Carl Jung, an eminent theorist in the realm of personality, old age begins at 65. Robert Havighurst (1972), a prominent developmentalist, labels the final stage in an individual's life span "later maturity" and states that it begins at age 60. Although various researchers have employed different chronological labels to designate old age, most are found within the 60- to 70-year-range. As the human life span increases and mandatory retirement becomes a thing of the past, it may be predicted that such chronological labels will change and reflect increased age. However, at this time, the most commonly used age classification to indicate old age is 65 years. Although it is somewhat arbitrary, for practical purposes of common reference and discussion, 65 years will be used in this book to denote the beginning of old age. The terms **old age** and **later maturity** will be used interchangeably in reference to that group of human beings who are 65 years and over because both terms are frequently encountered in popular and scientific literature.

What Does the 65 and Over Population Look Like Statistically?

Having defined old age in an objective manner, it may be useful to draw a brief statistical sketch of that group of individuals who are in the age category of 65 and over.

The elderly population within the **demographic** area of the United States is the focus of this statistical portrait. It should be noted that the characteristics of this population of older persons may be quite different from those of elderly members of other cultures. When a particular culture forms the basis for investigation and discussion, care should be taken not to mentally impose the attributes of one culture onto another. We must avoid making unwarranted cross-cultural comparisons or conclusions. What it means to age and to be old is, to a significant extent, determined by the culture in which the individual lives.

Proportion of the population

About one of every 10 United States citizens falls within the "65 and over" category—a total of more than 20 million people. This number is increasing annually, and it is estimated that by the year 2000, the elderly will make up between 16 and 20 percent (nearly 1 in 5) of the total population. During recent decades, a number of factors have contributed to this proportional increase in the aged population. These include a decreased birth rate, decreased infant mortality, and an increased average life expectancy. Looking even further into the future, we may anticipate a significant increase in the older population by the year 2015. The "baby boom" of the postwar decade will become the "aged boom" of the twenty-first century.

Life Expectancy

Our **life expectancy** is the number of years we can expect to live based upon statistical probability. According to the United States Bureau of the Census (1978), the average life expectancy of males and females in this country has constantly expanded from 1900 to 1976. A baby born in 1900 had a life expectancy of 47.3 years (46.3 for males and 48.3 for females). However, a baby born in 1976 is given an average life expectancy of 72.8 years (69.0 for males and 76.7 for females). The total increase in life expectancy for all individuals within the United States during the first three quarters of the twentieth century has been 25.5 years. This increase reflects an average increment of about 3.4 years per decade.

Although the average life expectancy of all human beings within the United States has increased during previous decades, the number of years that a black baby born in 1976 can expect to live is less than the average life expectancy of whites born in the same year. White males can expect to live 69.7 years and white females 77.3 years. However, black males are given a life expectancy of 64.1 years and black females can expect to live 72.6 years. In other words, in terms of current projections, black males may expect to live the least number of years and white females may expect to live the greatest number of years. However, as life-styles of blacks and women change within the United States, there is some question regarding the accuracy with which such predictions can be made.

Proportion of females to males

Although the proportion of the aged population is constantly increasing and the average life expectancy of human beings is continuing to expand, it is apparent that women tend to live longer than men and that the proportion of females to males does not remain constant with advanced age. The average life expectancy of the American female is approximately seven years greater than that of the American male. This difference in life expectancy between the sexes results in a **sex ratio,** the proportion of males to females, of approximately 72 males to 100 females in the 65 and over population. The probability that an older woman will become a widow is relatively high. Many women do, and will continue to, face the prospect of living their final years without the companionship, social support, and aid of a husband. According to demographic data gathered through the U.S. Census Office (1978), 41.1 percent of women in the 65–74 years age group were widows in 1977. A corresponding 9.3 percent of males in this age group were widowed at that time. When consideration is given to members of the 75 years and over population, differences between percentages of widowed males and females become more dramatic. In this advanced age group, 69.7 percent of the females are widowed and 24.3 percent of the males have survived their mates. Although these statistics reflect conditions within the United States, a similar pattern of differential life expectancy according to sex appears to be world-wide. Many psychosocial problems adhere from the reality of differential sex-related life expectancies.

Housing and income

Contrary to popular notion, the majority of elderly people do not live in nursing homes nor in any institutional setting. About 20 percent of the 65 and over group may expect to spend some time in a nursing or convalescent home, but such periods of confinement tend to be relatively short and are temporary. Less than 5 percent of the older population become permanent residents. About 90 percent of our older citizens live within, and continue to independently maintain, their own homes during later maturity.

Economically, the older population fares less well than other age segments within our society. The most recent statistics available from the U.S. Bureau of the Census (1978) indicate that about 14.1 percent of the aged population live on incomes considered below the poverty level established by the federal government. Older women tend to receive less average income than do older men, and the average income of blacks is slightly less than the average income of the entire older population. Economically, black females tend to fare least well in later maturity. Likewise, nonmarried older individuals tend to be economically less well off than those who are married. During the past several years, the extremely high rate of inflation experienced by our nation has posed great problems for older individuals who frequently must exist upon fixed incomes. Pensions are often inadequate, and social security payments have failed to keep pace with the rapid growth of inflation. Many people who thought they would be "rich" when they retired now have trouble making ends meet. Factors such as inflation, fixed incomes, and limited employment opportunities have effectively operated to impose financial hardship and economic stress upon many older adults.

Are You Stereotyping?

Before you read the next section, answer the following statements using *True* or *False*.

1. As people grow older, they become more alike.   T   F
2. If people live long enough, they will become senile.   T   F
3. Old age is generally a time of serenity.   T   F
4. Older people tend to show little interest in sex.   T   F
5. Older people tend to be inflexible.   T   F

6.	Most older people lack creativity and are unproductive.	T	F
7.	Older people have great difficulty learning new skills.	T	F
8.	When people grow old, they generally become "cranky."	T	F
9.	Most older people are lonely and isolated.	T	F
10.	As people become older, they are likely to become more religious.	T	F

There are a number of stereotypes or myths that surround aging and old age. A **stereotype** is a standardized picture or rigid perception of persons or things. The ten statements just presented were chosen because they represent stereotypic beliefs or perceptions concerning old age that are commonly found within our society and are often accepted by a significant segment of the total population (including the aged). If we hope to increase our knowledge of aging and old age, an important initial step toward achieving this goal is to dispel personal preconceptions or incorrect beliefs concerning the aging process and old age. With this end in mind, a brief discussion of these stereotypes may prove helpful.

Myth One: More alike

The idea that individuals become more alike as they grow older is perhaps the most widespread stereotype imposed upon older citizens by our society. Although people are quite willing to acknowledge the uniqueness of each child, this perceived uniqueness or individuality is not often extended to older adults. When faced with assessing the characteristics and qualities of aged adults, many people treat this particular segment of society as though they were a homogeneous group whose individuality has been lost as a function of time. Contrary to popular opinion, as we grow older, a commonality of characteristics does not develop. Just the opposite is true. With increased age comes increased diversity, individuality, and uniqueness. On all social, psychological, and biological measures, there are significantly greater variations among the scores of older groups of individuals than among those who are younger. Increased heterogeneity rather than increased homogeneity appears to occur with advanced age (Maddox and Douglas, 1974). Older people are less alike than their younger counterparts.

In an attempt to explain and better understand this increased age-related diversity among people, we must consider two developmental realities. First, as people grow older, their varied experiences exert a diversifying influence. With the passage of years, each individual learns different things, faces varied situations, and develops a unique pattern of response. In essence, as a person grows older, there is a constant and gradual accentuation of individuality and uniqueness. Diverse experiences create heterogeneity rather than homogeneity. Second, chronological age, or the number of years a person has lived, affects each individual differently. Some people are "old" at 65 and others are "young" at the same age. Also, within each individual various facets of aging are progressing at different rates. People do not just *age:* they age biologically, socially, psychologically, and chronologically. The potential for diversity within each aging process is enormous. The probability that any two individuals will become more alike as they grow older and follow identical patterns of aging is extremely remote. With growth comes change, with experience comes diversity. As people grow older, they become *less* alike.

Myth Two: Senile

Senile behavior is frequently considered synonymous with the behavior exhibited by people in old age. Inherent in this association is the belief that old age, in itself, constitutes some type of disease. Of course, this belief is highly erroneous. **Senility** is not an accepted clinical term or diagnosis. It is a term loosely used to describe certain pathological brain dysfunctions in which the primary manifestations are confusion, disorientation, forgetfulness, inability to concentrate or focus attention for significant periods of time, and possible hallucinations and delusions. Such pathological brain dysfunctions are labeled organic brain syndromes and are divided into two major categories: acute and chronic. Organic brain syndromes result in abnormal impairment of mental faculties that in no way reflect the normal changes in mental abilities sometimes occurring in old age. Organic brain syndromes are not a condition of normal aging. Behavior characterized as "senile" can be caused by a variety of physiological or psychological traumas, including drug misuse, intoxication, hypoglycemia (low blood sugar), congestive heart failure, infections, and metabolic disorders. All age groups are susceptible to such traumas and vulnerability is not restricted to the aged. Only about 2 to 3 percent of persons 65 and over develop symptoms associated with senility and are institutionalized for psychiatric or mental illness (Busse and Pfeiffer, 1977). In many instances the condition is correctable, depending on whether there is early identification and the provision of prompt, proper treatment. However, if senility is perceived as a normal result of advanced age, it is unlikely that prompt and effective treatment will be forthcoming. If we expect an elderly person to behave in a pathological manner and then such "expected" behavior occurs, we may make no effort to bring about change. In the absence of treatment, worsening of the pathological condition and progressive deterioration of the individual might be expected. However, in terms of probability, there is very little reason to expect an older individual to exhibit behavioral patterns characteristic of senility. The statistical probability of a person becoming senile as a result of achieving old age is extremely low.

Myth Three: Serene

With increased public awareness of the problems faced by many elderly people within our society, the myth of the "golden years" and serenity in old age is fast losing ground. Although images of the older generation happily occupied within an idyllic setting are imprinted upon much of the current adult generation, such images are quickly giving way to a more realistic assessment of the realities endured by many members of the older population. Such realities include poverty, fear of crime, lack of transportation, grief, physical disease, bodily decline, dramatic changes in life-style, loss of social power, and decline in status. No other age group faces and endures stresses and traumas comparable to those faced and endured by the elderly. Such stresses are both internal and external, physical and psychological, social and economic. Many stresses faced by the elderly can be alleviated through effective social intervention by family, public agencies, friends, or community helpers. However, regardless of intervention procedures employed, the alleviation of certain stresses encountered by the older adult may prove an extremely difficult, and at times impossible, undertaking. Within the United States the aged make up about 10 percent of the total population, yet 25 percent of all suicides are committed by individuals who are 65 years and over (Resnik and Cantor, 1970, p. 153). By itself, this statistic should effectively eradicate the myth of serenity in old age.

Myth Four: Sexless

Within our society, there is an unfortunate but pervasive belief that sexuality is the exclusive province of youth and that sexual activities, when engaged in by older adults, are inappropriate, if not lascivious, behavior. Such beliefs are often accepted by old and young alike and play an important role in determining how older adults are perceived by others and perceive themselves. To believe that our sexuality is lost with the coming of old age is to accept the philosophy that with advanced age individuals lose a significant portion of their humanity. To become "sexless," is to become less than "human."

The myth of lost sexuality in old age is psychologically harmful. If older individuals believe that sexual activities are abnormal or impossible, they may unnecessarily become resigned to a life devoid of sexual outlets. Moreover, if they do believe the stereotype and, in spite of it, continue to engage in sexual activities, they may suffer feelings of guilt, depression, and self-depreciation. In either situation the aged individual is the loser and psychological stress will be the probable result.

Until relatively recently, very little research has been done on sexual behavior in old age, chiefly because the subject was considered taboo. However, during the 1960s, the team of William Masters and Virginia Johnson (1966) investigated this sensitive subject. Their findings have done much to dispel popular misconceptions regarding the aged and sexuality. Although at this point we will not discuss their research methods and results in detail, their general conclusion warrants mention. Their findings were that sexual activities and sexual responsiveness, including orgasm, do not end with old age. The researchers found that individuals possess the capacity for sexual intercourse and orgasm to, and frequently beyond, the 80-year-age level. These conclusions were affirmed by a longitudinal study conducted by Duke University (Palmore, 1974). Among variables cited by Masters and Johnson as contributors to successful sexual functioning in later maturity were physical

health, a feeling of psychological well-being, the availability of a willing partner, and a history of interest and enjoyment in sexual activities. Likewise, a
number of factors that contributed to unsuccessful sexual functioning in old
age were identified. Among these were monotony or boredom with the same
partner, mental or physical fatigue, fear of failure, and overindulgence in
drink or food. As we examine the variables that contribute to either successful
or unsuccessful sexual functioning in later maturity, it becomes apparent that
these variables do not differ significantly from those that are conducive to
successful or unsuccessful sexual functioning during adolescence, early, and
middle adulthood.

Myth Five: Inflexible

Inflexibility refers to a psychological orientation characterized by rigid
resistance to change and the inability to adapt to new situations or circumstances. Some older people are indeed inflexible. Their behavioral patterns
are characterized by rigidity and they are very resistant to change. However,
it is accurate to say that some children, some young adults, and some middle-aged individuals are also characterized by inflexibility. Inflexibility refers to
a personality trait that may be manifested by individuals during any stage of
their development. In some cases, actual lack of available opportunities to
develop, grow, and change may be interpreted erroneously by the outside
observer as inflexibility in old age. It should be recognized that economic,
social, and physical restraints may prove significant barriers to change regardless of the elderly individual's personal inclination or ability to behave in
an adaptive or flexible fashion. However, lack of opportunity to change and
develop does not constitute, and should not be confused with, inflexibility.

Years accumulated or chronological age does not produce an inflexible
personality structure. Not only do older individuals change, but they must, by
necessity, adapt to major events that are frequent and expected accompaniments of later maturity—retirement, changes in income and status, loss of
loved ones, illness and disease, and changes in residence or life-style. Although research suggests that older individuals change attitudes and opinions somewhat more slowly than do younger people, changes noted among
older persons tend to mirror prevailing shifts observed in society-at-large
(Cutler and Kaufman, 1975). Happily, most older people remain open to
change throughout the entire course of later maturity. In the absence of this
quality, adjustment would prove extremely difficult, if not impossible.

Myth Six: Unproductive and uncreative

The myth of unproductivity and lack of creativity in old age probably stems
from our society's tendency to equate productivity and creativity with remunerative employment. Unless people are earning money, they are generally
viewed as unproductive and lacking in creativity in our society. In an attempt
to dispel this myth, we need only look at the number of individuals who have
made significant creative and productive contributions to society while in
their seventies, eighties, and nineties. Contributions of individuals such as

Sigmund Freud, Pablo Picasso, Eleanor Roosevelt, Bertrand Russell, Maggie Kuhn (founder of the Gray Panthers), Artur Rubinstein, Anne Morrow Lindbergh, and Anna Mary (Grandma) Moses serve to exemplify creativity and productivity in old age. However, unlike most of these individuals whose entire lives have been marked by conspicuous creativity and achievement, many people begin to discover and develop their special abilities and talents for the first time in old age.

During later maturity, many individuals have the freedom necessary to explore and pursue various creative undertakings. Such exploration may have been impossible when they were engaged in full-time formal employment. New interests develop and previously unidentified aptitudes may be discovered and cultivated. The productive activities and contributions of older individuals may be seen in a number of realms including artistic, political, educational, and religious. Although the majority of older individuals are not engaged in formal remunerative employment, it is erroneous to equate productivity and creativity with "holding down a job." Regardless of employment status, many older citizens continue to be productive, contributing, and creative members of society well into later maturity. If the creative potential of the 65-and-over population is denied, ignored, or suppressed by society, all members of that society will suffer a significant loss.

Myth Seven: Difficulty learning new skills

A popular maxim is "you can't teach an old dog new tricks." This saying reflects the attitude that with advanced age comes a loss in ability to grow, to change, to acquire new knowledge, and to develop new skills and abilities. The person who ascribes to this maxim is also likely to view older people as inflexible, unproductive, and lacking in creativity. **Learning** is a relatively permanent change in behavior resulting from experience. It would be incorrect to suggest that differences in learning rates and abilities do not exist between and among various age groups. We know that preschoolers learn differently than do older schoolchildren and that schoolchildren learn in ways that are different from those used by the young adult. However, notions of inferiority and superiority are not imposed upon such observed differences. As a person grows older, differences in learning, as reflected by performance, are noted. To assume that such differences represent a decrease in ability to acquire new information is a mistake.

Learning is an extremely complicated subject to study. It is complicated because no one has ever seen learning or has been able to directly observe the mental processes that result in learning or in mental acquisition. All learning must be inferred from performance. Unless a person actually emits behaviors, there is really no way to determine whether or not learning has taken place. Learning is also difficult to study because it is influenced by a vast number of internal and external factors, including environmental conditions, motivation, emotional state of the learner, experiential background, and performance requirements.

Researchers who attempt to compare learning rates or abilities of any two individuals, or groups of individuals, are forced to give attention to such factors and must be willing to make the assumption that such variables are held constant for both entities being compared. When individuals are drawn from different age groups for purposes of comparison, it is impossible to validly make this assumption. At the very least, to assume that individuals drawn from different age groups share common experiential backgrounds is ludicrous. For this reason, the making of valid comparisons between different age groups has proven to be a difficult, and at times impossible, task.

James Birren, who has investigated age-related changes in learning for more than a quarter of a century, studied the same individuals over a number of years in an attempt to determine what changes occur as we grow older in our ability to learn. As a result of this research, Birren and his associates (1963) concluded that deterioration of mental functioning or decline in ability to learn should not be expected in old age. According to their findings, mental deterioration is the result of pathology or disease rather than normal aging. Although this research revealed a natural slowdown of mental and physical reaction time as a consequence of normal aging, general mental abilities or the capacity to learn was not found to decrease. Most individuals can, and do, continue to acquire new information, to incorporate new experiences—to learn throughout old age.

Myth Eight: "Cranky"

The ability to get along with others, to maintain a pleasant social demeanor, and to compatibly interact with our fellow beings, is developed and refined throughout the life of every individual. The young adult or middle-aged person who is pleasant company, maintains a generally positive outlook, and is sensitive to the feelings of others, is likely to continue this particular social orientation throughout old age. Conversely, if a person is constantly fault-finding, difficult to please, and generally negative toward people and circumstances, there is little reason to expect that these characteristics will not continue to be exhibited during old age. Patterns of adjustment and social behavior exhibited by elderly individuals are similar to patterns and behaviors that were exhibited by these same individuals during early and middle adulthood (Botwinick, 1973). This researcher suggests that the proportion of individuals who have reached old age and are characterized by cranky, ill-tempered dispositions, does not differ significantly from the proportion of such persons found in other age groups. In itself, this observation is surprising because the elderly are subjected to more stress and problems than are the young. Exposure to such stress would presumably create a greater number of socially negative individuals during later maturity. However, such does not seem to be the case.

It would appear that most people develop certain characteristic ways of interacting socially, relating to the environment, and dealing with stress. Once developed, these characteristic modes of response tend to be maintained and continue into old age. Our unique social temperament or orientation tends to prevail regardless of advanced chronological age. If you are "cranky" now, in all probability, this characteristic will show itself in old age. Likewise, if you have developed a positive social orientation, there is little reason to believe that the addition of years to your age will eradicate this particular facet of your personality.

Myth Nine: Lonely

The results of a study conducted by Louis Harris and Associates (1975) suggest that a major misconception held by the public about the aged centers upon the subject of isolation and feelings of personal loneliness.

> Twelve percent of those 65 and over did feel that "loneliness" was a very serious problem for them personally, but a much higher 60 percent of the public considered "loneliness" to be a very serious problem for most people over 65. (Harris, 1975, p. 30)

In a study conducted by Dean (1962), about two thirds of the 65-and-over population stated that they were never or very rarely ever lonely or experienced feelings of loneliness.

A number of factors appear to contribute to a general lack of perceived loneliness among the majority of older individuals. Initially, it must be noted that frequent contact between elderly people and members of their immediate family is the rule rather than an exception within our society (Binstock and Shanas, 1976). Contrary to the beliefs of some, it is unusual for an older person to be "abandoned" by family members, to be forgotten, ignored, and rarely, if ever, visited. In addition to family, friends also make up a significant factor in warding off loneliness among the elderly. According to the previously quoted Harris study, approximately half the surveyed older population said that they spent a "lot of time" socializing with friends. Only 5 percent of the 65 and over population perceived "not enough friends" as a serious problem (Harris, p. 31). Additional research indicates that volunteer organizations, social clubs, church or synagogue groups, and community activities are instrumental in preventing loneliness or isolation in old age (Hausknecht, 1962; *Catholic Digest,* 1966).

Myth Ten: More religious

It is very tempting to agree with the idea that as people grow older, they are likely to become more religious. This temptation may be grounded in an intuitive feeling that as the reality of death becomes increasingly close, we are apt to become more interested in life after death, personal salvation, and metaphysical concerns. The temptation to agree with this idea may be grounded in personal observations that the present older generation tends to be more religious than the younger generation. However, regardless of intuitive feelings or personal observations, the fact remains that people generally do not become more religious as they grow old. It is a mistake to assume that age differences in religious orientations are a product of increased age or growing older. The older generation did not become more religious as they aged. When compared with the present younger generation, we find that the older population was more religious in their youth, received more religious training as they grew up, and have continued upon a religious path established during the early or formative years of their lives. Differences in religious orientation appear to be generational rather than age-related. On the basis of data derived from longitudinal studies, Balzar and Palmore (1976) found no indication of increased interest in, devotion to, or preoccupation with, religion as a function of aging. Although religious involvement appears to neither increase nor decline in later maturity, there is a tendency toward decreased church attendance in old age (Moberg, 1965). Of course, church attendance and religiosity cannot be equated. As a person ages, factors such as lack of transportation, poor health, and changes in residence may account for observed declines in regular church attendance. Essentially, there is no evidence suggesting that as people grow older they become more involved in religious activities, gain increased satisfaction from religion, or devote more time and attention to religious concerns.

What Is Ageism?

Although most of the population is familiar with the terms racism and sexism, the term ageism is not widely known or understood. When someone says that whites are naturally more intelligent than blacks, racism is immediately recognized. If someone says, "A woman's place is in the home," we regard such a statement as sexist or a reflection of sexism. However, when we hear elderly people referred to as inflexible, cranky, or senile, the general tendency is to accept such remarks with little or no thought.

Definition of ageism

The term ageism was coined in 1968 by Robert Butler, a physician. To some extent, previously discussed myths and stereotypes concerning old age illustrate a few beliefs underlying ageism.

As with sexism and racism, **ageism** represents a basically prejudicial orientation toward a particular segment of society based upon misconceptions, half-truths, apathy, and ignorance. This prejudicial orientation has at its foundation the belief that the elderly segment of our society is fundamentally different from all other segments and, by inference, inferior. Within the concept of ageism is the assumption that personality, character, behavioral, and social traits are determined by chronological age. This assumption is coupled inextricably with the belief that one age group is inherently superior to another.

Origins of prejudicial attitudes about the aged

In an attempt to explain or better understand ageism within our society, four factors should be considered. These are: (1) our attitudes toward youth, (2) limited contact with the elderly, (3) the media, and (4) ignorance.

Attitudes toward youth. First, and of fundamental importance, is the fact that ours is a youth-oriented society. We tend to glorify youth, place great value upon being young, and attempt to maintain our youthfulness regardless of cost.

> A kind of cultural attitude makes me bigoted against
> old people; it makes me think young is best; it
> makes me treat old people like outcasts.
> Hate that gray? Wash it away!
> Wrinkle cream.
> Monkey glands.
> Face-lifting.
> Look like a bride again.
> Don't trust anyone over thirty.
> I fear growing old.
> Feel Young Again! (Curtin, 1977, p. 88)

To be young, in itself, is considered an accomplishment. By placing great positive emphasis upon youth, society is saying two things: "Young is good." "Old is bad." When great value is placed upon one segment of society, it usually follows that any group representing the opposite of that segment must be devalued or held in relatively low esteem. The devaluation of old age encountered within our society is, of course, not a universally observed phenomenon. Anthropologists and sociologists have studied societies that bestow upon their older members extraordinary value, respect, and power. In such societies youth rather than old age tends to be the "loser." Only as a person grows old can he or she hope to achieve the envied status reserved for the elderly. In our particular society the opposite tends to be true.

Limited contact. Limited contact with the elderly is a second factor that creates ageism. Clair Townsend (1971) refers to old age as "The Last Segregation," a time in which older individuals are systematically separated from other members of society. Surprisingly few people do have personal contact for any *extended* periods of time with the elderly—or even with one elderly individual. Grandparents or parents may be visited, older people may be observed in passing as they shop or walk along the street, or one might periodically converse with an aged neighbor. However, many younger individuals possess neither the desire, nor perceive the necessity, to establish long-term or close relationships with any elderly person. Those who have little or no contact with members of a particular group are more likely to accept whatever myths or stereotypes society imposes upon that unfamiliar group. Essentially, as a result of personal segregation from older adults, many of us are forced to respond to this segment of society on the basis of what we have been told or have learned second-hand. Too often, all that we have learned are the stereotypes and myths with which we have been presented throughout our lives.

The media. To some extent, television, movies, and popular literature must be given credit for engendering and perpetuating an ageist orientation in our society. Relatively few old people are featured on television or in the movies (Northcott, 1975). However, when elderly individuals are portrayed, they are frequently presented in a stereotypic manner that reinforces pre-existing myths and misconceptions (Aronoff, 1974). In some cases—particularly situation comedies and variety shows—the elderly person is ridiculed (generally because of mental or physical incompetence), held up to scorn, and depicted as an amusing but pathetic figure. The elderly person has often been portrayed as forgetful, behaving in a foolish manner, easily outwitted, and generally without power or status. At the other extreme, the elderly are presented as all-knowing, all good, saintly individuals who hand out sage advice. Neither portrait accurately depicts any human being. Both represent stereotypes of what we think old people are or should be. Until very recently, there has been a general failure on the part of the media to address older subjects as viable, diverse human beings. Of course, in fairness to the media, it must be said that material presented generally reflects what the public wants or expects to see.

> The public is not, on the whole, critical of the way the media portray older people. This may mean simply that the media project and maintain the stereotypes the public already holds.
> Majorities of television watchers do feel, however, that television shows young people, not older people. (Harris, 1975, p. 196)

Ignorance. The fourth factor that creates ageism is ignorance. Until recently, very little information about the process of aging or old age was available. A century ago, the elderly population was extremely small and in no way formed a significant number of people relative to the total population. At that time virtually no interest in aging or the aged was exhibited by researchers. However, as the proportion of older individuals increased, so also did research interest in the field of aging. As interest grew in research, our fund of valid information concerning aging and old age began to accumulate.

Unfortunately, much information derived from these pioneering research efforts was later found to be invalid and misleading. The invalidity of these early findings could often be traced to the researchers' mistaken assumption that differences between age groups were differences attributable to aging. It was frequently concluded that if one age group scored differently from another on the particular measure, the observed difference resulted from aging. For example, if a group of 65-year-old subjects scored less well on a vocabulary test than did a 20-year-old group, it was assumed that vocabulary decreased as a result of increased chronological age. That observed differences could be attributed to such factors as educational background, culture, or socioeconomic status (for example, generational differences) was often ignored. As a result of the erroneous assumption that age group differences must result from the aging process itself, much misinformation concerning aging and the aged was initially accumulated, accepted, and circulated. It is ironic that ageism was given scientific support by early research efforts using questionable methods and deriving invalid conclusions.

Can We Eliminate Ageism?

Robert Butler (1969) referred to ageism as another form of bigotry and perceived it as a serious national problem. He stated that ageism is a powerful force that will not be readily accessible to modification.

> Ageism reflects a deep-seated uneasiness on the part of the young and middle-aged—a personal revulsion to and distaste for growing old, disease, disability; and fear of powerlessness, "uselessness," and death. (Butler, 1969, p. 245)

Although we can agree with Butler's concern regarding the seriousness of the social threat posed by ageism, during coming years a number of forces may operate to effectively reduce prejudicial orientations toward the elderly and change established misconceptions concerning old age. Probably the most important factor that may be expected to change this prejudicial orientation will be the increasing proportion of elderly people in the population. As the number of older individuals increases, several influential changes may be foreseen. Initially, it may be predicted that the frequency and duration of contact with older citizens by younger age groups will increase. With increased contact, it is to be hoped that greater understanding between age groups will result.

Secondly, as the proportion of elderly individuals grows, so also will their power and influence, politically, socially, and economically. The effectiveness of political power in changing ageist policies within the government and society-at-large has already been recognized by activist groups of older citizens such as the "Gray Panthers." Such groups represent a nucleus of old and young individuals who are acutely sensitive to the social and political forces operating against the personal well-being of the elderly. Presently, such groups are actively involved in bringing about changes in areas such as employment, housing, medical care, transportation, and nutrition for the elderly. In part, these groups may take credit for the establishment of nutrition centers for the elderly, the abolition of mandatory retirement for many workers, and government-supported medical care for large numbers of aged people. In all probability, major changes in attitudes toward the elderly will be initiated and realized through the efforts of the elderly themselves. As with racism and sexism, those who are the target of prejudicial attitudes and behavior must ultimately assume responsibility for changing such negative orientations and adamantly demand that stereotyping cease. Only when blacks demanded that prejudicial treatment cease was any significant progress made toward racial equality, and only when women demanded equal rights were such rights forthcoming. Increasingly, the older population will make up a powerful political and social force, will demand that ageist attitudes change, and will not be satisfied until this goal has been achieved.

Finally, we hope that efforts to eliminate ageism will be aided by those researchers who have in the past and will continue in the future to devote themselves to the study of aging and old age. The study of aging and old age is a relatively new discipline and the necessity to obtain valid information in the field of gerontology is widely recognized. In an effort to meet the need for such information, increasing numbers of investigators are becoming committed to the study of old age. If successful, such researchers will provide the scientific basis for dispelling many myths and stereotypes concerning later maturity. With knowledge may come enlightenment, and with enlightenment may come an end to ageism.

Summary

Gerontology is a multidisciplinary field devoted to the study of aging and old age. An adequate study of aging and old age must take into consideration psychological, social, and biological factors. Aging is an inevitable process to which all of us are subject. However, each individual grows older, matures, and develops at different rates and in different ways. Although 65 years and over is generally used to denote "old age," the classification is somewhat arbitrary and is employed for purpose of common reference.

One in every 10 United States citizens is in the 65-and-over population. This number is constantly growing, and the proportion of older people within the general population is becoming significantly larger. The average life expectancy of males and females in the United States has continued to increase during the past seventy years. Presently, the average life expectancy of an individual born in the 1970s is 72.8 years. However, men tend to die at a younger age than do women and females outnumber males by a ratio of 100 to 72 in old age. Relatively few elderly individuals reside within nursing homes or institutional settings. Most reside within their own homes and continue to function with relative independence throughout old age. The older population faces many hardships, not the least is economic. Approximately 25 percent of the older population live on incomes that fall below the federally established poverty level.

Various myths and stereotypes surround aging and old age. Among these are beliefs that old people tend to be alike, that old age brings senility, sexual inadequacy, negative personality characteristics, unproductivity, decreased learning ability, social isolation, and increased religious feeling. Such myths underlie and exemplify what is referred to as "ageism," prejudicial attitudes and behaviors directed toward elderly individuals. Possible reasons for the development of ageism are the limited contact many people have with the elderly, our society's youth orientation, and the lack of valid information for many concerning aging and old age. Factors that may operate to reduce or eradicate ageist attitudes and behaviors are the increasing proportion of older people, increased opportunities for contact between various age segments, political and social power that may be wielded by the older population, and increased scientifically based information derived from gerontological investigations.

Progress Check

1. Define gerontology.   (pp. 2–3)

2. Why is gerontology a multidisciplinary study?   (p. 2)

3. What is the difference between the process of aging and the process of development?   (pp. 3–4)

4. Why has the proportion of older people within our society increased during recent years?   (pp. 6–7)

5. What are three demographic characteristics of the 65 and over population?   (pp. 7–8)

6. Describe five myths or stereotypes commonly imposed upon the elderly within our society.   (pp. 8–16)

7. Explain why people become less alike as they grow older.   (pp. 9–10)

8. What are three characteristics commonly associated with senility? (p. 10)

9. Cite three factors that might influence rate of learning in later maturity. (pp. 13–14)

10. Define ageism.   (p. 16)

11. List three factors that might promote ageism within our society. (pp. 16–19)

12. Why has much age-related information derived from early research efforts turned out to be invalid and misleading?   (p. 18)

13. List two social factors that may operate to eliminate ageist attitudes. (pp. 19–20)

14. How would you define old age?

Recommended Readings

Butler, R. Age-ism: Another form of bigotry. *Gerontologist*, 1969, 14, 243–249. A well-written, stimulating discussion of prejudicial attitudes and behaviors toward the elderly. Considers the strength of biases toward old people and increases sensitivity to age discrimination.

Curtin, S. Aging in the land of the young. In S. Zarit, ed., *Readings in Aging and Death: Contemporary Perspectives.* New York: Harper & Row, Publishers, 1977. In this work, the author portrays five elderly individuals and attempts to capture the strength and character of these persons. Feelings of empathy and identification with old people are fostered by this selection.

2

An Overview of Aging

Preview ∽ *Several definitions of aging will be presented in this chapter. We will discuss the concept of aging and a number of basic ideas underlying this concept. We will also define different types of aging and consider certain theories used to explain the aging process. In this chapter the relationship between various internal and external forces and aging will be emphasized. Finally, we will focus upon the need for theoretical foundations in gerontology. This chapter provides an overview of the aging process(es) and contains a great deal of basic information to which the reader might refer throughout the course of the book.*

Gerontology is the science of aging. Although this is a straightforward definition that appears to communicate meaning in an unambiguous fashion, whenever aging *is used in such a definitive context, consideration must be given to possible connotations and interpretations attached to the term.*

In What Ways Can We Define Aging?

Aging carries with it a number of implicit and explicit meanings and no single definition of the term will be supported by all individuals. Likewise, as situational and contextual factors change, modifications often occur in each individual's interpretation of the term. Scientific and philosophic orientation, situational demands, and contextual reference will operate to influence the manner in which aging is defined.

During our discussion of aging and the aging process, no attempt will be made to arbitrarily impose one specific definition of "aging." On the contrary, several definitions will be presented for consideration and individuals will be left to extract and incorporate those meanings best suited to their needs. Each individual will be encouraged to critically analyze each definition with freedom to discard unsatisfactory portions and to elaborate upon those parts perceived as relevant and valid. In so doing, a personally acceptable and useful definition of aging may be formulated by each person.

> Aging is a decline in physiological competence that inevitably increases the incidence and intensifies the effects of accidents, disease, and other forms of environmental stress. (Timiras, 1972, p. 465)

> [Aging] is a dynamic process encompassing complex bodily changes, redefinition of social identities and adjustments in psychological functioning. (Hendricks and Hendricks, 1977, p. 23)

> [Aging] refers to a sequence of events that take place, or are expected to take place, during an individual's life course. (Bengtson and Haber, 1975, p. 70)

> Aging can be regarded simply as an accumulation of pathological processes, which eventually kill off the individual by interfering with a vital function of the body. (Bromley, 1974, p. 115)

> Aging: (a) to show the effect of or undergo changes with the passage of time, (b) to suffer with the passage of time a diminution of essential qualities or forces. (Webster's *Third New International Dictionary*)

Aging: On What Points Can We Agree?

Although there is lack of consensus within the field of gerontology regarding what constitutes an appropriate definition of aging, a number of basic concepts are generally accepted by most researchers and practitioners. The following ten concepts concerning aging tend to be universally accepted.

Complexity

Aging is an extremely complex phenomenon. Few people would fail to appreciate the self-evident nature of this statement. No human being possesses the knowledge or expertise required to understand or explain the numerous factors involved in aging. To illustrate the complex nature of aging, we need only enumerate a few changes that are inherent within the process(es). Aging involves changes in cellular structure, chemical activity, and hormonal production. It involves changes in behavior, cognitive functioning, sensory acuity, and personality. Social interactions, social roles, and social status change as a function of aging. Related to aging are modifications in patterns of work, leisure, and recreation. External and internal alterations in the physical characteristics of every human being is an accompaniment of aging. Because aging is an extremely complex phenomenon, most gerontologists must be satisfied to concentrate most of their efforts upon one or two specific facets, for example, learning, retirement, and cellular change. Rather than being experts on "aging," gerontologists possess varying degrees of expertise regarding some particular aspect or aspects of the aging process.

Types of aging

There are many different types of aging. The three major categories of aging are psychological, biological, and social. Within these categories are encompassed considerations of the various changes that accompany aging that were mentioned above. However, these three categories are merely representative and should not be construed as constituting a finite delineation of gerontological topics or concerns. By themselves, a relatively complete list of subjects relating to aging would fill a book. In addition to psychological, biological, and social aging, we may also talk about chronological, functional, normal, and pathological aging. In gerontology it is not sufficient simply to talk about "aging." It is mandatory that the type of aging to which reference is being made be defined. Generic allusions to aging and the processes of aging are usually of little practical use when precise gerontological information is sought.

Different rates

Different rates of aging occur among different people. Not only does aging take place along a number of different dimensions, but rates of aging along each dimension tend to vary from person to person. Whereas one individual may experience relatively rapid aging of some particular characteristic, another individual may experience extremely slow aging of the same characteristic. For example, we know that all people do not "look sixty" when they reach their sixtieth birthday and that all people do not maintain comparable levels of intellectual sharpness at age seventy. In youth, differential rates of aging are labeled "early and late blooming." In later maturity, such differences are often ignored. Acceptance of differential rates of aging between different people (regardless of age) is fundamental to our understanding of the aging process.

Individual differences

Within each individual, different types of aging progress at different rates. Just as differences in rates of aging are observed among individuals, so also are differential rates noted within each individual. Studying one particular human being, we will inevitably notice that rate of social aging will not exactly coincide with rate of physical aging and that rate of functional aging may not keep pace with psychological aging. For example, it would not be extraordinary to discover an individual who is "young" psychologically, "old" physically, and "middle-aged" socially. Each separate facet of aging within the individual may be conceived as analogous to separate participants in a cross-country race. During the course of the race, various participants may alternately take the lead or lag behind. However, the entire race is characterized by continued progression of all participants toward a specific goal or end. Likewise, each participant's relative movement toward that goal will, to a greater or lesser degree, persistently vary. Each human being is constantly aging in a number of ways. The rapidity with which each type of aging will occur or progress within each individual is likely to vary greatly.

Universality

Aging is a universal characteristic of living organisms. Although all living organisms may not reach maturity or grow old, aging, regardless of specific chronological age, is an inherent characteristic of life. Aging is not a phenomenon associated with some particular stage of life, rather it is a continuing process affecting people in different ways during the entire course of their life span. With human beings, aging begins at conception; with human beings, aging is terminated at death. Although the observable signs of aging may, at times, be negligible, at no time in a person's life can aging be denied.

Genetic and environmental factors

Genetic and environmental factors influence aging. It is widely recognized that some types of aging (particularly physical aging) are highly influenced by hereditary or genetic factors. For example, identical twins (monozygotic) tend to age physically in very similar ways. However, it is also commonly recognized that heredity alone is not sufficient to explain aging. Environmental factors such as exposure to harsh elements in the environment, nutrition, excessive smoking, consumption of alcohol, and prolonged sensory deprivation are among those influencing certain types of aging. Likewise, it may be theorized that learning within the social environment may operate to accelerate or retard certain aspects of aging. We may learn to behave in an "old" or "young" manner in accordance with lessons imposed by the external environment. Although the relationship between heredity and environment and aging is far from clear, it is widely believed that various types of aging are significantly influenced by an interplay of these two major variables and that manipulation of these variables may result in differential rates and types of aging. To some extent, this belief underlies many programs involving environmental intervention that are specifically designed to retard the progression of certain negative aspects associated with the aging process.

Change

Aging entails change. Changes associated with aging are neither good nor bad. They may be positive or negative depending upon the perceptions of the individual and externally imposed evaluations. Although most changes associated with aging occur in a subtle and frequently imperceptible manner, some changes occur with relative rapidity and function to place the individual in a position requiring swift adaptation and adjustment, for example, sudden loss of physical health, unanticipated (and anticipated) death of mate or friends, and retirement. It is said that "life is change." It may be said with equal certainty that "aging is change."

Irreversibility

Aging is irreversible. This statement does not imply that certain physical, social, and psychological manifestations of aging cannot be reversed. Wrinkles, loss of adult social roles, and depression, for example, can all be reversed to some extent. However, when aging is perceived as a natural accompaniment of the passage of time, the irreversible nature of the process(es) becomes clear. From a chronological perspective, aging is an absolute in that no one has ever grown younger, has reversed the temporal sequence, or has developed from maturity to early childhood. Although certain types of aging are amenable to change, as human beings, we are each moving along a number of progressive aging tracks upon which forward movement is obligatory. The effects of aging may be modified, retarded, accelerated, and ameliorated. However, aging itself cannot be reversed.

External signs

Aging progresses whether or not we can actually see it. Wrinkled skin, changes in skin pigmentation, and gray hair are observable signs of aging. However, the absence of such external signs is in no way indicative of an absence of aging. For example, although individuals may exhibit no observable signs of aging between 20 and 21 years of age, the process(es) of aging constitute no less a significant factor in their development. If we repeatedly look in the mirror and detect no change in physical appearance, it may be tempting to conclude that we remain untouched by aging. Likewise, if people keep in "perfect" physical condition, give close attention to nutrition, and do everything conceivable to retain a youthful appearance, they may come to believe that aging has ceased. However, aging never ceases and no person remains untouched by the process(es). Although certain measures can be taken to retard the rate of certain types of aging, it is a pervasive characteristic of all living things and cannot be eliminated.

Causes

The exact cause or causes of aging are unknown. Whereas it has been noted that definite relationships exist between hereditary and environmental factors and aging, no one really knows what causes a person to age. Some researchers have speculated that when the cause or causes of aging have been identified, the effects of aging may be greatly retarded or halted. However, at this time, such speculation is pure conjecture. Although a number of cause-and-effect relationships between various factors and aging have been successfully established, a definitive answer to the question, "What causes aging?" does not exist. We know that all human beings are constantly aging. However, reasons why we age remain obscure.

Summing up

To reiterate, the following general concepts concerning aging are commonly accepted by individuals devoted to the study of aging and old age. (1) Aging is an extremely complex phenomenon. (2) There are many different types of aging. (3) Different rates of aging occur among different individuals. (4) Within each individual, different types of aging progress at different rates. (5) Aging is a universal characteristic of living organisms. (6) Genetic and environmental factors influence aging. (7) Aging entails change. (8) Aging is irreversible. (9) Aging progresses whether or not we can actually see it. (10) The exact cause or causes of aging are unknown.

With these basic conceptual foundations in mind, let us now move on to a discussion of specific types of aging and specific manifestations of the aging process.

What Are Some Specific Types of Aging?

As previously mentioned, the three major categories of aging are biological, social, and psychological. Although researchers are usually forced by practical constraints to focus upon one or two relatively narrow subjects related to aging, no single category or topic may be viewed in total isolation if we hope to grasp the dynamic nature of aging or to better understand the extreme complexity inherent in the process(es). There is constant interaction among the three categories and change in one dimension is likely to result in change in the others. For example, as the number of brain cells decrease as a function of increased age (biological), changes in ability to solve problems (psychological), or to engage in certain community activities (social) may result. Regardless of whether interrelationships among the three categories of aging are pronounced or subtle, they constitute an ever present reality that must be considered and addressed by gerontologists.

Biological aging

Biological aging refers to anatomical and physiological changes that occur over time in the various systems of the body, including the central nervous system, and the digestive, reproductive, muscular, skin, skeletal, cardiovascular, respiratory, and excretory systems. Biological aging also refers to age-related changes in molecular and cellular structures, tissues, immunity to disease, hormones, metabolism, enzymes, and incidence of physical pathology. Because the subject of biological aging is so broad, our present discussion does not permit a detailed enumeration of those topics and concerns included within this category. However, it should be pointed out that researchers in the area of biological aging are drawn from a number of disciplines including chemistry, psychology, endocrinology, immunology, genetics, radiology, and pathology. Those interested in biological aging might address questions such as the following: "What is the relationship between RNA synthesis and cellular aging?" and "Why do people become increasingly vulnerable to disease as they grow older?" To summarize, biological aging refers to external and internal changes that occur within the structure or functioning of the physical organism as a correlate of aging.

Social aging

Researchers and practitioners whose major interest is social aging view the individual or group within the particular social milieu or environment in which they exist. Attention is focused upon socially imposed variables that infringe upon the individual or group as a correlate of aging and upon the changes that result from the imposition of such variables. Essentially, socially imposed variables are those potentially influential factors to which we are exposed in the course of interactions involving individuals, groups, and institutions, for example, family, educational, economic, religious, and political institutions. An example of a socially imposed variable is mandatory retirement. Social aging may be affected by such things as patterns of interactions among friends, family, and acquaintances, by formal and informal affiliations with established social institutions, and by social class, status, and ethnicity.

Social aging refers to age-related changes in the individual or group that result from (1) forces arising from the society in which the individual lives and (2) the individual's or group's responses to socially imposed forces. For example, although society may "expect" an elderly person to behave in a certain way, this socially imposed expectation may be internalized by some individuals and rejected by others. In either case a certain aspect of aging has been influenced. Subjects commonly addressed by individuals concerned with social aging are interpersonal dynamics, organizational affiliations, demographic characteristics, social prescriptions, norms and expectations, social roles and status, and specific age-related problems such as housing, use of leisure, medical care, transportation, widowhood, education, employment, poverty, and nutrition. Many people interested in social aging are actively involved in the planning, development, and implementation of intervention programs specifically designed to thwart the negative influences of certain social forces upon the aging process.

Psychological aging

Psychological aging refers to age-related changes in behavior and mental processes. Those who are involved in the study of psychological aging most frequently concentrate upon some particular aspect of one of the following broad topics: sensation, perception, learning, intelligence, thinking, language, memory, motivation, emotion, personality, psychopathology, psychotherapy, social behavior, and mental health. A major task of the individual investigating psychological aging is to observe behavior (usually in some systematic manner) and make inferences regarding cognitive or mental processes underlying observed behavior. Secondly, an investigator of psychological aging would, following observations and inferences, usually make probability-based predictions regarding future behavior. At the most rudimentary level, those concerned with psychological aging (1) look at behavior, (2) ask why observed behavior has been emitted, and (3) attempt to ascertain what behavior will be exhibited in the future. For example, in the process of studying psychological aging, an individual might observe that an elderly person is unable to solve any oral problems involving mathematical computation. Following this observation, the investigator may infer that such behavior may be the result of factors such as anxiety, motivation, or sensory decline. The investigator may then formulate a probability-based relationship between observed behavior and underlying mental processes. Finally, on the basis of previously established inferences, the investigator will predict how the individual's future behavior will be characterized (a) if inferred relationships remain unchanged, or (b) if changes are brought about between observed behavior and inferred mental processes. For example, how might we expect the elderly person to behave if anxiety is eliminated, motivation is increased, or sensory decline is corrected?

Psychological aging refers to changes in the individual's ability to adapt, to adjust, to cope effectively. It refers to age-related changes in the individual's responses to environmental contingencies and internal modifications. Whereas **psychology** is the scientific study of behavior, the psychology of aging, **geropsychology,** is the scientific study of behavior as a correlate of aging and old age.

Chronological and functional aging

In addition to the three major categories of aging previously discussed, a distinction must be drawn between chronological and functional aging. **Chronological aging** simply involves the accumulation of years or time units beginning at birth (or beginning at conception in cultures where children are considered to be one-year-old at birth). Functional aging is concerned with what an individual "can or cannot do." **Functional aging** refers to age-related changes in the ability of the individual to perform certain tasks, to engage in certain activities, to behave effectively, and to operate at a particular level of efficiency. Chronological age is an obvious constant; namely, with the passage of twelve months, we're all a year older. In contrast, great variations in functional age are noted among and within individuals. Examples of functional aging are changes in physical strength, decline of fine eye-motor coordination, decreased reaction time, and changes in vigor.

Although the distinction between chronological aging and functional aging would seem to be rather apparent, many misconceptions and stereotypes concerning later maturity may be grounded in our inability to differentiate between years accumulated and patterns of behavior or performance. If this distinction were clearly understood by all, it would be unlikely that any individual would ever begin a statement with the words, "All old people . . ." Probably chronological age—how old we are in time units—will become increasingly reduced in significance as functional age—what we can do—becomes more significant.

Normal and pathological aging

Normal aging involves changes that occur as natural results of the passage of time. One researcher refers to normal aging as the inevitability syndrome and encourages distinguishing between changes that occur as a natural result of aging and **pathological aging**—changes that result from pathology or disease (Tobin, 1977). However, the difficulty involved in clearly distinguishing between normal and pathological aging is great. In part, this difficulty may be traced to the fact that pathology or disease is a frequent companion of old age and its effects are superimposed upon the effects of aging. Also, some age-related changes in structure and function may appear pathological when comparisons are made between older and younger individuals. Because the old population is vulnerable, in varying degrees, to the same diseases that plague humanity as a whole, it would be impossible to describe every pathology that might strike the elderly. Therefore, in an attempt to distinguish between normal and pathological aging, it is useful to look at those changes that are typical accompaniments of increased age and are not indicative of abnormality.

A description of normal aging.   Ruth Weg, a biologist associated with the Andrus Gerontology Center at the University of Southern California, has provided a compilation and discussion of changes that occur within the human body as a function of increased age. Phenomena listed and elaborated by Weg are natural accompaniments of aging and are therefore descriptive of normal aging. None of the following characteristics of advanced age (see Table 2.1) should be viewed as pathological.

Although some changes listed and discussed by Weg may appear to be pathological, they occur in conjunction with increased age, are manifested by the majority of older individuals, and are, by definition, normal. These age-related changes may result in many physical/psychological problems and complaints, may increase our susceptibility to pathology, and may reflect a general pattern of reduced physical welfare. But such changes do not result from disease. Rather, they are a result of normal aging—the inevitability syndrome.

How Do Various Theories Attempt to Explain Aging?

No comprehensive theory of aging exists: No single theory has been formulated that (1) defines aging, (2) takes into account all processes involved in aging, (3) explains differences in types and rates of aging, (4) tells why organ-

Table 2.1:   Physical Changes That Accompany Normal Aging

1. Cell death is a time-related phenomenon of probable influence and significance in the physiological manifestations of aging.
    (a) The loss of cellular units by death in skin, blood, liver, gastro-intestinal tract, and bone marrow is partially compensated through replacement. However, the rate of destruction may exceed rate of replacement with increased age.
    (b) The loss of cellular units in the central nervous system, muscle, and kidney is representative of the kinds of loss in the kinds of cells that no longer have the power of cell division or regeneration. These may be most crucial in the aging processes. In the nervous system, for example, the functional neurons may be replaced but by nonfunctional glial cells. So we are talking about death of units and decrease in function of those that remain.

2. There is good agreement that there are changes in fibrous proteins. Elastin fibers become thicker and aggregate, and are less elastic. The collagen fibers become less soluble. These changes in turn influence the structure and composition of the skin, the vasculature, and those very important joints.

3. There is good evidence for changes in mineral metabolism. Calcium, for example, under dietary and hormonal changes, may leave the bone and invest the soft tissues. It may enter into the lining of arterioles and into the joint sacs, leading to narrowed blood vessels and pain. Stiffening the rib joints, there may be increased difficulty in breathing. Changes in the bone structure may cause reduction in height, the familiar stooped posture, and limitations in mobility—all earmarks of advanced years.

4. There is a measurable, progressive reduction of basal oxygen consumption by the aging person. This reflects the lowering of reserve in all body functions. Since we can only do that for which energy is available, we can't do as much as we get older. For example, necessary syntheses of the stuff of protoplasm decreases. More biochemical studies would provide information to substantiate these changes of time, exercise, and disease. Research could demonstrate the reduction in available oxygen and the use of O_2 even when it is available. The more molecular information we can gather, the closer we may come to a real understanding of basic aging processes.

5. There is evidence for measurable change in heart and blood vessel structure and function. Blood vessels narrow to cause increased peripheral resistance. Blood pressure increases with age, and can be modified by environmental, genetic, and cultural factors. There is a decrease in the capacity of the heart to respond to extra demands, to the stress of heavy work, and to emotional tensions. Any sclerotic changes in vessels of the brain may contribute to identifiable psychological symptoms.

6. We know that breathing may be less efficient due to changes in the muscles of the ribs and chest, arteriosclerotic changes in lung blood vessels, changes in elastic fibers, and/or changes in rib joints. As a consequence, less oxygen is available to reach all tissues of the body.

7. There is evidence for changes in the gastrointestinal tract. A number of frequently cited physical factors attest to this. There is a decrease in sense of smell and taste, a loss of teeth, problems with dentures, a reduced mobility of stomach and intestines, a reduced secretion of digestive juices, constipation, hemorrhoids, malnutrition, and a decrease in fluid intake. Unfortunately, there is an increase in desire for, and consumption of, sweets. Often this is in the role of fulfilling psychological needs, rather than essential hunger.

8. There is agreement that changes in the genito-urinary tract present the aging individual with new concerns and threats to his dignity and personality. There is an increase in urinary incontinence and in frequency of urination. With men, this is often related to the enlargement of the prostate. With women, this is often accompanied by

Table 2.1: Physical Changes That Accompany Normal Aging

infection of the urethra or the bladder. Atrophic changes of genital tissues in men and women are expected changes with time. Natural involutional changes accompany the decrease in gonadal secretions and lead to a gradual atrophy of vaginal tissues after menopause, a decrease in lubrication, and a decrease in the size of the uterus and cervix.

9. Some of the other endocrine glands also come in for gradual, measurable changes. There is a marked decrease in the ability to fight disease as well as an increase in autoimmune properties. This loss of recognition of self often leads to the destruction of one's own tissues.

10. There are notable changes in the nervous system, the chief coordinating, integrating mechanism of the human body. Reaction time and speed of movement slow down. This effect is common to different sensory modalities and several different motor pathways. Simple neurological function which involves few connections in the spinal cord remains virtually unchanged. It is the complex connections of the central nervous system that aging appears to affect mostly, contributing to memory loss, to difficulties with decision making, and to the decrease in homeostatic capacity. In any parameter we choose to monitor—heart rate, blood pressure, resistance to infection—the magnitude of the displacement is greater and the rate of recovery is slower.

11. And finally we find empirically that there is an increased susceptibility to disease, particularly chronic disease. There appears to be a statistically significant increase in death from causes that earlier in life would not have had that result. (Weg, 1978, pp. 9–12)

Source: From "Physiological Changes That Influence Patient Care" by Ruth B. Weg, Ph.D., from *Psychosocial Needs of the Aged: A Health Care Perspective*, edited by Eugene Seymour. Copyright © 1978 The Ethel Percy Andrus Gerontology Center. Reprinted by permission of The University of Southern California.

isms age, and (5) provides a basis for predicting the course of aging through-out the individual's life span. No single theory provides an all-inclusive conceptual foundation from which aging may be viewed, interpreted, and investigated. Furthermore, no such comprehensive theory appears to be forthcoming in the foreseeable future, and it is reasonable to suggest that such a theory may never become a reality. The enormous complexities involved in aging and the processes of aging operate strongly against the formulation of an all-encompassing, yet functional, theory.

In an attempt to explain what causes aging, a number of theories have been formulated and proposed. Some are grounded in biology, some in sociology, and some in psychology. Each theory is a product of scientific inquiries or everyday observations resulting in "common sense" hypotheses. Although each theory may contribute something to our understanding of some aspect of aging, different theories boast varying degrees of scientific support. Most theories of aging continue to be scrutinized by the scientific community and are always subject to modification.

Theories of biological aging

Among frequently encountered theories of biological aging are the following: (1) wear and tear, (2) metabolic waste, (3) autoimmunity, (4) collagen, and (5) mutation.

Wear and tear theory. The **wear and tear theory** of aging probably coincides most closely with our popular conception of why things get old, wear out, and finally are no longer usable. This theory views human aging as analogous to the aging and deterioration of a car, a dishwasher, or any other machine. It is postulated that as a result of use (wear and tear), various parts of the human machine (organs) finally become worn out. However, on the basis of our knowledge, we recognize that the analogy between the aging of human beings and machines cannot be carried to a satisfactory conclusion. We know that regular use of the human body tends to retard rather than hasten the aging process. People who exercise regularly, use up significant amounts of energy in physical activities, and continue working, tend to maintain physical functional capacity longer than individuals who are generally sedentary and maintain prolonged states of bodily repose. If the wear and tear theory of aging were valid, we would expect the opposite to be true. It appears that this theory of aging, although highly plausible on the surface, falls short of explaining why people age.

Metabolic waste theory. The **metabolic waste theory** suggests that aging occurs as injurious metabolic waste products gradually accumulate in the cells of the human body. One such waste product that progressively builds up in conjunction with increased age is **lipofuscin** or age pigment. Lipofuscins begin to accumulate in various physical systems (including the cardiovascular) long before they manifest themselves as **liver spots** on the skin. It is believed that the depositing and accumulation of lipofuscins results from age-related changes in the body's ability to metabolize or effectively process certain nutrients. If such is the case, metabolic waste accumulation may be a symptom of aging rather than a cause. Although the metabolic waste theory may be instrumental in explaining various physical changes that occur with increased age, it does not seem to attack the basic issue of "what causes aging?" In order to get closer to the root of the matter, we have to ask, "What causes metabolism to change with age?"

Autoimmunity theory. The **autoimmunity theory** suggests that aging results when various bodily systems begin to reject their own tissues. As a person grows older, there is an increase in autoimmune antibodies produced by the body. These autoimmune antibodies cause the body to behave in a self-destructive manner or to operate against itself. Autoimmune reactions have been observed in connection with various cardiovascular diseases, diabetes, and cancer. Each of these pathologies constitute major causes of death in later maturity. Moreover, a definite relationship has been established between autoimmunity and rheumatoid arthritis, an affliction that becomes increasingly prevalent as we grow older. For some unknown reason, it appears that with increased age there is a growing tendency on the part of the body to "turn on itself" and to function against the physical well-being of the human organism.

Collagen theory.   The **collagen theory** is based upon established relationships between changes in the body's fibrous proteins (collagen and elastin) and aging. Collagen and elastin fibers are extremely abundant within the body and are the two most common proteins in all connective tissues. These fibrous proteins are found in muscles, joints, bones, cartilage, ligaments, and vessels. With increased age, fibrous proteins become thicker, less elastic, less soluble, tend to mass, and replace existing tissues. Age-related changes in collagen and elastic fibers are associated with various external signs of growing older such as wrinkling of the skin, sagging muscles, and slower healing of cuts and wounds. Changes in fibrous proteins as a function of age are noted in many animals other than the human being. For example, at the dinner table, such changes can make the difference between a tender steak and a steak that you can hardly cut.

Mutation theory.   The **mutation (somatic mutation) theory** of aging is based upon the observation that as one grows older, cells exhibiting unusual or different characteristics tend to be noted with increased frequency. Such new cells are termed "mutants" and are believed to be the product of faulty genetic transmissions to dividing cells. Somehow instructions to dividing cells get messed up and atypical or abnormal cells result. The mutants may progressively take the place of previously existing bodily cells, may eventually die and be replaced by fibrous tissues (collagen and elastin), or may develop abnormally or in an erratic fashion characteristic of malignancy. According to this theory, when mutated cells are present in sufficient quantities, external and internal characteristics of growing old will develop. In addition, it is assumed that the death of the aged organism may ultimately be traced to the process of somatic mutation.

What causes biological aging? Although every theory of biological aging has not been addressed, it is probably sufficiently apparent that physical changes associated with aging can be traced to many sources. However, researchers have yet to discover a single definitive reason why human beings age biologically. We know that metabolic waste products accumulate, that autoimmune antibodies increase, that changes in fibrous proteins occur, and that cells mutate, but we do not know "why" this should be the case. What in the "nature" of the organism makes physical aging an inescapable requisite of life? When this riddle is solved, the entire complexion of human existence may be changed.

Theories of social aging

Two major theories are proposed to explain social aging: (1) the disengagement theory and (2) the role activity theory. Although numerous psychological considerations evolve from these major theories, they are placed under the heading "social aging" because both attempt to explain age-related changes as derived from the particular society in which the individual lives. A society's expectations about what is "normal" behavior for the aged operate to prescribe how an older person should act, to expect and demand that certain standards of behavior be observed, and to impose certain sanctions (rewards or penalties) when a person does or does not comply with social definitions of appropriate conduct. For example, if society says that an elderly woman should not date an eighteen-year-old man (prescription), we are not prepared to see such behavior (expectation), and when observed behavior is contrary to our expectations, we are likely to stare, snicker, or ostracize (sanctions) the offending individual in a number of ways. Society prescribes, expects, and sanctions certain behaviors. Those who conform to such prescriptions are rewarded or reinforced. Those who do not conform are punished or have rewards withheld. As a result, most societies are highly successful in controlling the behavior of most of their members.

Disengagement theory. The **disengagement theory** of aging was originally formulated by Cumming and Henry (1961). This theory proposes that as people approach and enter later maturity, there is a natural tendency to psychologically and socially withdraw from the environment. It is suggested that older individuals, of their own volition, choose to detach themselves from customary activities, to progressively take less interest in the external environment, and to increasingly exhibit lower levels of involvement with other people. It is further suggested that patterns of withdrawal are triggered or stimulated by increased consciousness of our own mortality, by acute awareness of the limited number of years remaining to live, and by recognition of personal declines in abilities and skills. This natural tendency to withdraw or disengage ourselves results from changes in certain internal processes and such changes are inherent factors of aging. Withdrawal or disengagement is therefore hypothesized to be a normal characteristic of growing old.

Almost immediately following presentation of this theory, fire was drawn from many quarters. Researchers argued that disengagement, rather than constituting a natural characteristic of aging, was in reality a socially imposed condition—society began to withdraw from the individual long before the individual began to withdraw from society. Opponents of the disengagement theory suggested that society, in the process of meeting the needs, expectations, and demands of the younger generation, gradually withdrew support, positions of status, social roles, available rewards, and opportunities for meaningful social interactions from the older generation. In so doing, society (overtly or covertly) presented the older individual with an environment that discouraged active, continuous involvement and, to a certain extent, punished attempts of older individuals to maintain customary levels of interaction within the social mainstream. In essence, such opponents viewed disengagement as a reaction to socially imposed prescriptions, expectations, and sanctions rather than a product of aging. At this point it is sufficient to state that whereas some evidence suggests that reduced involvement in later maturity in a natural accompaniment of aging, much evidence points to social imposition of withdrawal.

Role activity theory.   The **role activity theory** of social aging is based upon the premise that our social roles (mother, engineer, employer, student) form the basis of our identity and are critical to maintenance of positive feelings toward self. According to this theory, as we approach and enter later maturity, there is a tendency to become increasingly divorced from those activities or social roles that have been the foundation of self-identity (Who am I?) during a significant portion of adulthood. As this occurs, feelings of personal worth, value, and meaningfulness may greatly suffer. As role identity references are removed, acute demoralization may result.

The role activity theory of social aging suggests that if an elderly person is to maintain positive feelings toward self, new social roles must be adopted to replace those that have been lost. It is important that the elderly person becomes involved in new activities that might provide those *new* roles necessary for feelings of positive self-identity. In so doing, an assumption is that the older individual will, to a great extent, avoid the acute demoralization that frequently accompanies loss of significant roles. It is further assumed that higher activity levels provide greater opportunities for developing new roles essential to positive self-identity.

Although this theory of aging advocates activity as a means of maintaining self-identity through the incorporation of new social roles, activity in the absence of involvement and personal identification is not enough to promote morale, personal adjustment, and positive self-identity. Interest, commitment, and some degree of personal investment must be accompaniments of activity. For example, if an elderly person attends a particular social function on a regular basis, a fairly high level of activity may be shown. However, if this elderly person couldn't care less about what's going on, derives no gratification from the function, and does not become involved with those activities or persons with whom he or she is interacting, substitute roles with accompanying positive self-identity feelings are not likely to develop. No matter how frantic, activity in itself does not guarantee avoidance of the potentially demoralizing effects of role loss.

Upon contemplating the two major theories of social aging, a number of interesting relationships between disengagement and role activity might be formulated. Is it possible that disengagement or withdrawal is a product of the elderly individual's failure to develop new social roles to replace those that have been deprived? Likewise, it might be conjectured that inability to develop new social roles is the result of socially imposed constraints that limit opportunities to engage in interesting activities and promote withdrawal in later maturity. Finally, we might wonder what would happen to disengagement if society really tried to facilitate maintenance of accustomed adult roles into later maturity. With the abolition of mandatory retirement, researchers may have an opportunity to investigate possible relationships between continuation of customary work roles and disengagement, that is, the relationship between role activity and disengagement. If such research is undertaken, valuable information concerning social aging will undoubtedly be generated. It is even possible that a new dynamic theory of social aging might evolve.

Theories of psychological aging

As previously mentioned, although no specific theory of psychological aging exists, the disengagement and role activity theories have been used extensively by psychologists as bases for investigating and explaining age-related changes in behavior and mental processes. Until recently, psychology has concentrated most of its attention upon the behavior and development of the young individual and has given little consideration to maturity and later maturity. As a consequence, there is a general lack of theoretic input concerning psychological aging.

Although no comprehensive theory of psychological aging has been developed, Erik Erikson (1963) and Carl Jung (1933) have formulated theories of personality development that encompass the entire life span of the human being. Both Erikson and Jung are considered neo-Freudians (psychoanalysts who disagreed with Sigmund Freud's concept of personality development and functioning) and their theoretical contributions have mainly concerned the development, organization, and functioning of the **ego**—the concept of the self. Emphasis is upon adaptation and adjustment as products of ego or self-development.

Ego development theory. According to Erikson's **theory of ego development,** all human beings pass through a number of sequential stages during the course of their life span. At each stage, we are faced with a critical conflict or crisis that may be resolved in a satisfactory or unsatisfactory manner. If the crisis is resolved satisfactorily, the ego gains strength and expands. If unsatisfactory resolution occurs, skills and competencies necessary to effective coping and healthy adjustment do not develop. Put another way, the individual's strength or ego development will move in a positive or negative direction depending upon the manner in which each crisis or conflict is resolved. Erikson's eight stages of ego development with their accompanying psychosocial crises are: (1) first year—trust versus mistrust (crisis), (2) second year—autonomy versus shame and doubt, (3) third to fifth years—initiative versus guilt, (4) sixth year to onset of puberty—productivity versus inferiority, (5) adolescence—identity versus identity diffusion, (6) early adulthood—intimacy versus isolation, (7) middle adulthood—generativity versus self-absorption, (8) later adulthood—integrity versus despair.

Using Erikson's theoretical frame of reference, we might view differential patterns of psychological aging in terms of our success in resolving the psychosocial crisis faced in later adulthood. Unsuccessful resolution results in feelings of despair. Successful resolution results in feelings of integrity. In either case, psychosocial aging, viewed in terms of adjustment, adaptation, and ability to cope, is significantly influenced. Erikson's theoretical orientation will be discussed further in the chapter dealing with personality (see Chapter 6). Therefore, at this point, it is sufficient that consideration be given to the following possibilities. First, the concept of ego development as a factor in crisis resolution may be employed as a basis for considering psychological aging. Second, a relationship may exist between psychological orientation throughout later maturity and our success or failure in resolving the integrity versus despair crisis.

Analytical psychology. Carl Jung has also contributed to our understanding of psychological dynamics associated with later maturity. Again, personality is the focus of the orientation. Jung was the first theorist to distinguish between personality types characterized by **extroversion,** the tendency toward greater preoccupation with the external world than the internal self, and **introversion,** the tendency toward focusing upon the inner self, introspection, and withdrawal. Employing this distinction between basic personality types, Jung suggested that a natural movement toward introversion would be exhibited by individuals as they grew older and entered later maturity. That is, in old age we might expect an individual to become more introspective, more withdrawn, more philosophical, and less involved—and concerned—with society and social activities. Likewise, Jung suggested that as a person ages, there will be a natural restructuring of value priorities: What was valued and prized in youth may no longer hold any attraction for the individual. On the basis of personal observations, most of us would agree that each individual's value system does change, to a certain extent, with age and may therefore be an age-related phenomenon. However, the fact that we become progressively introverted with increased age is not accepted by all. This theoretic premise does, of course, have its counterpart philosophically in the disengagement theory of social aging.

Why does a person age psychologically? Why do age-related changes in factors as learning, intelligence, sensation, perception, and motivation develop? In order to formulate a theory of psychological aging, there is little doubt that significant input will be required from various social and physical sciences. Likewise, in all probability, no single theory of psychological aging will prove adequate to the task of explaining all age-related changes in behavior.

Summary

Aging may be defined in a number of ways depending upon circumstances, personal orientation, and pragmatic considerations. No definition of aging is universally accepted, but most people agree that (1) aging is an extremely complex phenomenon, (2) there are many different types of aging, (3) different rates of aging occur among different people, (4) within each individual, different types of aging progress at different rates, (5) aging is a universal characteristic of living organisms, (6) genetic and environmental factors influence aging, (7) aging entails change, (8) aging is irreversible, (9) aging progresses whether or not we can actually see it, and (10) the exact cause or causes of aging are unknown.

There are a number of different types of aging. The three major categories of aging are biological, social, and psychological. Biological aging refers to external and internal changes that occur within the structure or functioning of the physical organism as a correlate of age. Social aging refers to changes that result from social forces and the individual's response to social forces. Psychological aging refers to age-related changes in behavior and mental processes. In addition to biological, social, and psychological aging, consideration must be given to chronological, functional, normal, and pathological aging. Chronological aging refers to the amount of time the organism has lived. Functional aging focuses upon what the organism can and cannot do. Normal aging refers to natural results of increased age. Pathological aging refers to changes that may be traced to abnormality or disease. In many cases, it may be difficult to distinguish between normal and pathological aging. It may be more productive to concentrate upon natural changes that accompany aging rather than pathology.

Theories that attempt to explain aging arise from the social and physical sciences. However, at this time, no theory adequately explains aging and the aging process(es). Frequently cited theories of biological aging are: (1) wear and tear, (2) metabolic waste, (3) autoimmunity, (4) collagen, and (5) mutation. Social aging is most commonly explained in terms of the disengagement and role activity theories. Although no specific theory of psychological aging has been formulated, the work of Carl Jung and Erik Erikson provides a basis for conceptualizing personality changes in later maturity.

Progress Check

1. Using available information, define aging in your own words.   (p. 24)

2. Why is aging such a complex phenomenon?   (pp. 24–25)

3. List five generally accepted concepts related to aging.   (pp. 25–28)

4. List and define two specific types of aging.   (pp. 28–31)

5. What procedure is followed by the person who investigates psychological aging?   (pp. 29–30)

6. What is the difference between chronological and functional aging? (pp. 30–31)

7. List six characteristics of normal aging.   (Table 2.1, pp. 32–33)

8. Why might we confuse normal and pathological aging?   (p. 31)

9. List and define three biological theories of aging.   (pp. 34–35)

10. List and discuss two theories of social aging.   (pp. 35–37)

11. Why is the theory of disengagement criticized by some gerontologists? (p. 36)

12. List and discuss two personality theories that may be used to explain psychological aging.   (pp. 38–39)

13. What do you think is the major cause of aging?

Recommended Readings

Tobin, J. D. Normal aging—The inevitability syndrome. In S. H. Zarit, ed., *Readings in Aging and Death: Contemporary Perspectives.* New York: Harper & Row, Publishers, 1977.
Emphasizes the fact that aging is a continuous process that does not begin at one particular point in time. Considers differential rates of aging, individual differences in aging, and physiological declines associated with growing older.

Cumming, E. & W. Henry. *Growing Old: The Process of Disengagement.* New York: Basic Books, 1961.
An in-depth discussion and delineation of the social theory of disengagement. A good theoretical discussion of age-related behavioral changes.

Weg, Ruth. Physiological changes that influence patient care. In *Psychosocial Needs of the Aged: A Health Care Perspective.* The Ethel Percy Andrus Gerontology Center, University of Southern California, 1978.
An excellent theoretical and practical discussion of anatomical and physiological age-related changes. A clear and concise handling of biological aging.

3

Aging and Intelligence

Preview ◇ *In this chapter we will define the concept of intelligence, provide a conceptual foundation from which intelligence may be viewed, and differentiate between intelligence and IQ. We will also examine the influence of research methods and sampling techniques and present some illustrative studies concerned with the relationship between age and intelligence. Finally, we will suggest some conclusions concerning the effect of age on intelligence and discuss certain factors that may operate to improve intellectual performance in later maturity.*

Before discussing the subject of intelligence, and particularly the relationship between intelligence and aging, it is advisable that we be prepared to encounter a number of contradictions and a scarcity of pat answers. Since the birth of psychology as a formal discipline, intelligence has proven to be an extremely complicated subject that is influenced by numerous factors and susceptible to many sources of confusion and error. Moreover, intelligence, perhaps more than any other psychological concern, has prompted varying degrees of emotional involvement. If we wish to stimulate strong emotions, it is only necessary to assert the intellectual superiority of one major segment of society over another, for example, men over women, whites over blacks, young over old. We tend to be elated by references to our intellectual superiority and threatened by suggestions of inferiority. In general, such feelings are not evoked by comparisons involving memory, learning, motivation, or perception. For better or worse, feelings of self-worth and intelligence are closely allied, and assaults upon our intellectual ability are usually equivalent to assaults upon our self-worth. Whether individual or group comparisons are being made, most of us have difficulty maintaining an objective attitude on the subject of intelligence.

What Is Intelligence?

It should come as no surprise that no single definition of intelligence is embraced by all individuals. Even among psychologists, there is strong disagreement regarding definition. This is because intelligence is a hypothetical construct created by human beings in an attempt to explain individual differences in behavior. No person has ever seen, heard, touched, smelled, or tasted intelligence. Intelligence is an abstract idea. We assume its existence on the basis of observations that people exhibit different levels of abilities and aptitudes. Basically, the concept of intelligence provides a useful and convenient reference for explaining why some people do certain things well and other people do not.

It should be pointed out that we make statements and draw conclusions about a person's intelligence on the strength of actions and performance. In the absence of overt behavior and actions, it is impossible to make inferences regarding an individual's particular level of intelligence. For example, in an attempt to estimate your intelligence, you might be required to give information, solve a problem, or put together a puzzle; in doing so, you would be required to perform, take action, or demonstrate some behavior. On the basis of your performance, inferences about your intellectual level could be made. However, if you chose not to emit required behaviors, such inferences would be impossible. Only on the basis of behavior can inferences concerning intelligence be made.

Since conclusions concerning intelligence are based upon **inferences,** which are only guesses grounded in probability, by definition, such inferences are subject to error. What a person does, or how one behaves, may in no way accurately reflect mental abilities or intelligence. For example, if an elderly person enrolls in a college course and receives an *F* at the end of the semester, the inference might be made that he or she is lacking in intelligence. However, the elderly person who receives an *F* may indeed possess above-average intelligence but may have little or no motivation in reference to earning grades, or may feel no need to demonstrate to others knowledge or skill which has been mastered.

Absolute certainty is never a possibility when inferences are made concerning the relationship between behavior and mental characteristics. Observed behavior may be misinterpreted, misunderstood, or misperceived. Likewise, individuals may consciously or unconsciously choose to emit behaviors that are misleading or not representative of underlying psychological characteristics. Psychological inferences are statements of probability that should never be viewed as indisputable facts or realities. Although we may feel relatively sure that we know how "smart" another person is, we can never be absolutely positive.

Finally, it should be noted that no one has ever measured intelligence. Measurement of an abstract mental construct is a logical impossibility. Rather, measurements of intelligence are in reality estimates of intellectual level based upon measurements of behavioral samples. In an attempt to quantify the concept of intelligence, samples of behavior are obtained and numeric values are assigned to such samples. Because estimates of intelligence are dependent upon relatively few samples of behavior, there is always the possibility that selected behaviors may not provide an accurate indication of underlying abilities. Also, there is always the possibility that behavioral samples may reflect underlying psychological characteristics that are distinguishable from intelligence, for example, motivation, emotional state, or personality.

Before pursuing a more detailed discussion of intelligence and age-related trends in intellectual abilities, it is suggested that the following thoughts concerning intelligence be fixed in your mind. (1) Intelligence is an emotional subject about which few people maintain absolute objectivity. (2) Intelligence is a hypothetical construct created by human beings for purposes of explanation and reference. (3) Intelligence is inferred on the basis of observed behavior. (4) Inferences concerning intelligence can never be more than guesses based on probability. (5) Estimates of intelligence are derived from samples of behavior. (6) Behavioral samples may or may not be accurate reflections of intelligence. With these thoughts clearly in mind, maintenance of a highly critical attitude toward the subject of intelligence should be assured.

Is Your Intelligence the Same as Your IQ?

Intelligence is a hypothetical mental construct arising from inferences based upon observed behavior. The label most commonly used to represent intelligence is *IQ* or *intelligence quotient.* Your IQ is simply a numerical designation of intellectual level based upon performance standards established by similar individuals or norm groups. The average IQ is generally assigned the numeric label "100." If you receive a score of 100 on an intelligence test, this means that your performance on that specific psychological instrument was average when compared with other individuals with whom common characteristics, for example, sex, age, and education, are shared. **IQ** is a numeric representation of selected behavioral samples that have been measured in an attempt to ascertain underlying intellectual ability. The formula for IQ is mental age/chronological age $\times$ 100. However, variations on this basic formula are now available. IQ and intelligence are not synonymous. Just as assigned grades in school may not accurately reflect learning, IQ may not accurately reflect intellectual level.

Specific abilities

Intelligence is a many-faceted construct whose definition must encompass a multitude of specific and general abilities or aptitudes. For example, your intellectual ability may show itself in the form of verbal fluency, mechanical manipulation, spatial perception, abstract thinking, and information retention. Some people may be very talented mechanically but possess relatively little verbal aptitude. For others, the opposite may be true. However, it would be incorrect to assign labels of general intellectual inferiority or superiority to either group on the basis of such differences. Rather, evaluations would have to focus upon relative differences in specific intellectual abilities.

Intelligence is a composite of many different mental abilities that may manifest themselves to a greater or lesser extent depending upon internal and external factors influencing the individual. This composite view of intelligence has been defined as follows:

> Intelligence, operationally defined, is the aggregate or global capacity of the individual to act purposefully, to think rationally, and to deal effectively with his environment. It is aggregate or global because it is composed of elements or abilities which, though not entirely independent, are qualitatively differentiable. By measurement of these abilities, we ultimately evaluate intelligence. But intelligence is not identical with the mere sum of these abilities, however inclusive. There are three important reasons for this: (1) The ultimate products of intelligent behavior are a function not only of the number of abilities or their quality but also of the way in which they are combined, that is, their configuration. (2) Factors other than intellectual ability, for example, those of drive and incentive, are involved in intellectual behavior. (3) Finally, while different orders of intelligent behavior may require varying degrees of intellectual ability, an excess of any given ability may add relatively little to the effectiveness of the behavior as a whole. (Wechsler, 1958, p. 7)

Because intelligence is an aggregate mental construct composed of a number of abilities, consideration of changes in intellectual functioning must begin with a clear statement concerning what specific aspect of intelligence is under discussion. Although we may well ask, "Does intelligence decline in later maturity?" such a question is worthless from a research point of view. It is necessary that investigations concerning age-related intellectual changes begin with specific questions such as, "Does verbal fluency decline in old age?" "Does our ability to solve numerical problems change as we grow older?" or "What is the effect of aging upon abstract thinking?" When thought is given to age-related changes in intelligence, precise, operational definitions that identify the specific types of intellectual ability being considered are absolutely necessary. Does intelligence decline as we approach later maturity? In the absence of information pertaining to the specific type of intellectual ability to which reference is being made, no rational response to this question is possible.

What Research Methods Are Used to Test Intelligence?

The subject of age-related changes in intellectual abilities is characterized by contradictions, unresolved problems, and confusion. Few definitive statements concerning the subject can be made. Much confusion concerning the relationship between intelligence and aging may be traced to two sources: (1) research method employed—cross-sectional or longitudinal—and (2) sampling technique used—random or matched.

During the 1930s, 1940s, and 1950s, standardized intelligence tests were used extensively for the purpose of ascertaining changes in intellectual functioning as a result of the aging process. On the basis of much of this research, it became generally believed that intelligence reached its peak at a relatively young chronological age (teens or early adulthood) and thereafter was characterized by a gradual, but steady, decline. This deterioration hypothesis was generated from repeated observations that older individuals generally obtained lower IQs or intelligence scores on standardized tests than did their younger counterparts. Because older individuals scored lower than younger individuals, it was frequently assumed that intelligence declined with increased age. Until relatively recently, this age-related hypothesis of intellectual deterioration was not seriously challenged. Only during the past twenty years has it been vigorously suggested that observed differences among various age groups might be a product of research methodology rather than the aging process.

The cross-sectional research method

Most early (and recent) attempts to investigate age-related changes in intellectual performance used the **cross-sectional research method.** In this method, samples or groups of individuals are chosen from one or more categories under consideration and are studied or measured concurrently. For example, if a researcher is interested in different age groups (categories), samples of 20-year-olds, 50-year-olds, and 70-year-olds might be selected and administered an intelligence test at approximately the same time. Using measures of performance or obtained IQs, comparisons could then be made between the different age groups. If the 20-year-old sample obtained a higher average score than did the 70-year-old sample, the researcher could legitimately report the presence of an average IQ difference between the two age groups. Unfortunately, after noting the presence of such differences in intellectual performance, many researchers went one step further and concluded that observed differences between age groups were the result of the aging process. This conclusion inferred that as a person grew older, intellectual abilities declined.

The basic irrationality of this logic is exemplified by the researcher who went into an Italian American community and interviewed various age segments in an attempt to identify differences among such groups. After a great deal of investigation, the researcher observed that older individuals were more likely to speak with an Italian accent than were younger individuals. Excited by this finding, the researcher concluded that as people grow older, they will increasingly acquire an Italian accent. Although this example may appear to be somewhat farfetched, it should be recognized that similar thinking underlies all cross-sectional research that results in conclusions concerning intellectual changes as a function of the aging process.

Cohort differences. Rather than assessing differences attributable to aging, the cross-sectional method assesses differences between people born in the same generation, or **cohorts.** If differences are observed between the performance of a cohort born in 1910 and a cohort born in 1960, such differences may be attributable to variables such as education, social interactions, and general experiential background. There is little doubt that individuals born in 1910 and individuals born in 1960 were reared in vastly different worlds. Likewise, there is little doubt that background differences are eminently capable of exerting a significant influence upon intellectual performance. On the basis of cross-sectional research, it is impossible to segregate cohort from age effects. Both operate simultaneously to produce discrepancies in intellectual performance noted between different age groups.

Interpretations of cross-sectional studies. When cross-sectional research studies are encountered in the literature, the reader can avoid many interpretive pitfalls if the following realities are always remembered. (1) When the cross-sectional method is used to investigate intelligence and age, age declines tend to be intensified. In all probability, the combined effects of cohort and age operate to maximize differences between age groups. (2) On the basis of cross-sectional research, it is impossible to make statements concerning any age-related (or other) *changes* in the individual or group. You can't meet a person for the first time and say, "My goodness! You really have changed!" When conclusions concerning intellectual decline are generated from cross-sectional research, the investigator is, in essence, meeting a particular group of individuals for the first time and saying, "My goodness! You don't seem to be as smart as you used to be!"

The longitudinal research method

The probability of reaching valid conclusions concerning the relationship between aging and intellectual functioning is increased through the use of the longitudinal research method. When the **longitudinal method** is employed, some characteristic of *one* group of individuals is repeatedly measured at various intervals over an extended period of time. For example, measures of intellectual abilities may be obtained when a group is 20 years old, later when the same group is 40 years old, and again when the same group is 60 years old. The performance of one group is observed as its members actually grow older.

Although the longitudinal method is superior to cross-sectional research when investigations of age-related changes in intellectual functioning are being made, it is not free from potential sources of confusion and bias. Factors such as subject attrition, practice, and cultural effects may operate to distort results (Schaie, 1967; Botwinick, 1977). Perhaps the greatest source of potential error or bias inherent in longitudinal research is subject **attrition** or "drop-out." Research indicates that the less able and less intelligent individuals are more likely to discontinue participation in longitudinal research studies than are the more able and intelligent (Riegel, Riegel, and Meyer, 1967; Baltes, Schaie, and Nardi, 1971). Such selective subject attrition would result in observations of increased intelligence in conjunction with increased age. If less intelligent subjects do not continue to participate when follow-up or retest measures are being obtained, the average intellectual level of the remaining group will increase.

In addition to subject attrition, attention must be given to the potential effect of repeated measures upon test performance (Campbell and Stanley, 1963). To what extent are follow-up measures of intellectual performance influenced by previous exposure to test items? It is possible that some longitudinal gains in intellectual performance may be a product of practice rather than a reflection of genuine developmental change. Likewise, it is certainly possible, and probable, that previous exposure to a measurement instrument could influence subsequent test performance.

Whereas factors such as subject attrition and practice may operate to minimize or negate possible age-related patterns of intellectual decline, the combined effects of age and cohort tend to maximize "age-related" declines in intellectual abilities. If you care to project a rather pessimistic picture of age-related intellectual differences, cross-sectional studies would probably be emphasized. Likewise, a more optimistic picture would result from the citing of longitudinal studies. Basically, the probability of drawing faulty conclusions concerning the relationship between intelligence and age is relatively high when either cross-sectional or longitudinal methods are used. The only protection the individual has against such faulty conclusions is prior knowledge of the influence of methodology upon research data.

Sequential developmental methods

In an attempt to deal with difficulties arising from longitudinal and cross-sectional methods, Schaie (1965; 1970) has formulated sequential developmental methods (1977) of data collection and analyses. Sequential developmental methods incorporate both longitudinal and cross-sectional methods and are designed to differentiate between cohort and age influences. According to Schaie, Labouvie, and Buech:

> Based on the repeated drawing of cross-sectional samples at different times of measurements, the sequential strategies allow comparisons between longitudinal change sequences of single cohorts and differences in developmental level across many cohorts. (1973, p. 151)

Although there is some debate regarding the feasibility of ever separating age and cohort effects (Horn and Donaldson, 1976), sequential developmental methods promise to be very useful in the investigation of relationships between aging and intelligence. Presently, studies employing sequential developmental methods are appearing with growing frequency in the research literature. In time, it is not unlikely that sequential developmental methods will render longitudinal and cross-sectional methods archaic for purposes of age-related inquiries.

Sampling techniques

Another source of confusion concerning age-related trends in intellectual abilities can be traced to sampling techniques. Sampling refers to the manner in which individuals are chosen to participate in a particular research study. Two major sampling techniques are referred to as random and matched.

Random sampling. Using **random sampling,** subjects are drawn from a particular target population using procedures that will assure each individual an equal opportunity of being selected to participate. A rather obvious example of random sampling might be putting the names of every member of a population into a big barrel, drawing each name blindfolded, and including every fourth name in your sample. Theoretically, through the use of such a procedure, each member of the target population would have an equal chance of being selected to become a member of the sample. However, much more practical and sophisticated random sampling procedures are available to the researcher.

Matched sampling. When **matched sampling** is used, subjects are equated on the basis of one or more factors or variables considered significant by the investigator. For example, a researcher might like to compare 30-year-olds and 70-year-olds who have achieved comparable levels of formal education, share the same religion, and drive silver Fords. Although it is possible for groups to be matched on a large number of variables during the course of a single research study, practical considerations usually lead researchers to restrict themselves to one or two variables as a basis for matching. For example, it would be extremely difficult to obtain sufficiently large samples of 30-year-olds and 70-year-olds if matching were on the basis of the above mentioned three variables. Even if "drive silver Fords" were eliminated, the task would be great.

Some comparisons.   Investigating the relationship between sampling techniques and age differences in intellectual abilities, Green (1969) compared the performance of subjects who had been obtained through random selection to the performance of subjects who had been matched on the basis of educational level. When subjects were selected randomly, a pattern of overall age deterioration in intellectual abilities was manifested. However, when subjects were matched on the basis of educational level, the typical trend of general age decline was not noted. This research suggests that education (or some other variable) may constitute a more critical factor than chronological age when consideration is given to cohort or generational differences in intellectual functioning. Likewise, matching subjects on the basis of education attainment, Birren and Morrison (1961) found a stronger relationship between education and measures of intellectual abilities than between age and intelligence scores. According to another researcher:

> . . . if intelligence in the sense of capacity is meant, then the matched groups might be given emphasis. If intellectual ability as it is distributed currently in the "real world" is the concern, then random sampling is to be emphasized. Any random sampling of people of different ages would likely result in samples of decreasing education level with increasing age of group. This reality exists now; it may not exist in the future. (Botwinick, 1977, p. 582)

When matched samples are used to investigate the relationship between age and intelligence, cohort effects tend to be reduced. When samples are matched on the basis of one or more critical variables, the probability increases that differential effects of experiential background will be minimized. In addition, when comparisons are made between different age groups that have been randomly chosen, the probability increases that differential cohort effects will remain prominent.

At this point, a word of caution concerning sampling techniques and research involving elderly individuals is in order. Unfortunately, many elderly individuals are chosen to participate in research studies because of their ready accessibility. For example, samples of elderly individuals are often obtained from nursing homes and other institutional settings. Of course, such samples are not representative of the elderly population and data derived from such samples cannot be generalized to the normal aged population. However, attempts to make such generalizations are not uncommon and should be rejected when encountered.

It should be remembered that data derived from any research study are restricted in usefulness and applicability by the gathering procedures employed. When examining research concerning the relationship between age and intellectual abilities, close attention should be given to the research method and sampling technique used. In the absence of such careful attention, unsubstantiated conclusions may be uncritically accepted and erroneous inferences may be drawn.

Does Age Affect Our Intelligence?

When we give consideration to the concept of intelligence, we are impressed by the enormous number of behaviors that it may explain. For example, intelligent behavior may involve building a house, investing in the stock market, or learning to talk. The question among researchers focuses upon whether intelligence is a global concept that influences all behaviors equally or whether intelligence is composed of specific factors differentially influencing various behaviors. If intelligence is a global concept, the individuals should exhibit similar levels of proficiency on all tasks demanding intellectual ability. However, if intelligence is composed of specific factors, different levels of proficiency or aptitudes should be expected. Assuming the position that intelligence is composed of specific factors, Cattell has devised a model of intelligence incorporating two very broad ability categories.

The fluid and crystallized intelligence models

A theoretical model of intelligence that differentiated between "fluid" (intelligence) and "crystallized" (intelligence) was proposed by Cattell (1963). **Fluid intelligence** is the ability to shift our thinking, to attack problems from various angles, to adjust our problem-solving approach according to the demands of the situation, and to have the capacity for insight into complex relationships regardless of cultural content. If you were faced with a novel problem and had no experiential background to draw upon for its solution, fluid intelligence would be required. **Crystallized intelligence** refers to mental abilities that are acquired by the individual as a product of acculturation. Socioeconomic status, cultural environment, educational level, and social interactions influence crystallized intelligence. Classified under the heading of crystallized abilities would be general information, knowledge, and skills acquired through education and experience.

When Cattell differentiated between crystallized and fluid intelligence, he hypothesized that as people grow old and approach later maturity, a decline in both types of abilities would occur. Furthermore, according to Cattell, whereas the decline in crystallized abilities would probably be insignificant, a pronounced age-related decrease in fluid abilities would be noted. If people continue to operate within their accustomed environment (culture), there would be little reason to expect crystallized abilities to diminish greatly in later maturity. However, as a person grew older, ability to attack and solve novel problems in a flexible, efficient manner would definitely suffer.

Using a test of **omnibus intelligence** (measures of fluid intelligence, crystallized intelligence, and a composite of fluid and crystallized abilities labeled omnibus intelligence), Horn and Cattell (1967) executed a cross-sectional study designed to investigate the relationship between intellectual abilities and age. In Table 3.1 (see p. 54), a description of the major dimensions or components of fluid and crystallized intelligence may be seen. These descriptions are based upon Horn's (1975) subsequent conceptualization of the major dimensions of intelligence.

Figure 3.1: Cross-sectional age differences for different operational definitions of intelligence in adulthood (after Horn and Cattell, 1967).

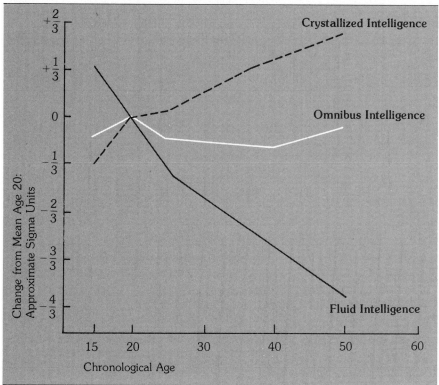

Source: From S. Gershon & Allen Raskin, "Aging and Intelligence," *Aging: Genesis and Treatment of Psychologic Disorders in the Elderly, 2*, p. 28. © 1975, Raven Press, New York.

In the omnibus intelligence study, subjects were randomly drawn from age groups ranging from mean (average) age 20 to 50. The results of this study are summarized in Figure 3.1.

It may be noted that the trend exhibited by fluid intelligence reflects the dramatic age-related decline predicted by Cattell. However, contrary to expectation, rather than remaining relatively constant, crystallized intelligence tended to increase as subjects were drawn from older populations. Omnibus or composite intelligence remained relatively constant across all age groups.

On the basis of results, a positive age-related cohort effect in reference to crystallized abilities may be hypothesized. In terms of crystallized intelligence, membership in an older cohort seems to have constituted an asset and membership in a younger cohort appears to have been a liability. However, it would seem that abilities not highly related to education and experiential background were not significantly influenced by cohort membership.

Table 3.1: *Measurement and Process Descriptions of Major Dimensions Indicated by Second-Order Factoring Among Primary Mental Abilities** *

I. Gf, Fluid Intelligence. Involving processes of perceiving relationships, reducing correlates, maintaining span of immediate awareness in reasoning, abstracting, concept formation, and problem solving, as measured in unspeeded as well as speeded tasks involving figural, symbolic, or semantic content but in which relatively little advantage accrues from intensive or extended education and acculturation. Good measures of the dimension include the following primary mental abilities.

   A. I, Inductive Reasoning, as measured in:
      1. Letter Grouping: Find the rule which relates three of four sets of letters and mark the one set that does not fit.
      2. Number Series: Select the number which should appear next in a progression.

   B. CRF, Figural Relations, as measured in:
      1. Matrices: Choose a figure to fill in an empty cell in a matrix in such a way that it maintains a relationship extant among the figures of the other cells of the matrix.
      2. Dominoes: Insert a domino into a pattern of dominoes in accordance with the rules of the game and in such a way as to extend the pattern.

   C. Ma, Associative Memory, as measured in:
      1. Recall Paired Associates: Picture-number. Recall a number that had been paired with a picture.
      2. Recognition Paired Associates: Landmarks-names. Match (recognize) names with landmarks, as previously paired.

   D. Ms, Span Memory, as measured in the tests indicated for factor M below:

II. Gc, Crystallized Intelligence: Involving processes of perceiving relationships, reducing correlates, reasoning, abstracting, concept attainment, and problem solving, as measured primarily in unspeeded tasks involving various kinds of content (semantic, figural, symbolic), but content which clearly represents relatively advanced education and acculturation either in the fundaments of the problems or in the operations which must be performed on the fundaments. Good measures of the dimension include the following primary mental abilities.

   A. V, Verbal Comprehension, as measured in:
      1. Synonyms Vocabulary: Select the best synonym for a word from among five choices.
      2. Information Recall: Provide the correct answers to a wide range of questions pertaining to matters of fact as reported through the mass media.

   B. Rs, Syllogistic Reasoning, as measured in:
      1. Nonsense Syllogisms: Indicate which conclusion follows from stated premises which, however, are nonsensical.
      2. Inference: Select the most justifiable conclusion to be drawn from a set of statements.

---

* There are a few other major dimensions that might be listed here. However, some, such as carefulness, have a more nearly temperamental or motivational quality than the qualities of an ability, and for others, such as Broad Auditory Ability, the factor analytic evidence is not yet sufficient to warrant conclusion that the ability is both broad and independent of the other dimensions noted above.

Source: From S. Gershon and Allen Raskin, "Aging and Intelligence," *Aging: Genesis and Treatment of Psychologic Disorders in the Elderly, 2,* pp. 23–24. © 1975, Raven Press, New York.

Table 3.1: *Measurement and Process Descriptions of Major Dimensions Indicated by Second-Order Factoring Among Primary Mental Abilities*

    C. R, General Reasoning, as measured in:
        1. Arithmetical Reasoning: Solve word problems of a kind similar to those presented in elementary algebra courses.
        2. Ship Destination: Use rules of a game and information about wind direction and velocity, ocean current direction and velocity to calculate time to port.

    D. Mk, Mechanical Knowledge (when sample is all male), as measured in:
        1. Tools: Indicate use intended for a wide range of tools.
        2. Mechanical Principles: Choose correct answer to indicate knowledge about mechanics, use of tools, etc.

III. Gv, Broad Visualization: Involving imagining the way objects may change as they move in space, maintaining orientation with respect to objects in space, keeping configurations in mind, finding the Gestalt among disparate parts in a visual field, and maintaining flexibility concerning other possible structurings of elements in space. Good measures include the following primary mental abilities.

    A. Vz, Visualization, as measured in:
        1. Punched Holes: Show how holes in folded paper would appear after paper is unfolded.
        2. Clocks: Indicate how clock would look after having been rotated in several ways.

    B. Cs, Speed of Closure, as measured in:
        1. Gestalt Completion: Write the name of an object depicted only in part.
        2. Peripheral Span: Identify letters flashed in the periphery of the field of vision.

    C. Cf, Flexibility of closure, as measured in:
        1. Embedded Figures (Gottschaldt Figures): Indicate whether or not a given geometrical figure is embedded in a complex pattern.
        2. Hidden Pictures: Find shapes and forms hidden in the lines and shadows of a drawing.

IV. Gs, Broad Speediness: Involving quickness in simple repetitive writing and checking tasks in which there is little complexity. Good measures are

    A. P, Perceptual Speed, as measured in:
        1. Finding Letter "a": In columns containing four-letter words, check words containing the letter "a."
        2. Number Comparisons: Indicate whether two multidigit numbers are the same or different.

    B. N, Number, as measured in:
        1. Adding: Add up sets of numbers.
        2. Checking: Check sums, products, subtractions to see if they are correct.

    C. W, Writing Speed, as measured in:
        1. Copying: Copy by writing a simple sentence as many times as possible in a time limit.
        2. Printing: Print a set of words as fast as possible.

V. F, Broad Verbal Fluency: Involving a facility in quickly bringing many ideas, words, word parts, sentences, and paragraphs from long-term memory into immediate awareness. Good primary ability measures include

Table 3.1: *Measurement and Process Descriptions of Major Dimensions Indicated by Second-Order Factoring Among Primary Mental Abilities*

   A. Fa, Associated Fluency, as measured in:
     1. Controlled Associations: Write as many words as possible similar in meaning to a given word.
     2. Associations of a Pair: Produce a word similar in meaning to two given words.

   B. Xs, Spontaneous Flexibility, as measured in:
     1. Uses: List as many uses as possible for a common object (e.g., a brick).
     2. Object Naming: List as many objects as possible belonging to a certain class.

   C. Fe, Expressional Fluency, as measured in:
     1. Letter-Star: Write as many k-word sentences as possible when the first letter of each word is provided.
     2. Simile Interpretations: Complete sentences so they will express idea analogous to that in another sentence.

VI. M, Immediate Memory: Involving an ability to immediately reproduce (within less than 30 seconds) information presented either auditorily or visually. Good measures include

   A. Ms, Memory Span, as measured in:
     1. Auditory Digits Backward
     2. Visual Letters Backward

   B. Mr, Nonsymbolic Recognition Memory, as measured in:
     1. Tonal Memory: Indicate whether or not a second tone is the same as a prior tone.
     2. Chords: Chose from among three piano chords the one that is the same as a test chord.

In this study measures of crystallized intelligence were more highly dependent upon verbal abilities than were measures of fluid intelligence.

Cross-sectional studies using PMA and WAIS tests

Schaie (1958) administered the Primary Mental Abilities (PMA) test to subjects ranging from age 20 to 70. Fifty subjects were drawn from each of ten 5-year intervals (20 to 25, 26 to 30, and so forth), resulting in a total of 500 participants. In this cross-sectional study, the five subtests administered were verbal meaning, space, reasoning, number, and word fluency. Performance differences among the various age groups on the five measures may be seen in Figure 3.2. It may be observed that no significant age-related decline is exhibited on any subtest until approximately age 50. However, all subtests show an overall pattern of age-related deterioration. Likewise, a systematic pattern of decline may be seen in the composite of the five measures presented in Figure 3.3. Again a pattern of steady, uninterrupted decline does not manifest itself until approximately age 50.

Many age and intelligence studies have used the **WAIS (Wechsler Adult Intelligence Scale)** to measure verbal and performance abilities (Doppelt and Wallace, 1955; Eisdorfer, 1963; Eisdorfer, Busse, and Cohen, 1959; Har-

Figure 3.2: *Performance differences among various age groups in the Primary Mental Abilities test.*

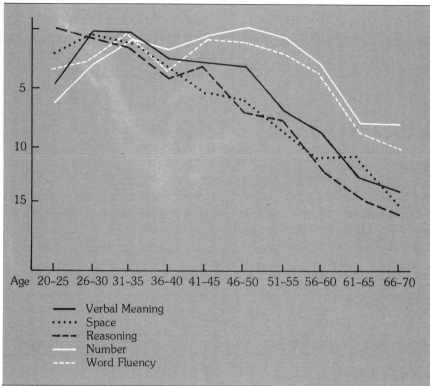

Source: From K. Warner Schaie, "Rigidity-flexibility and intelligence: A cross-sectional study of the adult life span from 20 to 70 years," *Psychological Monographs, General and Applied, 72,* No. 9, Whole No. 462, 15. Copyright 1958 by the American Psychological Association. Reprinted by permission.

wood and Naylor, 1971; Birren and Morrison, 1961). The WAIS is an individual intelligence test composed of 11 subtests; 6 subtests are verbal and 5 are performance. Combined verbal and performance scales result in full-scale measures from which full scale IQs are computed. Examples of verbal subtests are information, comprehension, and vocabulary. Examples of performance subtests are object assembly, picture completion, and block design. Success on performance subtests, unlike the verbal subtests, is not highly dependent upon the individual's linguistic ability. Performance measures tend to reflect what has been defined as fluid intelligence. Verbal measures are largely measures of crystallized intelligence.

On the basis of many cross-sectional studies using the WAIS, a classic aging pattern in reference to verbal and performance abilities has evolved. This classic aging pattern is characterized by declines in both verbal and performance measures in conjunction with increased age. However, performance decrements are significantly more pronounced than are verbal. It was concluded that although the overall performance of elderly individuals is

Figure 3.3: Age changes in the Primary Mental Abilities test.

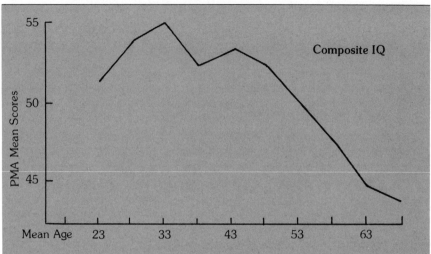

Source: From K. Warner Schaie, "Rigidity-flexibility and intelligence: A cross-sectional study of the adult life span from 20 to 70 years," *Psychological Monographs, General and Applied, 72,* No. 9, Whole No. 462, 14. Copyright 1958 by the American Psychological Association. Reprinted by permission.

inferior to that of younger cohorts, verbal abilities tend to be less sensitive to age than are performance abilities. This superiority of verbal over performance measures has been observed repeatedly among older populations and is replicated in many studies. The classic aging pattern derived from WAIS measurements is shown in Figure 3.4 (page 59).

Schaie's 1956 longitudinal study

In 1956 Schaie and his associates began a longitudinal study designed to investigate the intellectual functioning of the same individuals over an extended period of time. Thirteen measures of intellectual ability were initially obtained from 500 subjects whose ages ranged from 21 to 70 years. Using the same measures, 301 subjects (significant attrition occurred) were assessed 7 years later in 1963. Upon completion of the 1963 testing, two sets of 13 scores had been obtained from each subject who had continued in the study. Using factor analysis (a statistical technique), four relatively independent intellectual dimensions were generated from the 13 measures of intellectual ability. These dimensions were labeled and defined as follows:

1. *Crystallized intelligence* encompasses the sorts of skills one acquires through education and acculturation, such as verbal comprehension, numerical skills, and inductive reasoning. . .

Figure 3.4: Mean sums of verbal, performance, and full-scale scores for age groups in national and old-age samples.

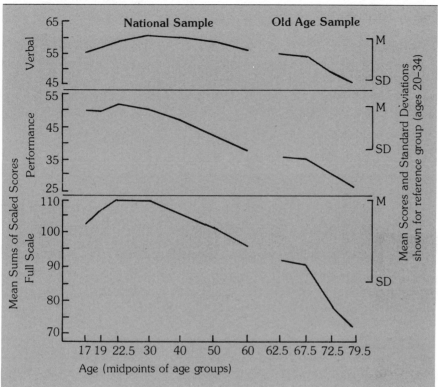

Source: Doppelt, J. E., & Wallace, W. L. Standardization of the Wechsler Adult Intelligence Scale for older persons. *Journal of Abnormal and Social Psychology,* 1955, *51,* 323.

2. *Cognitive flexibility* measures the ability to shift from one way of thinking to another, within the context of familiar intellectual operations, as when one must provide either an antonym or synonym to a word, depending on whether the word appears in capital or lower-case letters.

3. *Visuo-motor flexibility* measures a similar, but independent skill, the one involved in shifting from familiar to unfamiliar patterns in tasks requiring coordination between visual and motor abilities, e.g., when one must copy words but interchange capitals with lower-case letters.

4. *Visualization* measures the ability to organize and process visual materials, and involves tasks such as finding a simple figure contained in a complex one or identifying a picture that is incomplete. (Baltes and Schaie, 1974, pp. 35–36)

In Figure 3.5, longitudinal age-related patterns of performance on these four ability dimensions are shown. Focusing upon the dark, unbroken lines, it would appear that all measured intellectual dimensions decline as a function of increased age. Likewise, the unbroken line used to graph data obtained

Figure 3.5: Comparison of cross-sectional (1956, 1963) and 7-year longitudinal gradients on four ability dimensions.

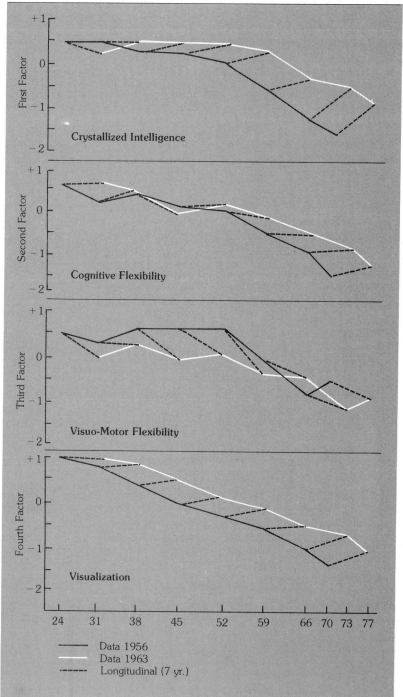

Source: Nesselroade, J. R., Schaie, K. W., & Baltes, P. B. "Ontogenetic and generational components of structural and quantitative change in adult cognitive behavior." *Journal of Gerontology*, 1972, 27, No. 4, 225. © 1972, Gerontological Society.

from the follow-up testing in 1963 appears to show a pattern of intellectual loss as a result of aging. However, these unbroken lines do not indicate intellectual changes that result from the aging process: they represent differences in intellectual performance between various age groups or cohorts. Viewed in this manner, it is apparent that older subjects tended to perform less well on all measures of intelligence than did younger subjects. However, this information has been obtained repeatedly from numerous cross-sectional studies. The critical finding of this study is represented by the broken lines or dashes that connect the two unbroken lines. These broken lines are used to compare the earlier and later performance of each age group with itself. Upon close examination of these connecting lines, we can see distinct improvements in measures of crystallized intelligence and visualization across the entire age span under consideration. That is, upon retesting 7 years later, the performance of each age group improved in terms of these dimensions. Although cognitive flexibility does not appear to be highly related to age across the entire age span, definite improvements are noted as individuals approach and enter later maturity. Only the visuo-motor flexibility dimension shows a definite age-related decline. This might suggest that as an individual grows older, he or she may become progressively handicapped when required to execute tasks demanding rapid changes involving visual-motor coordination.

A subsequent report on the previously discussed longitudinal study reported in detail by Nesselroade, Schaie, and Baltes (1972) is important to our understanding of the relationship between aging and intelligence for a number of reasons. Initially, findings indicate that many intellectual differences observed between various age groups cannot be attributed to growing old. Rather, such differences may reflect cohort or generational characteristics. Secondly, data suggest that the normal aging process does not diminish an individual's ability to solve problems, to employ novel approaches, or to adopt an attitude of mental flexibility. According to Baltes and Schaie:

> On at least *some* dimensions of intelligence, particularly the crystallized type, people of average health can expect to maintain and even increase their level of performance in old age. (1974, p. 36)

As a result of this study, previously accepted beliefs concerning age-related intellectual decline have been seriously challenged. Is it possible that intellectual decline in later maturity is largely a myth? Finally, this study has prompted gerontologists and developmentalists to scrutinize previously accepted research methodology and to further examine established "truths" concerning old age.

Other longitudinal studies

Although convincing evidence in opposition to age-related decrements in intelligence has been put forth by the longitudinal research of Schaie and his associates, certain longitudinal studies add credence to the age decline hypothesis. Eisdorfer and Wilkie (1973) administered the WAIS to two groups of subjects (ages 60 to 69 and 70 to 79) on four occasions over a period of ten years. On each occasion, verbal, performance, and full-scale scores were obtained for each subject. At the start of this study, 61 subjects were in the 60 to 69 sample and 37 subjects were in the 70 to 79 sample. For the younger group 35 subjects were available for all testing sessions. For the older group 15 individuals were able to participate throughout the entire course of the study. The results of this study generally agree with the intellectual age-decrement hypothesis. Between the initial and final testing sessions, significant declines on full-scale scores were exhibited by both age groups. For the younger sample (60–69), declines on performance measures were significantly greater than were declines on measures of verbal abilities. However, for the older sample (70–79), declines on both verbal and performance scales were significant but not markedly different from each other. Data derived from this research point to an age-related pattern of intellectual decrement with verbal abilities proving more resistant to decline than performance abilities. Results also suggest that a general decline in all intellectual abilities may occur in conjunction with advanced old age.

Evidence from sequential developmental studies

Using sequential developmental techniques (combined cross-sectional and longitudinal methods), Schaie, Labouvie, and Buech (1973) executed a 15-year study of intellectual functioning in which data were obtained from subjects tested in 1956, 1963, and 1970. From the original 1956 sample (N–500), 161 subjects were available for testing in 1970. In this study measures of verbal meaning, space, number, reasoning, and word fluency from the PMA test were obtained. In addition, motor-cognitive rigidity, motor speed, and personality-perceptual rigidity were measured. The results of this study indicated that some intellectual abilities decline in association with increased age and suggested that the hypothesis of intellectual decline could not be rejected absolutely. According to the researchers:

> Three of the primary mental abilities, verbal meaning, space, and reasoning, exhibited a consistent rise indicating that successive cohorts achieve higher performance on these abilities. This positive generational change was less dramatic for number. Word fluency, in contrast to the other primaries, exhibited a reversed pattern: There appears to be negative generational change over the 1889 to 1910 birth years . . . Educational aptitude, as was true for its component abilities verbal meaning and reasoning, also showed a consistent rise from earlier to more recent cohort levels . . . Two of the factors, personality-perceptual rigidity and motor-cognitive rigidity, again showed positive gains from cohort to cohort . . . Psychomotor speed, exhibited similarly to word fluency, a dramatic dual pattern of both negative and positive generational change. As on word fluency, there were successive performance losses from 1889 up to the 1910 cohort; then, the gradient showed a drastic reversal with impressive cohort-to-cohort gains for the 53-year-olds. (Schaie, Labouvie, and Buech, 1973, pp. 161–162)

According to Horn and Donaldson (1976), some results obtained by Schaie and associates are compatible with the previously discussed theory of fluid and crystallized intelligence. Viewing verbal meaning and number as representative of crystallized intelligence and reasoning, space, and flexibility as indicative of fluid intelligence, Horn and Donaldson argue that a differential age-related change in the two major dimensions can be detected.

> . . . there is suggestion that for V [verbal meaning] and N [number] there is at least some upward development in the early adulthood period (through age 50), but that for R [reasoning] and S [space] the curves are more consistently and steeply downward. Assuming that these latter represent fluid abilities, the results might be interpreted as indicating a somewhat later decline in Gf [fluid intelligence] than has been indicated in most previous research. Thus, a modification in the Gf-Gc [fluid intelligence–crystallized intelligence] theory might be called for. (p. 710)

On the basis of this study, Schaie and his associates were also forced to modify their stance in reference to the relationship between aging and intelligence. No longer could the notion of age-related decline in intellectual functioning be categorically rejected. Certain developmental changes were clearly demonstrated. However, in contrast to the previously established and generally accepted pattern of early intellectual decline (beginning in early adulthood), results indicated that age-related decrements appear relatively late in life.

> When age and cohort differences are compared over 7-year intervals, it becomes evident that reliable age changes (with the exception of the highly speeded word fluency measure) cannot be observed prior to age 67. (Schaie and Parham, 1977, p. 650)

Conclusions

On the basis of cited research, what conclusions may be drawn concerning the relationship between age and intelligence? Although few if any definitive conclusions can be reached, evidence tends to support a number of broad hypotheses concerning age-related changes in intellectual functioning. First, it would appear that the following statement made by Baltes and Labouvie (1973) may be accepted without reservation:

> The evidence presented is not sufficient to make precise statements about the nature of ontogenetic [developmental] changes in intellectual performance, but is certainly rich enough to seriously challenge the often-stated stereotype of a general performance decrement during later adulthood and old age. (p. 171)

Overall intellectual decline can no longer be perceived as an inherent aspect of growing old. Some measured abilities manifest no pattern of decline in later maturity; indeed, some abilities seem to improve with increased age. At this point, there appears little reason to believe that we must anticipate a general loss of intellectual acuity with the approach and onset of old age.

Second, evidence suggests that perceptible age-related decrements in intellectual abilities are not likely to be exhibited until the fifth or sixth decade of life. It would seem that the hypothesis of overall intellectual decline beginning in early adulthood might be replaced with a hypothesis of differential change with selective declines occurring in later maturity.

Third, on the basis of available data, it would appear that certain abilities are more sensitive to aging than are others. In general, performance abilities are more likely to suffer age-related declines than are verbal abilities. However, although performance abilities appear relatively susceptible to the effects of aging, pronounced declines in these abilities frequently are not manifested until advanced old age.

Finally, it may be stated that many intellectual differences previously attributed to the aging process are, in reality, reflections of differences between various cohorts. Although older generations often obtain lower scores on measures of intelligence than younger generations, such performance discrepancies cannot be explained in terms of increased chronological age.

What Factors Might Affect Our Intelligence As We Age?

How we behave or perform is influenced by a number of factors. Our behavior might be influenced by factors such as time of day, persons with whom we are in contact, noise level, or hunger. Because such factors influence performance, they also influence measures of intelligence. However, although our behavior is affected by various factors, is it accurate to assume that our intellectual abilities are also influenced? Recognizing that a number of significant factors affect performance, close attention must be given to the effects of intrinsic and extrinsic variables that may operate to change or modify performance upon tests of intellectual ability. When intelligence tests are administered to the elderly, potentially influential factors should be noted and given consideration. Among such factors are response speed, level of education, test-taking sophistication, general health, social forces, and environmental conditions.

Response speed

Many measures of intelligence are dependent upon an individual's ability to respond to a physical or mental stimulus with speed and accuracy. Most tests of intelligence also impose strict time requirements and give no credit for correct answers if such answers are not emitted within a specified time period. For example, if an individual completes a WAIS block design item correctly but exceeds the allowed time limit, that person is given no credit for successful performance. The score given that individual would be the same as that given the individual who could not complete the design successfully. When employed to assess intellectual abilities, could tests requiring subjects to respond with speed operate to the disadvantage of the older population?

Likewise, could such tests reflect an inaccurate picture of the actual intellectual abilities of the older person?

As a person ages, a physiological change occurs that results in a slowing down of reaction time or an increase in time required to respond to various stimuli. With advanced age, neural impulses that had previously traveled at approximately 140 miles per hour gradually slow to approximately 110 miles per hour. As a result of this physiological change, sensory cues or information are received, processed, and reacted to more slowly. We do react more slowly as we grow older. However, in terms of intellectual functioning, we must ask whether increased reaction time can legitimately be equated with diminished mental abilities. This is a subject of debate among various researchers.

Are intelligence tests that demand speeded responses generally unfair to the elderly population? Addressing this question, Doppelt and Wallace (1955) administered the WAIS to older subjects (age 60 to 75) using speeded (timed) and unspeeded (untimed) procedures. On the basis of this study, no significant differences were noted between the performance of elderly individuals who worked under time restrictions and those who did not. Again using the WAIS, Klodin (1976) repeated Doppelt and Wallace's study but extended it to include young subjects (average age 22 years). Under untimed conditions, it was observed that the performance of younger subjects did not improve as much as the performance of older subjects (average age 73 years). However, even under conditions that did not impose strict time requirements, the performance of older subjects did equal that of younger subjects. It was suggested that on selected performance subtests of the WAIS, elimination of speeded conditions may function to reduce the absolute magnitude of differences between various age groups. However, relative age group differences persist regardless of time impositions.

Educational level

A second factor that may operate to modify performance on intelligence tests is educational level. Research (Birren and Morrison, 1961; Green, 1969) indicates that educational level and intellectual performance are more highly correlated than age and intellectual performance; that is, the performance of individuals of similar educational backgrounds, regardless of age, tends to be more alike than the performance of individuals drawn randomly from the same age category. The relatively high correlation between educational level and intellectual performance may be traced to initial similarities in ability level as reflected by educational attainment. This correlation may be traced, in part, to the fact that many tests of intelligence are strongly weighted with items that draw upon information obtained within formal learning situations.

In some situations there may be confusion between physical ability to perform certain intellectual tasks and mental ability to execute these tasks. Thus intellectual performance may be modified by physical handicaps unrelated to intrinsic cognitive functioning. In this context, handicap refers to any internal condition that may operate against the individual's optimal performance upon whatever task is undertaken. A common example of such a performance handicap is fatigue. As an individual becomes tired within the testing or performance situation, behavior is likely to suffer. However, such an observed decline in functioning is the result of fatigue rather than basic changes in intelligence. Although we know that elderly people tend to become fatigued more quickly than do younger people, this factor is often ignored when attention is given to age-related changes in cognitive functioning. A person who is tired will behave less effectively than a person who is not tired. When individuals who become fatigued at different rates are compared, those who tire more quickly have a definite performance handicap. By ignoring this, and similar handicaps, there is always the possibility of obtaining faulty data from age-intelligence research.

Test-taking sophistication

Another factor that may function to modify intellectual performance is the degree of test-taking sophistication. Within our society, degree of test sophistication tends to be a function of age. Older people often have had less formal education than have younger people, have had less exposure to controlled evaluation situations, and lack familiarity with the demands and procedures of standardized testing. Lack of familiarity with testing procedure and requirements could result in less than optimal performance among the elderly. If you can remember your first test using computerized response sheets, you should be able to appreciate what is meant by the effect of test sophistication upon performance. In most cases, such first "computerized" attempts prove confusing and result in less than maximal performance. Although you may have known required material, your ability to present it was negatively influenced by your lack of test sophistication. However, your inability to effectively present required material in no way altered the fact that you had mastered it. There was, nevertheless, a resulting discrepancy between performance and ability.

Health, social conditions, and intellectual environment

In old age, individuals who have chronic physical disabilities, particularly those resulting from strokes or any condition involving a progressive reduction of blood to the brain, will usually exhibit a marked decrease in intellectual acuity. **Arteriosclerosis,** or hardening and narrowing of the vascular system (which can affect young as well as old), is a major cause of intellectual decline in old age. Some researchers believe that when the disease is conquered, our entire concept of mental loss in old age will undergo radical change.

In addition to health, social conditions may operate to hasten intellectual decline. If a person becomes isolated from other people, has little opportunity for meaningful interpersonal contacts, and becomes generally divorced from accustomed social interactions, in all probability, mental abilities will show evidence of decline. In part, intellectual decline resulting from social deprivation may be traced to accompanying changes in personality, motivation, and reality orientation. Older people who remain in the mainstream of life, who continue to pursue and initiate normal social contacts, and who remain personally involved with others, are far less likely to experience intellectual decline than are elderly individuals who are cut off from others and endure prolonged periods of social isolation. The previous statement is equally valid when applied to most human beings regardless of chronological age. We are social animals, need the company and companionship of other people, and when deprived of social contact will tend to react in a negative manner.

Finally, the characteristic degree of environmental complexity which affects the elderly person appears to be related to changes in intellectual functioning. Individuals who continue to operate within a stimulating, challenging environment, who maintain an active interest in learning, and remain involved in a variety of interesting and rewarding activities, are less likely to manifest signs of mental deterioration in old age. Moreover, individuals who live within an environment characterized by deprivation or a general lack of stimulation are more likely to experience a decline in intellectual functioning. It is important that a relatively interesting or stimulating environment be maintained throughout later maturity. Recognition of this fact has provided the impetus for many social, educational, and religious programs specifically designed to supply learning experiences, create a challenging atmosphere, and provide a variety of stimulating activities to those who have reached old age.

Summary

Certain fundamental concepts concerning intelligence are basic to our understanding of this mental construct: (1) Intelligence is an emotional subject about which few people maintain absolute objectivity. (2) Intelligence is a hypothetical construct created by human beings for purposes of explanation and reference. (3) Intelligence is inferred on the basis of observed behavior. (4) Inferences concerning intelligence can never be more than guesses based on probability. (5) Estimates of intelligence are derived from samples of behavior. (6) Behavioral samples may or may not be accurate reflections of intelligence.

Although intelligence and IQ are separate concepts, some individuals mistakenly perceive them as synonymous. IQ is the numeric label most commonly used as a designation of intelligence. IQ may or may not provide an accurate estimate of intelligence. Because intelligence is composed of many abilities, investigations concerning relationships between age and intellectual functioning must begin with precise definitions of those intellectual abilities under consideration.

There is much confusion concerning the subject of intelligence and aging. Much of this confusion may be traced to research methods and sampling techniques used to investigate the relationship between aging and intelligence. An understanding of the differential influence of various research methods and sampling techniques upon data obtained and conclusions drawn is fundamental to our interpretation of age-intelligence literature.

On the basis of cited research, the following conclusions concerning the relationship between age and intelligence can be drawn: (1) Overall intellectual decline cannot be perceived as an inherent aspect of growing old. (2) Perceptible age-related decrements in intellectual abilities are not likely to be exhibited until a person is 50 or 60 years old. (3) Certain intellectual abilities are more sensitive to aging than other abilities. (4) Many intellectual differences previously attributed to the aging process are reflections of differences between generations.

Many factors may operate to modify measures of intellectual performance. Among such factors are response speed, educational attainment, test-taking sophistication, physical condition, social deprivation, and environmental stimulation. The extent to which such factors may affect performance is not always exactly known.

Progress Check

1. Why is intelligence called a hypothetical construct?   (p. 44)

2. Why are estimates of intelligence always subject to error?   (pp. 44–45)

3. What is the difference between intelligence and IQ?   (pp. 45–47)

4. Why is it impossible to make statements concerning age-related changes in intelligence on the basis of cross-sectional data?   (p. 48)

5. What factors might confuse or bias results derived from longitudinal studies?   (p. 49)

6. What is the difference between random and matched sampling? (pp. 50–51)

7. How might sampling techniques influence data derived from age-intelligence studies?   (p. 51)

8. On the basis of available data, defend the proposition that intelligence does not decline as a function of increased age.   (pp. 52–64)

9. What is the difference between crystallized and fluid intelligence? (p. 52)

10. Cite five factors that may influence performance on psychological instruments estimating intelligence.   (pp. 64–67)

11. On the basis of your knowledge, what do you think is the relationship between intelligence and age?

Recommended Readings

Baltes, P. B. & K. W. Schaie. Aging and IQ: The myth of the twilight years. *Psychology Today*, 1974, 7, 35–40.
The authors suggest that the widespread assumption that intelligence declines with increased age may be quite erroneous. Various factors that operate to produce the appearance of age-related intellectual decline are discussed and criticized.

Horn, J. L. Psychometric studies of aging and intelligence. In S. Gershon & A. Raskin, eds., *Aging, Vol. 2: Genesis and Treatment of Psychologic Disorders in the Elderly.* New York: Raven Press, 1975.
The author presents his conceptualization of the major dimensions of intelligence (crystallized and fluid) and presents research evidence in support of age-related differential declines.

4

Aging and Learning

Preview ∾ *In the following chapter we will introduce the concept of learning, differentiate between learning and performance, and examine the effects of certain noncognitive factors upon performance. We will also consider the role of transfer in learning and emphasize the relationship between learning and memory. Memory will be introduced as a three-stage process, two types of memory and retrieval will be discussed, and various factors that may hinder memory in old age will be presented. Finally, procedures designed to enhance memory in later maturity will be discussed. The major intent of this chapter is to promote a critical attitude toward age-related research in learning and memory.*

Exactly what is learning? Let us consider first a definition drawn from Webster's Third New International Dictionary.

> *Learning: (a) To gain knowledge or understanding of a skill in a study, instruction, or experience; (b) to develop an ability to, or readiness of, by practice, training, or repeated experience; (c) to become aware; (d) to acquire through experience, practice, or exercise.*

How Can We Define Learning and Performance?

The preceding definition of learning emphasizes acquisition of some quality (knowledge, understanding, ability, awareness) as a function of some experience (study, instruction, practice, exercise). Learning is an internal process resulting from external influences. Although this definition of learning is adequate for use in most situations, for purposes of research and psychological investigation, learning must be defined in terms of some performance criteria that can be used as a basis for inference regarding internal cognitive changes. Cognitive changes are those involving intellectual and mental experiences and processes. Because we cannot observe learning directly, scientific inquiry demands the presence of some observable feature upon which statements regarding learning may be founded. With this in mind, the following definition of learning will be employed for purposes of discussion.

> Learning refers to the change in a subject's behavior to a given situation brought about by his [or her] repeated experiences in that situation, provided that the behavior change cannot be explained on the basis of native response tendencies, maturation, or temporary states of the subject [e.g., fatigue, drugs, etc.]. (Hilgard and Bower, 1975, p. 17)

This definition emphasizes the **performance** (external acts or behavior) aspects of learning rather than the inferred internal processes that may underlie changes in behavior. Likewise, it focuses upon a number of factors (fatigue, drugs, maturation) that may influence behavior but do not, in themselves, constitute learning.

The need to differentiate between learning (internal) and behavior (external) is fundamental to all research concerned with age-related changes in learning. According to Botwinick (1973), failure to make this distinction has resulted in erroneous conclusions regarding learning ability in later maturity.

> Much of what in the past has been regarded as a deficiency in learning ability in later life has more recently been seen as a problem in the ability to express learned information. In other words, much of what has been thought of as a deficiency in the internal cognitive process is now seen as a difficulty older people have in adapting to the task and in demonstrating what they know. (p. 218)

Does Performance Always Reflect Learning?

Although researchers must use behavior as a gauge of learning, it is generally recognized that our performance may or may not constitute a valid representation of learning ability or mental acquisition. However, this contingency is handled within our definition by the qualifier, "provided that the behavior change cannot be explained on the basis of native response tendencies, maturation, or temporary states of the subject" (Hilgard & Bower, 1975, p. 17). Woodruff and Walsh (1977), in an attempt to explain discrepancies that may occur between observed behavior and internal learning process, make a distinction between **cognitive** (intellectual or mental) and **noncognitive** (not related to intrinsic intellectual and mental experiences and processes) factors influencing performance.

> The observer can see only the act and not the process; he [or she] must infer that learning ability is poor when—little or no improvement [is observed] in performance after training. It is possible for this inference to be wrong because the poor performance may be a result of noncognitive factors such as poor motivation, lack of confidence, or poor conditions of training. The extent to which we have information about such noncognitive factors will lead us to be more correct in our inferences regarding learning. (p. 425)

These researchers suggest that some observed age-related changes in learning may be a function of noncognitive performance factors rather than exclusively a product of internal cognitive processes.

Psychologists and other investigators concerned with the subject of age-related changes in learning are faced with a dilemma. Briefly stated, learning is an internal process that cannot be observed directly. For this reason, inferences concerning learning must be derived from observations of behavior or performance. However, depending upon a variety of noncognitive factors, our behavior may or may not accurately reflect internal cognitive or mental processes (learning). Upon consideration of this dilemma, it is suggested that individuals interested in studying learning must be interested in studying performance. In addition, those interested in performance must be concerned with individual and environmental factors that could render behavior an invalid indicator of learning.

Learning, like intelligence, is an extremely broad concept that encompasses many categories of behavior and demands many inferences regarding the operations of various mental processes. We do not simply learn in a general sense. We learn specific tasks, information, and skills, such as to talk, to swim, to solve abstract problems. Depending upon the type of learning undertaken, different cognitive strategies and abilities will be employed. Moreover, personal and situational variables will operate to produce learning environments that are somewhat unique to each individual. That is to say, there is no way to be sure that the learning environments of any two people are identical, or even comparable. For these reasons, questions concerning age-related changes in learning ability must focus upon specific types of learning with special consideration given to the environment in which each occurs. Can "old" people learn as well as "young" people? It all depends upon what is being learned and what are the conditions of learning.

As recently as 1960, most research in adult learning reinforced the notion that general ability to learn inevitably declined as a function of advanced age. Until that time, drastic age-related declines in learning ability had been reported repeatedly in the literature. However, in conjunction with such reports, little attention was given to noncognitive factors that might influence performance. Variables that might produce discrepancies between internal mental processes (learning) and external manifestations of internal processes (performance) were generally ignored. Likewise, few researchers suggested that perceived declines in performance were not necessarily indicative of declines in learning ability. For example, Gilbert (1941) tested a number of age groups using various tasks involving learning and memory. When compared to their younger counterparts, a performance deficit on all tasks was noted among older subjects. The most marked decline was exhibited on tasks requiring **paired-associate learning**—learning associations or relationships between pairs of verbal cues—for example, woman/lamp, tree/basketball. Without consideration of noncognitive factors or the possibility of discrepancies between performance and learning ability, it was concluded that learning ability declines with age. For decades, this, and similar conclusions, were accepted without serious question or reservation. As a result, the negative stereotype regarding age-related decrements in learning ability gained credibility and was endowed with scientific respectability.

What Are Some Noncognitive Factors That Affect Performance?

During recent years, most age-related studies in learning have incorporated the manipulation of one or more variables in an attempt to ascertain the influence of noncognitive factors upon task performance. Among the noncognitive factors considered have been pacing, anxiety, the meaningfulness of the learning material, differences in learning procedures, and distraction within the learning situation.

Pacing

Pacing refers to variations of rate and speed within the performance situation. A number of different variations are possible. Canestrari (1963), using paired-associate tasks, investigated the effect of pacing (time permitted to respond) upon performance. The performance of younger (17–35 years) and older (60–69 years) subjects was measured under three pacing conditions (1.5 seconds, 3.0 seconds, and self-paced). When subjects were self-paced, unlimited time to respond was allowed. In addition to varying task pacing, a distinction between **errors of omission** (no response at all given) and **errors of commission** (incorrect response given) was made. Upon comparing the performance of younger and older subjects, it was found that fewer mistakes were made by younger subjects under all experimental conditions. However, as pacing was slowed (1.5 to 3.0 seconds), older subjects showed greater improvement than did younger subjects. Moreover, when self-pacing was permitted, age differences were smallest. Focusing upon differences in types of errors, Canestrari observed that older subjects showed more improvement in errors of omission than did younger subjects under the self-paced conditions. However, both age groups made less errors of omission under the 3.0 second condition than under the 1.5 second condition. Commission errors were not significantly influenced by pacing.

Studying the relationship between pacing and task performance, Eisdorfer (1965) manipulated two experimental variables, time permitted to study and time permitted to respond. Using serial learning tasks (learning a list of items in a specified order, for example, floor, metal, green, happy, cat, and pencil), it was observed that the performance of older subjects improved as a function of less rapid pacing of study and response conditions. Also, errors of omission decreased as time permitted to respond increased. However, the positive relationship between decreased errors of omission and increased time to respond did not continue beyond the 10 second mark. Essentially, subjects who were unable to respond correctly within 10 seconds were unlikely to exhibit successful performance regardless of additional time taken.

In another study conducted by Eisdorfer (1968), the relationship between pacing (time permitted to respond), time taken to respond, and errors of omission was investigated using serial learning tasks. This study confirmed the previous finding that under conditions of slow pacing, errors of omission declined among the elderly. However, perhaps the more interesting finding of this study was that under slow pacing conditions subjects were generally able to respond within time limits imposed by rapid pacing conditions. That is, when older subjects were allowed unlimited time to respond, this allowance did not increase time taken to respond. Under slow pacing conditions, rapid paced responses were the rule. This finding led researchers to assume a relationship between rapid pacing and the imposition of debilitating anxiety. Could rapid pacing induce high levels of anxiety among the elderly and result in decreased rates of response?

Using paired-associate tasks and permitting self-paced responses, Canestrari (1968) investigated the relationship between rate of presentation of materials to be learned and task performance. In this study, each verbal pair was presented for one second but intervals between presentations were varied according to experimental conditions (0.0, 0.5, or 5.0 seconds). Although the performance of younger and older subjects improved when the presentation rate increased from 0.0 to 0.5 seconds, only the performance of older subjects exhibited continued improvement within the 5.0 second experimental condition.

Kinsbourne and Berryhill (1972), studying the relationship between presentation rate (pacing) and performance, varied time permitted to view (**inspection interval**) paired-associates (2, 4, and 6 seconds). Time between presentations or time permitted to respond (**anticipation interval**) was held constant at 2 seconds. Results of this study may be seen in Figure 4.1. Initially, it may be observed that the performance of the younger subjects was superior to that of the older subjects regardless of inspection interval. In addition, moving from the 2 second presentation to the 4 and 6 second

Figure 4.1: Correct responses under three conditions of pacing over trials (elderly and young subjects).

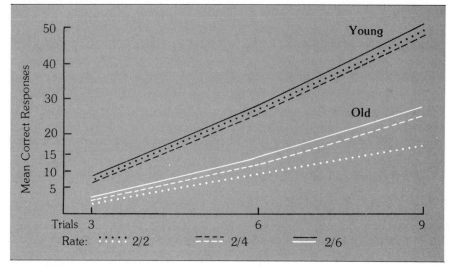

Source: From Marcel Kinsbourne and Judith L. Berryhill, "The nature of the interaction between pacing and the age decrement in learning." *Journal of Gerontology*, 1972, *27*, No. 4, pp. 471–477. © 1972, Gerontological Society.

presentations, a slight improvement in the performance of the elderly sample may be noted. However, this improvement in performance was not significant and no age-related pacing effect on performance was found in association with varied inspection intervals. Amount of time permitted to view materials to be learned did not differentially affect the performance of younger and older subjects. On the basis of this study, the researchers concluded that "rate of acquisition of new information decreases with advancing age" (p. 476).

Varying length of anticipation and inspection intervals, Monge and Hultsch (1971) studied age-related differences in paired-associate learning. In this study, there were two age groups (20–39 and 40–66 years), three anticipation intervals (2.2, 4.4, and 6.6 seconds) and three inspection intervals (2.2, 4.4, and 6.6 seconds). As usual, the performance of the younger group was generally superior to that of the older group—even though the older subjects were middle-aged rather than elderly. Data suggested that length of the anticipation interval was significantly related to observed age differences. The performance of younger subjects was not significantly affected by varying the anticipation interval. The performance of older subjects, however, exhibited a decline under conditions of reduced anticipation (2.2 seconds). However, an age-related difference in conjunction with varied inspection interval was not demonstrated. Regardless of age, performance improved when trials involved longer inspection intervals. According to Monge and Hultsch:

. . . the two intervals (anticipation and inspection) interact neither with each other nor jointly with age. This implies that the total time available per item (i.e., the sum of the anticipation and inspection intervals) is not differentially important to people of different ages. Only that portion of total time allotted to the anticipation interval makes for age differences. (1971, p. 161)

This study suggests that one critical age-related, noncognitive factor affecting performance may be time permitted to respond rather than time permitted to learn. This significant relationship between age and anticipation interval had been noted in earlier studies (Eisdorfer, Axelrod, and Wilkie, 1963; Arenberg, 1965) and constitutes an important contribution to our understanding of the relationship between age and learning.

Age and pacing conclusions. Although all questions pertaining to interactions between age and pacing have not been answered (or posed), the critical nature of this noncognitive factor in reference to learning is strongly supported by available research evidence. Several investigations show that the performance of older subjects is usually inferior to that of younger subjects regardless of pacing. Investigations also show that whereas errors of omission are affected by pacing, commission errors are not significantly influenced. Under conditions of slow pacing, errors of omission tend to decline among the elderly although time taken to respond does not increase significantly. When time permitted to respond or time between presentations (anticipation interval) is increased beyond an absolute minimum, performance of older and younger subjects improves. Yet when anticipation intervals are further expanded, performance continues to improve among the older subjects but not among the younger subjects. A significant relationship appears to exist between anticipation interval and age. No such relationship, however, has been noted between inspection interval and age. This suggests that response time, rather than study time, is an important age-related factor influencing performance. Finally, research shows that among the elderly, best learning performance is exhibited under conditions of self-pacing.

Anxiety

In addition to pacing, another noncognitive factor that is known to influence learning performance is anxiety. As previously stated, it has been suggested that performance declines among the elderly under rapid pacing conditions may, in part, be attributed to elevated levels of anxiety that negatively affect behavior. Investigating the relationship between anxiety level (arousal) and learning performance, Powell, Eisdorfer, and Bogdonoff (1964) used serial learning tasks. In this study, free fatty acid (FFA) levels, measures of heart rate, and measures of galvanic skin responses were used as indicators of arousal or inferred anxiety. Blood samples to be analyzed for FFA were taken from subjects before, during, and after participation in the learning situation. Throughout this experiment, higher FFA levels were observed among older subjects than among younger subjects. Moreover, throughout this experiment, the performance of older subjects was inferior to the performance of younger subjects. Following the learning task, it was observed that though FFA levels of older subjects continued to rise, FFA levels of younger subjects did not. Powell et al. concluded that the older sample was more involved in the learning task than the younger sample and therefore experienced a higher degree of arousal (autonomic activation). It was suggested that older people may experience more anxiety (arousal) within experimental learning situations than do younger people and that such anxiety may prove an impediment to optimal performance.

A link between age and anxiety. Eisdorfer, Nowlin, and Wilkie (1970) conducted an experiment in which an attempt was made to eliminate anxiety or arousal as a factor influencing learning performance in old age. In order to accomplish this goal, a sample of elderly men were administered the drug Propranolol which blocks or suppresses autonomic activity without modifying cognitive or mental processes. Another group of elderly men (controls) were given **placebos** (sugar pills) which would have no inherent effect upon performance. Again, FFA levels were used as measures of arousal. The investigators found that following administration of the drug, FFA levels dropped and learning performance improved (errors decreased). Such changes were not exhibited by the control (placebo) group. The idea that reduced arousal would result in improved learning performance was substantiated. The performance, as measured by number of errors, of the placebo group was inferior to the performance of the drug group. The placebo group made more errors. It was concluded that many learning deficits observed among the elderly may be attributed to overarousal within the experimental learning situation. Because a sample of younger subjects did not participate in this study, no conclusions concerning age-related differences could be drawn.

In a study by Powell, Buchanan, and Milligan (1975) blood pressure was used as an indicator of arousal. In this, as in most previously cited studies, overall task performance of older individuals was inferior to that of younger individuals. However, not in keeping with Eisdorfer's findings, data indicated a positive correlation or relationship between superior performance among older subjects and elevated measures of arousal. Superior performance among the elderly was found in association with higher blood pressure levels. Although results derived from this study may appear to contradict previous studies involving FFA levels, it should be remembered that anxiety cannot be observed directly and must be inferred. For this reason, anxiety may be operationally defined in different ways. At the present time, although specific physiological responses are clearly indicative of autonomic arousal, it is not clear which specific physiological responses are indicative of anxiety. Although physiological changes may be noted and measured, anxiety and its effects upon performance must be inferred. On the basis of cited studies, a relationship between arousal and performance may be conjectured. However, it would appear that the general concept of arousal can be employed with equal force to explain either inferior or superior performance exhibited by older individuals within the learning situation.

Meaningfulness of learning material

A third noncognitive factor that may affect performance is meaningfulness of learning material. A problem inherent in many laboratory learning experiments is the lack of meaningful material to be learned. In such contrived or experimental situations, tasks are frequently boring, tedious, and devoid of personal significance. In general, verbal learning tasks such as those previously discussed (paired-associates and serial) are not reflective of "real life" learning situations and may not inspire maximum personal commitment and involvement. In the absence of personal commitment and involvement, task performance is unlikely to be a valid indication of learning ability. Hulicka (1967) found that elderly subjects were much more likely than younger subjects to "drop-out" of learning situations involving nonmeaningful or "nonsense" material; for example, learning paired associations between stimulus letters such as *SP* or *PM* and words such as "happy" or "plant." In this study, the drop-out rate among elderly subjects reached 80 percent. Reluctance to exert themselves in the pursuit of nonsense learning was generally expressed. However, when material was made more personally meaningful (replacing stimulus letters with significant names), older subjects willingly participated and persevered. Still, it must be noted that even under "meaningful" conditions, the performance of the older sample did not equal that of the younger.

Witte and Freund (1976) conducted research in which younger and older subjects were presented with concrete (more meaningful) and abstract (less meaningful) paired-associates. In this study, as may be observed in Figure 4.2, the concreteness effect was greater for the older than for the younger sample. Within the elderly sample, performance under concrete conditions was superior to performance under abstract conditions. This difference was not observed within the younger sample. Again, under both experimental conditions, overall superior performance was exhibited by the younger group.

In studies involving the acquisition of meaningful and nonmeaningful materials, age-related discrepancies in performance tend to decrease when meaningful material is introduced. This would suggest that when younger and older individuals are compared on tests such as rote learning of nonsense syllables, the performance of the younger group will be far superior to that of the older group. However, when different age groups are compared using meaningful material such as performance in a university course, learning a new card game, or mastering directions to a new location, discrepancies should diminish. At the present time, there is a need for age-related research involving the learning of materials that are truly meaningful as opposed to those that are artificially contrived. On the basis of available data, it would appear that when older individuals perceive a learning task as person-

Figure 4.2: Mean correct responses per trial to paired-associates with concrete and abstract stimuli (elderly and young subjects).

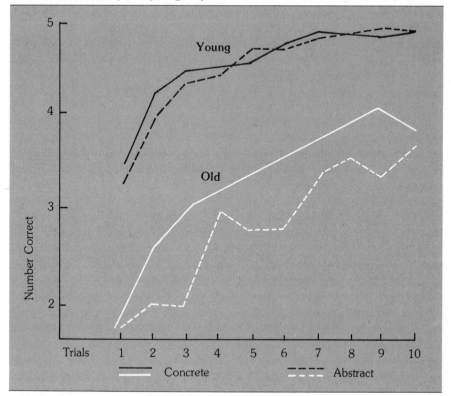

Source: Witte, K., & Freund, J. "Paired-associate learning in young and old adults as related to stimulus concreteness and presentation method." *Journal of Gerontology*, 1976, *31*, 190.

ally meaningful, they tend to exhibit greater interest, sustain better long-term effort, and utilize experiential background more effectively.

Differences in learning procedures

Research also suggests that performance discrepancies between younger and older subjects may, in part, be traced to differences in learning procedures employed by various age groups. Hulicka and Grossman (1967) found that older subjects were less likely than younger subjects to use **mnemonics** (techniques used to aid memory; for example, remembering *Every Good Boy Does Fine* in order to learn the treble scale). Other studies indicate that elderly individuals are less likely than younger individuals to use visual and verbal mediators or relationships in associative learning (Hulicka and Grossman, 1967; Rowe and Schnore, 1971). It has been conjectured that older people have greater success with concrete rather than abstract tasks because the demand for mediators is less pronounced when associations are made between concrete pairs. Canestrari (1966) found that paired-associate learning among the elderly improved as associations between pairs became stronger. For example, an individual would be more likely to learn "good/bad" with greater ease than "good/green." Also, the overall performance of elderly subjects improved significantly when verbal or visual mediators were provided within the learning situation. Yet, despite improvement with the provision of mediators, performance of elderly subjects did not equal that of younger subjects. It would seem that although differences in learning procedures and strategies may partially account for discrepancies between the performance of younger and older subjects, such differences, by themselves, do not totally explain age-related decrements in task performance.

The importance of instructions.   Ross (1968) investigated the effects of challenging and supportive instructions on the verbal learning of older individuals. In this study, two age groups (18–26 years and 65–75 years) were given paired-associate tasks using three experimental conditions (neutral, supportive, and challenging instructions). In the supportive condition, the following instructions were given.

> I need your help with a research project that I am doing for Columbia University. . . . I am interested in finding out something about the characteristics of words. Your performance is *not* my main concern. My purpose in asking you to do this task is just to find out which words go together more easily and which do not. (p. 263)

In the challenging condition, the following was said.

> I am doing a research project for Columbia University. . . . The ability to learn this material is a good test of your intelligence, not of what you know but of how well you can learn *new* things. It's to your advantage, then, to do your best to show how capable you are, how bright you are in relation to people of your own age. Listen carefully and do your best, for your score will be compared with those of other subjects. (p. 263)

Two learning tasks involving easy (common) and difficult (uncommon) pairing were given to each subject.

In this study, the task performance of the older sample was inferior to that of the younger sample under all instruction conditions. However, of greater interest is the fact that under challenging conditions, elderly subjects exhibited a significant drop in performance on the difficult or uncommon task. This drop was not demonstrated by younger subjects. In her discussion, Ross suggested a link between performance decrements and anxiety.

> The increasing insecurity and susceptibility to stress of aging individuals become particularly evident when they are placed in an evaluative situation and told that their performance will be compared with that of others. (p. 265) . . . Although it cannot be presumed that anxiety per se was responsible for the discrepancy in age groups, it does appear that the older person reacts with nonadjustive behavior in an evaluative situation where his [or her] performance is to be compared with that of others. (p. 266)

Distraction within the learning situation

Finally, it must be mentioned that older individuals are more susceptible to the negative influence of distraction within the learning situation than are younger individuals (Welford, 1958; Broadbent and Heron, 1962). With this in mind, researchers concerned with age-related differences in learning must, of necessity, give special attention to the physical characteristics of the learning environment that may operate to differentially distract subjects and modify behavior. For example, Is the physical environment too hot or too cold? Is lighting adequate? Are there distractions such as noise, movement, and interruptions? Is the learning environment comfortable or uncomfortable, attractive or unattractive, personal or impersonal, intimidating or secure? Although it may be impossible to identify and deal effectively with every factor that may function differentially to influence performance among various age groups, recognition of the relationship between age and susceptibility to distraction should prompt investigators to attempt to control as many potentially distracting variables as possible.

Conclusion

Certain representative studies using human subjects have been discussed with the goal of focusing upon various noncognitive factors that may produce discrepancies between learning and performance. In addition, certain studies have been reviewed with the goal of focusing upon the critical role noncognitive factors play in promoting observed performance differences between various age groups.

Most investigations pertaining to age-related differences in learning and performance involve verbal tasks (Botwinick, 1973). Paired-associate or serial learning tasks are usually employed within such studies. The extent to which information derived from such contrived experimental learning tasks reflects upon the "real" world is not known. A consistent observation from age-related research dealing with verbal learning is that elderly individuals perform poorer than do younger individuals. This situation persists regardless of experimental manipulation of selected noncognitive factors. However, research involving the experimental manipulation of various noncognitive factors suggests that certain age-related differences in performance are not necessarily indicative of age-related differences in learning ability.

Pacing and performance. A number of studies have established a relationship between pacing and performance with the observation that older subjects generally do better under self-paced conditions. However, under conditions that are not completely self-paced, time permitted to respond appears more critical to performance in old age than time permitted to study. When time permitted to respond is increased, performance among the elderly improves. Yet, increased time permitted to respond does not result in increased time taken to respond. This suggests that strict response time demands may involve the imposition of another noncognitive factor, anxiety, that negatively influences performance. Rather than aiding performance, "hurrying" an elderly individual within a learning situation may prove to be impairing. However, there is little reason to believe that failure to hurry an elderly person will increase time taken to execute a task. Just the opposite seems to be true.

Investigations show the differential effect of pacing upon types of errors manifested by the elderly. Under conditions of slow pacing, errors of omission decline and commission errors remain relatively constant. When given more time, the number of responses emitted by elderly subjects increases. This increase is not noted among younger subjects. Hurrying an elderly person to respond may increase the probability that no response will be forthcoming. Conversely, if we want to increase the probability of receiving a reply or response from an older individual, we should reduce time pressure as much as possible. For the best performance, we should permit elderly individuals to work at their own pace.

Anxiety and performance. It would appear that the performance of elderly individuals is more sensitive to the effects of anxiety than is the performance of younger individuals. This is not to suggest that certain levels of anxiety do not affect the learning performance of all individuals regardless of age. However, within objectively similar anxiety-provoking situations, the debilitating effects of anxiety are more likely to be reflected in the performance of older people than in the performance of younger people. However, it is quite possible that objectively similar anxiety-provoking situations may not be subjectively similar. For example, in the presence of a snake (objective anxiety situation), some people experience great anxiety and others experience none (subjective anxiety). It seems that elderly individuals experience more anxiety within the experimental learning situation than do younger people. This difference could be traced to a number of factors such as educational level, previous exposure to testing situations, or familiarity with the learning environment and experimental personnel. If different age groups actually experience different levels of anxiety within the experimental setting, it would be impossible to establish a definite relationship between anxiety and age-related task performance. Unless provoked anxiety is subjectively equal for all age groups, differential age-related effects upon performance cannot be ascertained. At this time, no evidence suggests that levels of anxiety have been held constant for various age groups participating in studies concerned with relationships among age, anxiety, and performance. Within the learning situation, it would appear that experimentally induced anxiety among elderly subjects results in decreased performance efficiency. This is particularly true when learning involves the acquisition of material that is relatively difficult. Nevertheless, high levels of anxiety negatively affect high level learning ability regardless of age. Essentially, it would seem that no definitive statement concerning age-related relationships between anxiety and task performance can be made at this time.

Meaningfulness and performance. Upon consideration of "meaningfulness" as a noncognitive factor affecting performance, it should be recognized that the probability of incorporating truly meaningful experiments is rather low. Indeed, we may ask whether the rote memorization of pairs or lists of words could ever constitute a personally meaningful task. Although studies show that the relative performance of elderly subjects improves when concrete words are substituted for abstract words, do such substitutions make the task more meaningful? It is also debatable whether meaningfulness is increased when words take the place of nonsense syllables. It is suggested that research concerned with age-related relationships between meaningful material and performance concentrate, in the future, upon real-life situations and tasks that have obvious relevance to the learner. Although age-related performance differences have been noted in the acquisition of various verbal cues, to attribute such differences to the presence or absence of meaningful material seems rather arbitrary and somewhat naive.

On the basis of available evidence, we conclude that within the experimental learning situation, (1) task performance of elderly subjects tends to be persistently inferior to that of younger subjects; (2) age-related differences may, in part, be attributed to certain noncognitive factors that operate differentially to influence task performance; (3) whereas noncognitive effects may account for some relative differences in task performance, absolute age-related differences in performance cannot be explained in terms of noncognitive factors.

How Does Transfer Affect Learning Performance?

Research indicates that elderly individuals may be handicapped in the learning of new material by their own previously acquired skills and knowledge (Canestrari, 1966; Zaretsky and Halberstam, 1968). Essentially, what has been mastered and incorporated in the past may function to hinder or interfere with present learning. The interfering effect of past learning upon new learning is referred to as **negative transfer** and may be a major barrier to effective learning in later maturity. With the passage of time, older people have developed and refined long-standing patterns of response that have proven effective over the years and will be called upon within new learning situations. If long-standing patterns of response meet the demands of the new learning situation, there will be **positive transfer**—learning will probably be facilitated. Unfortunately, such established habits may become obstacles to effective performance when the response demands made by the new learning situation are contrary to patterns established within the individual's behavioral repertoire. When this occurs, the elderly individual may repeatedly emit previously acquired behaviors that were effective in the past but now have little utilitarian value. When the elderly learner is confronted with familiar material that is presented in an unusual or unaccustomed manner, the handicap imposed by previously acquired knowledge or skills is likely to become most pronounced. This situation is exemplified by the person who has used a manually operated can opener for 50 years, is presented with a new electric model as a birthday gift, and experiences great difficulty learning to operate the new gadget. After a number of unsuccessful attempts to master the intricacies of the electric can opener, the elderly person finally gives up and returns to the old manual model. Basically, a previously established skill functioned to hinder or impede acquisition of another skill. If the concept of negative transfer is kept in mind, we are more likely to understand the tendency of many older adults to admire, appreciate, and then carefully store away modern devices and appliances that are received as gifts. If the modern appliance serves the same function as something to which the elderly individual is already accustomed, the probability is high that it will never be used. This behavioral pattern exhibited by many older people often produces feelings of frustration and dismay in family members who want the latest and best for elderly members of the clan. However, even in the face of encouragement, criticism, or cajoling, many a grandmother will continue to wash her dishes in the sink as her beautiful new dishwasher stands idly by. Although the age-related effects of negative transfer are not fully understood, it would appear that older adults are more handicapped by previous learning than are younger adults. It is possible that patterns of response that are used over a longer period of time become stronger, prove more resistant to modification, and gradually exert a more potent influence upon behavior than do patterns of shorter duration. Likewise, differences in education, experiential background, and learning set (tendency to approach a task in a particular manner) may also be used to explain negative transfer. Although explanations abound, the relationship between age and negative transfer is not clearly understood.

How Are Memory and Learning Related?

An apparent and close relationship exists between memory and learning. If you are unable to learn, few memories are likely to be stored and available for retrieval. Likewise, a memory deficit will be exhibited in your reduced ability to learn. All research concerned with verbal learning is irrevocably tied to considerations of memory. In addition, most learning research involving human subjects requires individuals to recall from memory some information that has been acquired within a specific experimental setting. From a practical and research standpoint, learning and memory are frequently indistinguishable and usually inseparable.

Distinguishing between learning and memory

Melton (1963) provided an operational basis for distinguishing between learning and memory. According to Melton, learning could be conceptualized in terms of behavioral change resulting from a number of trials or experiences. Memory, however, refers to modification of behavior as a function of time intervals between trials or experiences. In a common learning experiment, number of trials required to master a task is used as a gauge of learning ability. Amount of material retained and retrievable following a specified period of time is often used as a measure of memory.

Although some distinction between learning and memory is necessary for purposes of research, the separation of the two mental constructs tends to be based in utility rather than reality. Memory affects learning and learning affects memory.

Defining memory

Memory is a complex phenomenon not fully understood by psychologists, physiologists, or physicians. It is widely believed that memory is a three-stage process involving the input of sensory impressions **(acquisition),** the recording and storage of such impressions **(retention),** and finally the extraction of that which has been stored **(retrieval).** Depending upon a number of variables, memory may be enhanced or diminished at any point in this three-stage process. It is further believed by many researchers that two distinct types of memory are involved in the remembering of past events. These two types are referred to as **short-term memory** (STM) and **long-term memory** (LTM). Short-term memory is involved in the acquisition, retention, and retrieval of material that is within the temporally immediate environment of the individual, for example, the process involved in remembering a telephone number or oral directions for a relatively brief period of time. Long-term memory is involved when the individual retrieves information that has been acquired and stored in the relatively distant past, for example, remembering what happened on your last birthday, what happened yesterday, or recalling childhood events. Factors such as interference, meaningfulness of material, degree of learning, and motivation will influence both short-term and long-term memory.

In addition to distinguishing between types of memory, a distinction is made between processes involved in the retrieval of information or material. The two major types of retrieval are **recognition** and **recall.** Recall refers to the process of pulling from memory specific information without the aid of contextual cues. Conversely, retrieval requiring the process of recognition simply involves the identification of some information to which one has been previously exposed. When memory is tested using a recognition procedure, the individual may be presented with an array of information and be required to extract from this array those parts that are correct or pertinent. The multiple-choice examination exemplifies memory retrieval requiring recognition. The essay examination demands recall. When asked to choose, most students will opt to take a multiple-choice rather than an essay examination. This preference is probably based upon an intuitive feeling that it is easier to identify material that has been acquired than it is to remember such material without the benefit of cues. Research indicates that this intuitive feeling is quite valid. That is, memory is facilitated if the retrieval technique employed involves recognition rather than recall.

What Happens to Memory in Old Age?

Although it is popularly believed that noticeable memory loss or decline is an inevitable accompaniment of old age, loss of long-term memory is not a characteristic of normal aging. Rather, pronounced memory loss is usually restricted to cases involving physical or mental pathology.

Long-term and short-term memory in old age

For most older people, long-term memory (defined as recognition or re-call of distant events) tends to remain quite stable and the ability to recount incidents that occurred decades before is not unusual. When age-related differences in memory are noted, such differences usually involve short-term memory. That is, people may experience increased difficulty remembering material to which they have been exposed in the relatively recent past. Al-though it is not clear whether decrements in short-term memory can be traced to the acquisition, retention, or retrieval stage, research suggests that age-related declines in short-term memory may be a function of increased susceptibility to interference within the input or acquisition stage (Botwinick, 1970).

A major requirement of short-term memory is that it must be exposed to little or no **interference** (an intervening event or factor that hinders mem-ory). For example, most individuals can remember a telephone number long enough to write it down or to dial if nothing distracting occurs during that time period involving conscious retention of that specific bit of information. However, if prior to committing the number to memory, someone starts a conversation, the doorbell rings, or a cup of coffee is spilled, it is highly probable that the telephone number will be irretrievably lost as a result of interference. Much short-term memory loss noted in later maturity could be ameliorated if attention were given to the minimizing of distractions within the environment of the elderly. By reducing distractions, acquisition would, in all probability, be improved.

The evidence

The critical relationship between learning (acquisition) and memory was demonstrated in research conducted by Moenster (1972). In this study, five age groups ranging from 20 to 94 years were tested using recall of para-graphs of meaningful reading material. Initially, it was observed that learning and memory scores declined as a function of increased age. However, when adjustments for learning scores were made, age differences in memory were no longer exhibited. That is, differences in memory scores appeared to result from different levels of mastery or learning rather than from age. This study suggests that observed age-related differences in memory may in actuality be evidence of learning differences. If this is the case, attention must again be focused upon the potential significance of the acquisition stage upon all memory performance. Is it possible that elderly people remember less because they acquired, mastered, or learned less within the experimental environment? In an attempt to answer this question, research concerned with age-related differences in memory must take care to equate individuals on the basis of learning. In the past, most studies have failed to do this.

Whereas acquisition is highly relevant to consideration of memory in old age, a number of research studies have pointed to retrieval as the critical factor underlying age-related differences in memory (Schonfield and Robertson, 1966; Johnson, 1972; Thomas, 1972). Performance differences on recall and recognition tasks strongly suggest that declines in memory that happen with increased age may be traced to problems occurring at the retrieval rather than the acquisition stage. When older and younger subjects are compared on the basis of recalled material, a pronounced age-related decline inevitably results. Yet, when recognition rather than recall is used to retrieve memories, age-related memory decrements become insignificant and are frequently nonexistent.

It would appear that sensory cues contribute more to the memory performance of older individuals than younger individuals. Moreover, these age-related discrepancies usually become more pronounced when memory tasks are characterized by a complete absence of retrieval cues. At all ages, memories are more accessible when retrieval involves recognition rather than recall. However, in later maturity, the relative facilitating effect of recognition becomes more apparent as age-related deficits in recall become increasingly prominent.

How Might We Improve Memory in Old Age?

There are a variety of ways in which memory might be improved in old age. Four practical methods are (1) to reduce interference, (2) to rely on recognition rather than recall, (3) to make learning materials meaningful, and (4) to allow additional time.

Reduce interference

Short-term memory might be improved in old age if care is taken to reduce interference or distractions during the period in which information is being presented or conveyed. For example, if an older person is talking on the telephone, he or she should avoid leaving radios or televisions operating within the same room. Likewise, when information is being communicated, short-term memory may be enhanced if such information is conveyed within a relatively quiet or nonstimulating setting, for example, within a physician's office rather than in the waiting room or at the receptionist's desk. Provision of an environment that permits complete focus upon pertinent information or material may prove highly conducive to promoting improvements in short-term memory.

Rely on recognition rather than recall

When recognition rather than recall is used to retrieve memories in old age, deficits in memory diminish. Perhaps the most simple and effective use of recognition to aid memory retrieval is exemplified by written reminders such as notes, lists, and schedules. Elderly individuals might keep a pencil and tablet in some convenient location and make immediate note of events, obligations, and demands requiring future recall as they are brought to their attention, for example, medical appointments, birthdates, items needing to be purchased, and social commitments. In so doing, elderly people provide themselves with an accurate memory aid to which reference can be made when needed. Similarly, it is important that the environment of the older individual provide sensory cues that will automatically operate to facilitate memory of potential sources of danger. For example, an elderly person may be less likely than a younger person to remember the presence of a step down or elevational change in his or her walking path. In an attempt to promote recognition of the presence of such a potential source of danger, environmental cues such as lights, brightly painted lines, or signs might be provided. Such cues may effectively work to provide retrieval of information that is pertinent to that particular location and may be needed if the probability of safe functioning within the environment is to be increased.

Make material meaningful

As noted earlier, age-related memory deficits tend to disappear when learning is held constant. With this in mind, it may be suggested that factors operating to improve learning will also operate to improve memory. For example, if meaningful material facilitates learning, meaningful material should enhance memory; that is, material perceived by the individual as meaningful is more likely to be learned and remembered than is material that lacks meaning. With the goal of promoting retention through the facilitation of learning, care should be taken to avoid presentation of nonmeaningful material. In most cases, material or information to be learned may lack meaning for two major reasons: (1) It may be personally meaningless because of an individual's disinterest in the subject or activity under consideration. (2) Information may be presented in such a way that the individual is actually unable to understand or grasp what is being presented. If a person perceives information as boring or lacking relevance, it is unlikely that such information will be learned or retained for any significant period of time. Likewise, if information is presented in a manner that is inappropriate to the individual's educational or experiential background, the probability of learning and retention is significantly reduced.

Enhancing learning and memory. A number of steps may be taken in an effort to enhance learning and memory through the provision of meaningful material. Information presented to elderly persons might, when possible, be related to activities or events in which they are genuinely interested or to which they have a personal commitment. Although adherence to this suggestion is not always feasible, information can always be presented in an understandable and clear fashion. Care can be taken to use vocabulary and terminology that is appropriate to an individual's comprehension level. This level of comprehension or degree of experiential sophistication will, of course, vary from one elderly person to another. It is a grave mistake to assume that you must communicate with all older people using similar vocabularies or on relatively equivalent planes. It should be remembered when communicating with elderly people that they tend to be even less alike than younger people. What is meaningful to one person may in no way be meaningful to another. When possible, the ability of each elderly person to comprehend information should be informally determined prior to attempting to transmit specific information. When this is not possible, try to initiate verbal interactions using everyday language or the vocabulary you would employ within casual social situations—converse as though you were simply communicating with a friend. Within a relatively short period of time, you should be able to determine whether or not your attempts to communicate or transmit information are being met with success. At that point, any needed changes in level of communication may be made. What is important to remember is that when information is presented in a manner appropriate to the comprehension of the elderly individual, meaningfulness will increase and memory will subsequently be enhanced.

Take more time

Finally, in an attempt to better understand and improve memory in old age, it is important that the reality of increased reaction time be recognized and that allowances be made for this observed decline. In later maturity individuals tend to be physically less able to acquire, process, and retrieve information as rapidly as they could during earlier years. Information may have to be presented somewhat more slowly, additional time may be permitted for the processing of information, and increased time may be allotted for retrieval of material previously committed to memory. Just as changes in reaction time may result in mistaken impressions concerning intellectual and learning abilities, so also may such physiologically based changes operate to produce distorted pictures of memory functioning in old age.

Summary

Learning is a relatively permanent change in behavior resulting from experience. Because learning cannot be observed directly, it must be inferred on the basis of performance or behavior. Research concerned with the relationship between learning and age has focused upon a number of noncognitive factors that affect behavior and may promote observed performance differences between age groups. Examples of such noncognitive factors are pacing, arousal or anxiety, meaningfulness of tasks, learning orientation, and distractibility. On the basis of available research, it may be concluded that certain age-related differences in task performance are attributed to the differential influence of noncognitive factors. However, even when noncognitive effects are taken into account, age-related differences in task performance persist. Within the experimental learning situation, elderly individuals consistently perform on a lower level than do younger individuals.

To some extent, elderly individuals may be handicapped in the learning of new material by their own previously acquired skills and knowledge. Negative transfer refers to the interfering effect of previous learning upon new learning. The effects of negative transfer become most apparent in situations demanding unusual or unaccustomed responses to relatively familiar material. Although the relationship between age and negative transfer is not clear, it would generally appear that elderly individuals are more hindered by previously acquired learning than are younger individuals.

Memory is a three-stage process involving acquisition, retention, and retrieval. Two distinct types of memory are short-term and long-term. Retrieval may involve recall or recognition. Although learning and memory refer to different mental constructs, they are, in reality, inseparable. Memory affects learning and learning affects memory.

In later maturity, declines in short-term memory are commonly noted. Age-related decrements in short-term memory may be a function of increased susceptibility to interference, different degrees of learning or mastery, and methods of retrieval. Short-term memory might be enhanced in old age if (1) interference during the acquisition stage is reduced, (2) recognition rather than recall is used to retrieve memories, (3) material is presented in a meaningful manner, and (4) increased time is permitted for acquisition, processing, and retrieval of material.

Progress Check

1. Explain why learning and performance are not synonymous. (pp. 72–73)

2. List three reasons why estimates of learning based upon performance may be incorrect.   (pp. 73–74)

3. List and discuss the effects of two noncognitive factors upon performance.   (pp. 74–80)

4. Discuss the relationship between pacing and types of errors exhibited in later maturity.   (pp. 74–77)

5. In what way might anticipation interval influence performance on intelligence tests?   (pp. 75–77)

6. How might anxiety influence test performance?   (pp. 77–79)

7. Why is it difficult to control anxiety within a test situation? (pp. 78–79; 83)

8. Based upon available studies, how does meaningful material influence performance in later maturity?   (pp. 79–80)

9. List two reasons why the elderly may be more handicapped by negative transfer than the young.   (pp. 84–85)

10. What is the relationship between learning and memory?   (pp. 85–86)

11. Discuss the relationship between short-term memory and interference. (pp. 86–87)

12. List three factors that might negatively affect memory in old age. (pp. 87–88)

13. List three ways in which memory might be enhanced in old age. (pp. 88–91)

Recommended Readings

Canestrari, R. E. Jr. Age changes in acquisition. In G. A. Talland, ed. *Human Aging and Behavior.* New York: Academic Press, 1968.
   The author discusses age-related changes in acquisition as a function of pacing and the use of mediators. A good summary of age-related research involving pacing and mediators is presented in the introduction.

Woodruff, D. and D. Walsh. Research in adult learning: The individual. *The Gerontologist,* 1977, 17, 424–430.
   An excellent analysis of age-related learning research is presented in this article. Particular attention is given to noncognitive factors that operate differentially to influence performance.

5

Aging and the Senses

Preview ≈ *In this chapter we will discuss the relationship between sensory decline and increased chronological age. Age-related changes in hearing, vision, taste, smell, and touch will be considered. We will suggest certain compensatory measures that may be taken to alleviate the negative effects of sensory decline in later maturity. Potential consequences of sensory deprivation resulting from losses in sensory acuity will be considered. We will also introduce the concept of perception, distinguish between sensation and perception, and examine certain age-related differences in perception.*

Each individual's sense organs represent a link between self and the world. Information obtained by human beings from the environment is received by way of one or more of the five senses—sight, hearing, taste, smell, and touch. From these senses, we obtain pleasure, acquire knowledge, receive messages, and derive information we need to maintain our proper orientation within time and space.

What General Sensory Changes Occur?

As an individual grows older, all the sense organs begin to lose efficiency or are negatively affected in some way. With advanced age, our ability to see, hear, taste, smell, and feel declines. No sensory modality becomes increasingly efficient or acute as a result of growing older. The gradual, ongoing process of sensory decline occurs over a number of years and subtle changes in sensory functioning tend to occur imperceptibly. However, for most individuals, accumulated deficits in sensory acuity usually become noticeable at about age 60 and continue to become increasingly pronounced during later maturity.

Unless corrected, any decline in the efficient functioning of one or more of the sense organs will be accompanied by a reduction of information available to the individual from the environment. In some instances, the individual may compensate for reduction in information derived from one sensory modality by making better and more efficient use of those sense organs that remain less impaired. For example, if you lose the ability to see, increased sensitivity to auditory or sound cues may result. This is not to suggest that your ability to hear will actually improve. Such compensatory behavior should not be misconstrued as evidence of increased auditory functioning. Rather, it should be interpreted as evidence of attention shifting from visual to sound sensations. For example, if you close your eyes, within a relatively short period of time you will become aware of sounds of which you were not previously aware. In this situation you have readjusted or refocused your attention. However, your ability to hear has certainly not improved as a result.

The reactions of individuals to declines or losses in sensory functioning are extremely varied. Some individuals successfully compensate for such losses and continue to lead relatively normal lives. Others perceive sensory losses as insurmountable barriers to successful functioning and may become increasingly withdrawn and isolated. Losses in sensory efficiency may be accompanied by feelings of depression, anger, anxiety, and helplessness. Along with declines in sensory functioning, a number of psychological or physical problems may develop. However, no direct causal relationship exists between sensory decline and such negative side effects. To a great extent, psychological or physical problems that accompany declines in sensory acuity are traceable to the unique personality characteristics of each individual, that is, to our ability to successfully cope with life, to constructively deal with stress, to face reality, and to adjust effectively to change. Although sensory decline is a universal reality of later maturity, reactions to such declines tend to vary with the individual.

What Happens to Our Vision As We Age?

As a person ages, four major functions performed by the eye change: (1) **accommodation,** or the ability to see clearly those objects that are far; (2)

acuity, or the ability to see small objects or details clearly; (3) **adaptation,** or the ability to make adjustments to dark and light; (4) **color discrimination,** or the ability to accurately identify, differentiate between, or match colors (Bischof, 1976).

Accommodation

Presbyopia or "old" sightedness (far-sightedness) is a visual deficiency involving loss of accommodation and characterized by inability to attain sharp focus for near vision. Presbyopia is caused by diminished elasticity and increased thickening of the lenses of the eyes (McFarland, 1968; Corso, 1971). These changes result in the progressive inability of the lenses to change slope in order to accommodate for near and far vision. Changes in accommodation that ultimately culminate in presbyopia begin in early childhood and generally continue until approximately age 60 with the sharpest decline occurring between 40–55 years (Brückner, 1967). As a person ages, there is a tendency for reading materials and other matter requiring visual inspection to be held further from the eyes. It is not uncommon to observe a middle-aged or older person holding a newspaper at arm's length in an attempt to help in reading. Such behavior is seldom observed among children or young adults. After about age 60, relatively few individuals experience additional decline in ability to accommodate visually until the advent of advanced old age. However, by the time a person is 60 years old, visual deficiencies involving accommodation usually pose a significant handicap and require correction. In most cases prescriptive eyeglasses prove sufficient to lessen visual losses involving accommodation.

Acuity

Except in instances of disease or pathology, the visual acuity of most adults remains more or less constant until approximately age 40 to 45. However, at that time, most individuals note a marked decline in ability to see small objects or small details clearly (Bischof, 1976). By the time the seventieth birthday is reached, corrective aids designed to improve visual acuity are needed by most individuals. Declines in visual acuity that occur in conjunction with the aging process are attributed to a gradual loss of transparency in the lenses of the eyes accompanied by a progressive reduction in pupil size. As the pupil size decreases and the lenses become increasingly yellow, less light is permitted to enter the eye and a predictable decline in visual acuity results. Aids to visual acuity such as eye and magnifying glasses do much to effectively counter the negative effects of these physiological changes upon the individual's ability to see small objects clearly. In addition, the visual acuity of most older individuals may be improved through the use of proper lighting or intense illumination when needed. However, regardless of specific corrective aids or procedures used, it is not presently possible to restore to an elderly individual the same degree of visual acuity enjoyed during younger years.

Adaptation

Although deficiencies in accommodation and acuity can be lessened using various visual aids, losses in adaptation or the ability to make adjustments to dark and light are not presently correctable. As a person enters later maturity, a greater period of time will be required to adapt to darkness or to become visually acclimated within environments characterized by different intensities of illumination (Bischof, 1976; McFarland, 1968). For example, an elderly person who enters an unlighted room or a dark theater will require significantly more time to become accustomed to the darkness than will a young individual. In addition, the level of adaptation ultimately achieved by the elderly person will not be comparable to that achieved by the young person (Domey, McFarland, and Chadwick, 1960; Birren, 1964; McFarland, 1968). Changes in adaptation may be traced to age-related decreases in pupil size and changes in the functioning of the central nervous system (McFarland, 1968). Although no specific aids (eyeglasses) are available to correct losses in adaptation that occur in old age, a number of measures may be taken to ease the impact of this loss. When an elderly person is moving into an area of intensified illumination, it may be helpful to put on dark glasses before leaving the area of lower illumination. By so doing, required adaptation time will be reduced and the probability of experiencing visual discomfort will be lowered. Likewise, it is recommended that an elderly person sleep in a room that is moderately illuminated (a night light) and that comparable illumination be present in all areas of the home (halls, bathrooms, and kitchen) through which he or she might travel at night. Finally, it is suggested that elderly individuals and those who interact with them recognize and make allowances for changes in adaptation time—take time to wait until delayed adaptation to different intensities of illumination has been achieved, provide intensified lighting to those areas that may pose a potential source of hazard, and travel more slowly when entering or leaving areas characterized by discernible differences in illumination.

Color discrimination

As with adaptation, we can compensate for losses in color discrimination but cannot correct for such losses. During all stages of development, the ability of the human being to discriminate certain colors is superior to discrimination of other colors. Our ability to discriminate greens, blue-greens, and violets is inferior to our ability to discriminate reds, oranges, and yellows regardless of our age. This knowledge underlies the use of reds, oranges, and yellows on warning signs, raincoats worn by children, and most signals demanding rapid and accurate discrimination. During later maturity, the ability of the individual to discriminate reds, oranges, and yellows shows relatively little decline. However, with advanced age (approximately age 70) comes a pronounced decline in ability to discriminate colors that fall within the blue, blue-green, and violet range (Gilbert, 1957). In advanced old age (85+), this deficiency in color discrimination becomes extremely pronounced (Dalderup and Fredericks, 1969). Although the relationship between aging and changes in discrimination is not clearly understood, the yellowing of the lenses of the eyes noted in conjunction with old age may, to a great extent, be responsible for decreases in color discrimination. As a result of this yellowing, light waves of different lengths are differentially filtered; that is, shorter light waves at the blue end of the color spectrum are filtered more than longer light waves at the red-yellow end. As a result of visual deficiencies in color discrimination, some elderly people may have difficulty coordinating color schemes, choosing compatible wardrobe items, and accurately perceiving and identifying objects that display those colors that are most susceptible to discriminatory loss. For this reason, it is advisable that signs designed to direct elderly persons, particularly warning and danger signs, should be prominently placed and executed using red, yellow, and orange—colors that suffer little discriminatory decline in old age. Likewise, some elderly individuals may welcome, and profit from, advice concerning interior decoration and wardrobe coordination. Finally, increased illumination may operate to compensate for some loss in color discrimination occurring in old age. To a certain degree, discrimination of blues, blue-greens, and violets may be improved through the use of intensified lighting.

Summary of changes in vision

Deficiencies in vision exhibited in old age may be traced to a number of physiological changes that take place in the eye. Among such changes are reduced pupil size, loss of lens transparency (yellowing), and reduced lens elasticity. Certain corrective measures may be taken to aid various visual deficiencies. Among such measures are eyeglasses, increased illumination, provision of increased adjustment time, and effective choice of color schemes. Although in most cases, vision cannot be restored to an efficiency level comparable to that experienced in younger years, through the use of various aids and procedures, many changes in vision that occur as a result of the aging process can prove to be little or no handicap to the effective functioning of the elderly person.

What Happens to Our Hearing As We Age?

Of all the senses, sight and hearing exhibit the greatest decline in conjunction with increased age. **Presbycusis** is a general term used to refer to losses in **audition** (hearing) that are observed in old age. As with visual losses, decrements in ability to hear generally progress gradually over a number of years and are frequently so subtle that the individual may not recognize that any loss has occurred. Complete loss of hearing or total deafness is unusual in old age.

Frequency and pitch discrimination

Auditory losses found in conjunction with increased chronological age tend to be selective and are evidenced in declines in sensitivity to a specific

frequency (a physical property of sound) or **pitch** (the psychological correlate of frequency). Generally, most auditory decrements noted among the elderly involve losses in ability to discriminate frequencies or tones that fall within the higher range of hearing. For this reason, older people may have more difficulty understanding what is said by persons whose voices are high pitched than by persons with low pitched voices. For example, an elderly person who has suffered a loss in high frequency discrimination may have more difficulty understanding the higher pitched voice of a child than the lower pitched voice of an adult. Likewise, higher pitched female voices may prove more difficult to understand than lower pitched male voices.

Loss of high frequency sensitivity may show itself in decreased ability to discriminate or perceive certain high frequency consonants such as z, s, g, f, and t (Sataloff and Vassallo, 1966). When this occurs, the elderly person will hear "ave," "ame," "alk," and "pa" when the words "save," "game," "talk," and "pat" are spoken. When confronted with words having two or more high frequency consonants such as "gaze," "first," "stop," and "grass," the ability of the elderly person to accurately discern that which is being said may further deteriorate. As a result of normal speech modulation, the sounds actually heard by the hearing-impaired elderly individual may prove quite incomprehensible.

Physiological and experiential factors

Although men experience significantly greater auditory loss than do women, all adults hear less well as they grow older. This decline in ability to receive auditory messages can be traced to physiological changes that occur within the actual structure of the ear and within the central nervous system. Such changes usually begin at about age 25 and are presently considered inevitable. However, decrements in auditory ability associated with old age are a function of experiential factors as well as predictable physiological changes. Individuals who have been exposed to relatively high intensity noise throughout their life span are more likely to suffer pronounced hearing losses in old age than are those who have lived within relatively quiet or less stimulating auditory environments. For example, persons who have lived within rural settings throughout the course of their lives tend to exhibit less loss of frequency and speech discrimination than do those who have lived within the more noisy urban atmospheres. This relationship between experiential background and loss of hearing ability in old age underscores the concerns of many experts who see the younger generation exposed for prolonged periods of time to high intensity, high frequency music. In all probability, the full effects of such exposure will remain unknown for 50 years.

Measures to improve communication

During the course of communicating with the hearing-impaired elderly, certain measures can be taken to improve understanding. Although it is commonly believed that the auditory comprehension of the hearing-impaired elderly individual will improve if we shout or speak in a loud voice, such is not always the case. Because shouting tends to elevate voice frequency, the ability of some older people to understand what is being said may actually suffer as a result of such behavior. Rather than shouting, a conscious effort might be made to speak using a lower tone of voice, to enunciate clearly, and to slightly reduce rate of speech if necessary. In addition, ability to understand oral messages may be improved if elderly individuals are able to compensate for hearing losses by supplementing auditory cues with visual cues. It is likely that the ability of some elderly people to understand what is being said will improve if they are able to clearly see the lips of the person who is speaking. In situations that make such visual compensatory behavior difficult or impossible, the hearing deficit of the elderly person might become increasingly noticeable and more personally handicapping. In an attempt to facilitate successful compensation for hearing loss, while engaging in conversation, you should take care to directly face the hearing-impaired elderly person or to be situated in such a manner as to assure direct visual contact. Communication and compensatory behavior will be better facilitated by an environment characterized by little background noise or disruption. When communicating, it may be advisable to eliminate sounds from televisions, radios, appliances, or anything that produces noise extraneous to the conveyed message. In so doing, auditory interference will be reduced while making allowance for the increased distractibility frequently noted in later maturity. In group situations characterized by inordinate levels of background noise, it is particularly important that hearing-impaired elderly individuals be seated in a location that permits direct visual contact with the source of communication and minimizes visual and auditory distractions. If this is done, the ability of the elderly individual to accurately perceive messages should improve.

Because hearing losses occurring in old age tend to progress quite subtly, some elderly persons may fail to recognize that a loss has occurred. Decreased ability to perceive what is being said or communicated may be attributed to speech characteristics of those with whom the elderly person is interacting. Others may be accused of not speaking clearly, of mumbling, or of speaking too softly. Naturally, if a person fails to recognize that a significant loss of hearing has occurred, there will be a predictable and understandable failure or reluctance to seek and obtain correction for this deficit. If hearing loss becomes apparent, it may therefore be necessary for those who are close to an elderly person to suggest and encourage the seeking of professional evaluation and help. Corrective devices or aids usually prove highly effective in counteracting the effects of age-related hearing losses.

Finally, it should be noted that though reduced auditory acuity is a pervasive characteristic of old age, hearing loss does not constitute a significant handicap for most elderly persons. Although our relative ability to hear declines in conjunction with increased age, absolute ability to hear usually does not fall below the threshold requisite to normal functioning.

Summary of changes in hearing

The following general statements concerning the relationship between hearing and old age can be made.

Hearing losses that become noticeable in later maturity are the end product of physiological changes that have progressed over the life span of the individual. At this time, such physiological changes are considered inevitable. Changes in auditory ability that become pronounced in later maturity tend to be selective rather than total. Most deficiencies involve losses in frequency or pitch discrimination. Elderly persons who have experienced a hearing loss tend to hear parts of words and may have difficulty accurately perceiving words that have high frequency consonants.

Most hearing losses that occur in later maturity can be corrected. However, if an older individual fails to recognize the presence of a hearing deficit, there may be failure to seek professional help. Many older individuals successfully compensate for losses in auditory acuity by making greater and more efficient use of visual information or cues. Those interacting with the elderly should take care that provision is made for visual cues when needed. In an attempt to facilitate hearing in later maturity, interactions demanding auditory acuity should take place within environments that are relatively free from distractions. Also, those who speak with the hearing-impaired elderly should take care to lower voice pitch, speak at a slower rate, and enunciate clearly.

Hearing losses noted in old age are probably the product of both developmental and experiential factors. The extent to which experiential or environmental factors affect age-related changes in hearing is presently a subject of concern to many investigators.

Finally, though older people do not hear as well as younger people, age-related changes in hearing are usually not handicapping to most elderly persons.

What Happens to Our Sense of Taste and Smell As We Age?

Although taste (**gustation**) and smell (**olfaction**) are separate senses that involve different sensory receptors, they are frequently treated jointly because of the strong functional relationship that exists between the two. We know that our ability to taste various substances is related to our ability to accurately smell such substances. Taste sensitivity declines as a result of losses in sensitivity to smell. The relationship between taste and smell is recognized by most people who have suffered from head colds, temporarily experienced a decline in their ability to smell, and concurrently found their food had become rather tasteless and unappealing.

Smell and taste sensitivity

As a person ages, the ability to smell becomes increasingly susceptible to loss as a result of illness. An elderly individual may often suffer a pronounced and permanent loss of taste and smell sensitivity in the aftermath of an acute illness that has affected the sense of smell (for example, influenza, serious colds, or respiratory ailments). Such losses in taste sensitivity are directly attributable to changes occurring in olfaction rather than changes in gustation. However, it is interesting to note that decrements in the sense of smell that occur in conjunction with illness are not reflected in actual atrophy or deterioration of the neural receptors related to smell. Although a person may no longer be able to detect and identify odors accurately, the physiological cause underlying this change in sensitivity is not apparent.

Relatively little deterioration occurs in olfactory receptors or nerves as a function of growing older. During later maturity, although some evidence points to age-related atrophy of olfactory cilia (sensory receptors related to smell), pronounced physiologically based changes in the ability to smell are not noted (Liss & Gomez, 1958; Corso, 1971). No specific age-related effects upon the sensory receptors responsible for smell have been discovered. Because no relationship between olfactory decline and physiological change seems to exist, little can be recommended regarding correction. At this point, prevention rather than correction must be emphasized concerning olfactory loss in old age.

Relationship between taste and smell

The close relationship between taste and smell was demonstrated in a study conducted by Schiffman (1975). In this study, it was observed that older individuals (average age 76) exhibited less sensitivity to various odors than did younger individuals (average age 19). Likewise, it was noted that the ability of the older individuals to accurately identify various foods was significantly improved when the food odors were artificially intensified. That is, when odor rather than flavor was modified, ability to taste changed. This study suggests that the ability to taste is influenced by many factors and that the bond between taste and smell may be, for practical purposes, indivisible.

The four taste sensations are sweet, sour, bitter, and salty. Each of these taste sensations is received by the human being by way of specialized taste receptors located mainly on various parts of the tongue. A number of experiential factors may operate to accelerate losses in a person's sense of taste. Among these are heavy cigarette smoking, habitual eating of highly seasoned foods, and illness. However, although experiential factors may hasten and intensify loss of taste sensitivity, actual age-related losses in ability to taste may be attributed to a real numerical diminution of sensory receptors or taste buds that occurs in conjunction with growing old. By the time individuals are 70 years old, they have approximately one half the number of functioning taste buds as does the young adult. This loss of functional taste buds begins at about age 50 and often results in a noticeable decline in ability to taste beginning at about age 60 (Cooper, Bilash, and Zubek, 1959). Losses continue throughout later maturity and nothing can presently be done to reverse or halt this process of taste bud deterioration.

Although losses in sensitivity to sweet, sour, bitter, and salty substances occur as a result of the aging process, sensitivity to sweet substances appears to suffer the most marked decline (Bourliere, Cendron, and Rapaport, 1958). As an individual enters later maturity, a tendency to demand greater amounts of sweetening in foods and to consume much greater amounts of sweet substances such as candy, cakes, and pies may be exhibited. Foods that seem inordinately sweet to the young adult may be experienced as quite palatable to the elderly individual. Losses in sensitivity to sweet substances accompanied by dietary modifications may, of course, pose a potential health hazard to the older person. If possible, this increased demand for sweeter foods should be met by naturally sweet edibles such as dates, raisins, or honey rather than by highly processed confections such as cookies, cakes, and pies. The judicious choice of sweets in old age is important if nutritional requirements are to be met and health maintained.

Effect on eating habits

A number of problems may accrue from losses in sensitivity to taste that appear in old age. Food may become less appealing or appetizing and the elderly individual may no longer experience eating as an enjoyable or pleasurable sensation. Consequently, a marked loss of appetite may result and basic nutritional needs may suffer. Without encouragement, some elderly individuals may lose interest in preparing meals, in eating at regular intervals, and in maintaining a balanced diet. A tendency to pick at food, to periodically skip meals, and to supplement the diet with nutritionally valueless foods may develop. As a result of such eating habits, the elderly individual may experience various negative side effects of a physical or psychological nature. The problem of decreased sensitivity to taste is further compounded by the fact that many older individuals are required to stay on diets devoid of seasonings and condiments to which they have become accustomed (for example, salt- and sugar-free diets). Such dietary restrictions operate to further reduce the potential pleasure derivable from eating. Older individuals, when faced with such dietary restrictions, may be required to eat foods that are relatively tasteless (according to most people's evaluation) or contrary to their accustomed patterns of eating. In such situations, a predictable loss of interest in the consumption of food may result.

Essentially, nothing can be done to correct deficiencies in taste that occur in later maturity as a result of physiological changes in taste receptors. No corrective devices such as those available for hearing and vision are available. In an attempt to compensate for declines in taste sensitivity, the older individual may become more liberal in the use of seasonings, adding increased amounts of salt, pepper, sugar, and other condiments. Such dietary modifications may operate effectively to increase the intensity of taste stimuli and may result in a subjective taste experience comparable to that derived from less seasoned foods in earlier years. If no dietary restriction is placed upon the increased use of desired seasonings, their liberal use can do much to promote the attractiveness of food and to encourage maintenance of positive eating habits. To assume that an elderly person desires or can tolerate only bland food is a mistake.

Summary of changes in taste and smell

Basically, it is recognized that pronounced changes in taste and smell frequently occur in later maturity. Changes in taste are directly traceable to physiological changes in sensory receptors related to taste. A well-defined physiological link to declines in ability to smell, however, has not been established. Both olfaction and gustation may be subjectively improved through the provision of intensified sensory stimulation. However, at this time, deficiencies in taste and smell cannot be corrected and declines in these two sense modalities appear to be inevitable.

What Happens to Our Sense of Touch As We Age?

Specialized neural receptors responsible for the **tactile** sense (touch) are located within the three layers of the skin. For this reason, the skin is often referred to as the sense organ responsible for touch. However, it is more accurate to think of the skin as a housing for sensory receptors rather than as an actual sense organ. Specialized neural receptors located within the skin are sensitive to five types of stimulation: cold, heat, touch, pain, and pressure. Thus, three types of receptors are sensitive to tactile stimulation and two types of receptors are sensitive to temperature stimulation. In this context, sensitivity to touch refers to a specific tactile quality involving the perception of an object as a result of bringing it briefly in contact with the body. The use of the term "touch" in this context should not be confused with the more generic use which encompasses all five tactile and temperature sensitivities.

Of the five major sense modalities—vision, hearing, taste, smell, and touch—least is known concerning the physiological dynamics underlying modifications in the sense of touch that occur as a result of aging. Most available information regarding age-related changes in the sense of touch is derived from subjective reports from elderly and young individuals. The majority of research concerning our ability to detect temperature and tactile stimuli has been dependent upon personal reactions, subjective evaluations, and individual opinions. To some extent, the extremely subjective nature of such research casts doubt upon the validity of its results and conclusions. At the present time, there exists a great need for empirically based research concerned with the sense of touch and its relationship to the aging process.

Sensitivity to pain

Based upon subjective reports concerning sensitivity to various touch stimuli, it is currently believed that sensitivity to pain shows the greatest decrement in old age. This decreased sensitivity to pain begins to become noticeable at about age 60 (Schludermann and Zubek, 1962). In old age an individual may become less able to perceive externally imposed stimuli that cause pain. When sensitivity to pain decreases, the probability increases that when an elderly person is accidentally injured, this injury may pass unnoticed until incidentally brought to his or her attention. For example, while working in the house or garden, the elderly individual may suffer a bruise or scratch and continue to work unaware that any damage has occurred. It is not unusual for an elderly person to notice a cut or burn on the hand and to be unable to remember when or how it was incurred. As a result of decreased sensitivity to pain, the elderly individual may fail to attend to minor injuries when they happen, may not become alerted to potential sources of harm, and may repeatedly incur similar injuries.

Sensitivity to cold and heat

Whether our sensitivity to temperature increases or decreases as a function of advanced age is presently a subject of debate. However, on the basis of subjective reports and informal observations, it is believed that age-related changes in sensitivity to cold and heat are manifested in three major ways: (1) reduced ability to tolerate extreme temperatures, (2) reduced ability to adapt quickly and efficiently to changes in temperature, and (3) reduced ability to maintain a subjective feeling of body comfort within an environment characterized by moderate and unchanging temperatures. In old age a person may become increasingly subject to fluctuating feelings of warmth and cold even when environmental temperature is held constant.

In later maturity our subjective experience of heat and cold is likely to differ significantly from that of younger individuals. People of different ages "feel" the heat and cold differently. Attempts to compensate for changes in sensitivity to temperature may involve the wearing of clothing that may be taken off or added with ease, for example, sweaters or jackets, changing of thermostat settings during the course of the day, and the addition of special protective apparel when faced with the prospect of extreme temperatures. By employing such simple procedures, it is likely that the elderly individual will experience little or no discomfort as a function of decreased ability to adapt effectively to temperatures that fluctuate or remain constant.

Touch sensitivity

Studying touch sensitivity, defined as ability to accurately identify or perceive objects brought in contact with the hands, Thompson, Axelrod, and Cohen (1965) compared the performance of younger subjects (18–34 years) with that of older subjects (60–77 years). Subjects were required to examine by touch a number of objects and to match these objects with representations that were visually displayed. In this study, older subjects were less able to accurately match tactually examined objects with visual representations than were younger subjects. However, because other variables were incorporated in this study, for example, ability to match and ability to visually scan, the extent to which the observed deficit may be attributed to decrements in touch sensitivity is not clear.

Changes in the sense of touch that occur in conjunction with the aging process tend to be specific to each of the five separate types of neural receptors and occur at different rates and in different intensities. For example, changes in sensitivity to pain may progress more rapidly than do changes in sensitivity to heat or cold. Likewise, changes in the five separate types of neural receptors responsible for the sense of touch tend to vary among individuals according to race, sex, and experiential background.

Summary of changes in touch sensations

Relatively little is actually known about age-related changes in the five touch sensations. No relationship has been established between physiological factors and modifications in tactile or temperature sensitivity. Attempts to study age-related changes in touch are confounded by the fact that pain, cold, heat, touch, and pressure are subjective rather than objective experiences. Likewise, pain is a highly subjective concept that is difficult, if not impossible, to quantify or objectify. Stimuli perceived as highly painful by one person will be considered harmless by another. Research concerned with age-related changes in touch are further confounded by the fact that various factors will influence reports of subjective experiences. Some people may have been taught to tolerate pain and say nothing about it. Others may have learned to complain loudly at the first sign of discomfort. Factors such as cultural background, sexual identity, and self-concept may critically influence subjective reports concerning touch sensations. At this time, completely objective research concerned with age-related changes or differences in touch sensitivity is not yet possible.

What Are Some Potential Consequences of Sensory Decline?

The potential consequences of the generalized declines in sensory efficiency that so often accompany old age can be quite devastating. Following is a discussion of a few of the possible changes.

Isolation and psychological adjustment

A major consequence of decrements in sensory acuity is the separating of the elderly individual from experiences that had previously constituted major sources of enjoyment in life. Eating may no longer be the pleasurable experience it previously was. The older person may no longer be able to derive customary enjoyment from watching television, reading books, listening to music, conversing with friends, and engaging in various social functions. As a result of declines in sensory efficiency, the older person may become increasingly isolated from the social and physical environment. A tendency to turn inward or to live within oneself could develop as sensory losses progressively cut off the elderly person from social contact. If the older individual is increasingly deprived of sensory stimulation from social contacts or the physical environment, the probability of developing maladjusted behavioral patterns and personality problems may increase. Psychological maladjustment is a major accompaniment of acute sensory decline among older persons. In many instances providing a highly stimulating environment has proven to be very effective in easing some psychological problems encountered in old age.

Mental acuity

It is well known that optimal functioning of the brain requires that a certain minimal level of sensory stimulation be maintained. When sensory stimulation falls below a minimal level requisite to optimal functioning, our ability to function mentally in an efficient manner will decline. As a result of reduced sensory or informational input, the deprived individual may become confused, have difficulty focusing upon a specific topic or problem, have difficulty maintaining a reality orientation, and, in extreme cases, begin to experience delusions and hallucinations. It is possible that some changes in psychological adjustment and mental ability noted among some elderly people may be the result of decreased sensory stimulation rather than actual developmental changes that occur in conjunction with advanced chronological age.

A definite connection appears to exist between psychological adjustment, mental acuity, and sensory stimulation. Our perception of many personality and cognitive changes that occur in association with old age may undergo alteration with the development of devices that permit efficient functioning of the five sense organs throughout our life span. If losses in sensory acuity can be eliminated, it is quite possible that many problems found in conjunction with old age will vanish.

Sensation and Perception: Two Sides of the Same Coin

Sensation and perception, like learning and memory, are basically inseparable processes. **Sensation** refers to the input or experiencing of physical stimuli, for example, sound or light waves. **Perception** is the processing, mental organization, or interpretation of sensory input, for example, attaching meaning to a word or interpreting certain light waves as the color blue. Although physical stimuli necessary for sensation may be carefully controlled or held constant, perceptions of identical stimuli often vary from individual to individual. For example, a mother may ask her teenager to turn down the record player because it's too *loud;* the teenager may complain that it's already too *soft* to be heard. However, both individuals are simultaneously being exposed to identical physical stimuli. Moreover, if three people are placed in a 70 degree room, one may feel hot, one may feel cold, and the other may feel quite comfortable. Again, sensory stimuli are not varied, but perception is. Although it is generally recognized that individual differences in perception exist and constitute an important factor in considerations of human behavior, causes underlying such differences are not well understood and, in many instances, are unknown. We know that learning exerts a critical influence upon perception, but learning, by itself, does not adequately explain all observed differences. Maturation, health, and temporary mental state also affect how environmental stimuli are perceived. However, these too fall short of providing an adequate explanation for all individual differences in perception. To some extent, perceptual differences in the face of identical environmental stimulation may be explained in terms of each individual's unique ability to receive incoming stimuli by way of the five senses. It is apparent from the preceding discussion of age-related changes in sensory functioning that modifications in the effectiveness of the various sense organs will produce modifications in perception. For example, perception of words will be affected by loss of high frequency sensitivity. Recognizing that little of a definitive nature is known concerning causes underlying differences in perception, care should be taken not to abruptly establish a cause and effect relationship between chronological age and perceptual characteristics when consideration is given to age-related differences in perception. Although perceptual differences among various age groups are frequently reported, the reasons for such differences are far from clear.

Is There a Relationship Between Age and Perception?

Most research concerned with the relationship between age and perception has been executed within the controlled laboratory setting and has concentrated upon vision and hearing. *Flicker fusion* and *illusions* have frequently been employed in studies concerned with visual perception. In studies investigating auditory perception, *click fusion* and *paced transmissions* are commonly used.

Flicker fusion studies

In flicker fusion experiments, the rate of presentation and duration of flashing lights are varied until perceived as a steady or constant beam. The point at which the light appears constant is referred to as critical flicker fusion (CFF). When comparisons are made between younger and older adults, it is repeatedly noted that the point at which flashing lights are perceived as a constant beam is reached sooner for older than for younger people. That is to say, a decrease in CFF threshold characteristically occurs in conjunction with increased age. Reviewing several studies concerned with flicker fusion, Weale (1965) suggested that age-related differences in CFF threshold may be attributed to physiological changes in the lenses and pupils of the eye that are exhibited in later maturity. Lenses become less transparent and pupil size diminishes as we grow older. Although the critical influence of such physiological changes is generally accepted, other factors appear to affect CFF threshold. Some studies (McFarland, Warren, and Karis, 1958; Coppinger, 1955) have established a relationship between levels of illumination, relative duration of dark and light presentations, and CFF. Coppinger found that age-related differences in CFF thresholds were reduced as a function of increased illumination with younger subjects reaching fusion more quickly under conditions of increased illumination. McFarland et al. observed that age-differences in reaching CFF threshold were reduced when the duration of light presentations in relation to dark presentations increased. In experimental conditions involving long light presentations, the CFF thresholds of younger and older subjects were not significantly different. Presently, evidence suggests that age-related differences in CFF may reflect physiological changes that are, to a greater or lesser extent, subject to the influence of various extraneous factors. Likewise, on the basis of flicker fusion research, evidence suggests that the perceptions of youth may constitute a more accurate reflection of reality than do the perceptions of the old.

Click fusion studies

Experiments focusing upon auditory fusion involve presentation of sound clicks to both ears simultaneously. In such research, two sound clicks are presented in rapid succession and subjects are requested to indicate when the two clicks fuse or are perceived as one. As with research involving visual fusion, older adults reached the critical auditory fusion threshold sooner than younger adults. Fewer clicks were noted by older than by younger subjects and inability to discriminate discrete sounds was shown earlier by older individuals. Again, perceptions of younger individuals more closely approximated stimulus reality than did perceptions of older individuals. However, the extent to which auditory fusion differences between age groups is a function of aging is not clear. In a study executed by Weiss (1963), fusion differences tended to disappear when the perceptions of young males were compared with the perceptions of elderly males who were in first-rate physical condition. However, differences persisted when young subjects were compared with older subjects of normal health. It should be remembered that normal or average health in old age does not mean excellent health or an absence of disease. On the basis of this study, it may be concluded that auditory differences that appear to be age-related may be a function of pathology as well as increased age.

Pacing studies

The decreased ability of many older individuals to perceive discrete sounds presented in rapid order is demonstrated in studies concerned with the relationship between speech intelligibility and oral pacing. In old age, the extent to which speech is comprehendible is more highly related to speed of delivery than in youth. With increased age, decrements in intelligibility of speech occur in association with rapid pacing of words. However, no decline in ability to understand ordinary speech or messages that are conveyed under conditions of normal pacing is exhibited. Essentially, in the absence of hearing-impairment, there appears to be little need to promote compensatory behavior in elderly individuals through the use of slow speech. When marked hearing loss is not present, some loss of ability to understand normally paced speech is not noted among the elderly.

Visual illusion studies

Various studies concerned with age-related differences in perception have used visual illusions as a basis for investigation. **Illusions** are special types of perceptions that are inconsistent with physical stimuli from which they are produced. For example, if a group of people look at a level foundation and believe that it is sloping, this is an illusion. Likewise, the reflection of the sky produces an illusion of blue water. Illusions, as misperceptions or misinterpretations of objective stimuli, result from specific qualities within or surrounding what is being perceived, and are influenced by characteristics of the perceiver. Finally, illusions are very special misinterpretations of the real or objective world in that they may be consensually validated, that is, there will be widespread agreement regarding the correctness of the misperception. Figure 5.1 illustrates a few of the more common geometric illusions used in psychological research (see p. 112).

Age-related differences. Age-related differences in susceptibility to illusions are repeatedly encountered in research literature (Pollack, 1969; Wapner, Werner, and Comalli, 1960; Gajo, 1966; Eisner and Schaie, 1971). Using the Müller-Lyer illusion, Wapner, Werner, and Comalli (1960) found that the perceptual accuracy of children and old people was more influenced by illusions than was that of young and middle-aged adults. In this study, individuals were asked to manipulate the line segment with the angles pointing out until it was perceived as corresponding to the line segment with the angles turned inward. Differences between objective stimuli and perceived reality were then determined. Differences between perceived and objective reality were greatest among individuals over 50 years and under 10 years. Using the Müller-Lyer illusion, similar results were obtained by Gajo (1966) and Eisner (1971). In Gajo's study, it was found that a greater susceptibility to visual illusion was exhibited by older adults (60–77 years) than by two groups of middle-aged subjects (30–44 and 45–59 years). A pattern of developmental change in perceptual susceptibility to visual illusions has been observed in various studies using the Müller-Lyer illusion. The effectiveness of the Müller-Lyer illusion appears to decrease from childhood to early or middle-adulthood, but the influence of this illusion upon perception seems to increase as old age is approached and reached.

Figure 5.1: Common geometric illusions used in psychological research.

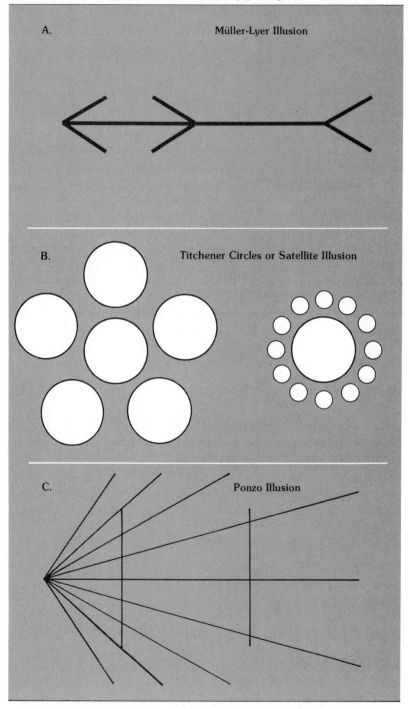

Summary of illusion research. Most research using the Müller-Lyer illusion provides evidence of increased perceptual susceptibility to illusion in old age. Research using the Titchener Circles or satellite illusion has produced contradictory results. In the previously cited study conducted by Wapner, Werner, and Comalli (1960), changes in susceptibility to the Titchener Circles illusion were also investigated. Using the Titchener Circles illusion, an actual decrease in perceptual susceptibility to illusion was exhibited by older subjects. In studies executed by Leibowitz and Judisch (1967) and Farquhar and Leibowitz (1971), a similar decrease in the effectiveness of this illusion was exhibited by older individuals. However, no age-related differences in perception of the Titchener Circles illusion was noted in research conducted by Eisner and Schaie (1971). To further confuse matters, Gajo (1966) reported an increase in susceptibility to this illusion among the elderly. Although the diverse results derived from research using the Titchener Circles illusion may be explained in terms of specific instrumentation, differences in sampling procedures, or variations within the experimental setting, the failure of investigators to consistently replicate results precludes conclusions concerning age-related susceptibility to this illusion. At this time, no definitive relationship can be established between increased age and perceptual acquiescence to the Titchener Circles illusion.

It should be noted that previously discussed studies involving flicker and click fusion are, in essence, studies concerned with differential susceptibility to illusions. Thus, when discrete light flashes or sound clicks are perceived as a single, indistinguishable whole, our perception does not accurately interpret objective reality and is, by definition, illusory. Viewing flicker and click fusion as types of illusions, a clearer relationship may be established between susceptibility to illusions and increased age. Data derived from fusion studies tend to be rather clear-cut. Studies show that with increased age, the illusion of visual and auditory fusion occurs more rapidly and definite age-related differences in susceptibility to illusion are manifested. However, the extent to which perceptual changes occurring in association with variable stimuli may be generalized to static stimuli is unknown. The dynamics underlying susceptibility to illusions arising from static and variable stimuli may be quite similar or entirely different.

Summary

In old age all five senses—sight, hearing, smell, taste, and touch—become less efficient. Decrements in sensory functioning are often noticeable by age 60 and become increasingly pronounced during old age. Although corrective devices (for example, eyeglasses and hearing aids) may effectively counteract the negative effects of certain sensory deficits, some deficits may evoke compensatory behavior in the elderly individual. Through the use of corrective devices and compensatory techniques, adaptation to declines in sensory functioning is achieved.

In later maturity four major functions performed by the eye manifest change: (1) accommodation or the ability to see clearly those objects that are either near or far, (2) acuity or the ability to see small objects or details clearly, (3) adaptation or the ability to make adjustments to dark and light, and (4) color discrimination or the ability to accurately identify, differentiate between, and match colors. Corrective measures designed to ease visual deficiencies include provision of increased adjustment time, eyeglasses, increased illumination, and effective use of color schemes.

Auditory losses found in conjunction with increased age tend to be selective and are frequently exhibited in declines in sensitivity to specific frequencies. Most auditory decrements involve losses in ability to discriminate frequencies that fall within the higher range of hearing. The use of hearing aids may benefit hearing-impaired elderly individuals. Other measures designed to facilitate auditory acuity include elimination of distractions, assuring direct visual contact during communications, and conscious lowering of voice frequency.

The senses of taste and smell are closely related. However, though physiologically based changes in the ability to taste are noted, pronounced physiologically based changes in the ability to smell are not. Although nothing can be done to correct deficiencies in taste or smell, intensification of gustatory and olfactory stimuli may provide some compensation for declines in sensitivity. Problems centering upon health and nutrition may be related to changes in taste and smell.

The sense of touch encompasses sensitivity to cold, heat, touch, and pain and pressure. The physiological dynamics underlying changes in the sense of touch that occur in association with increased age are not well understood. Research concerned with touch is confounded by the fact that pain, cold, heat, touch, and pressure are subjective experiences that are influenced by various personal variables. Although subjective age-related differences in touch sensitivity have been reported, the relationship between age and changes in touch sensitivity is far from clear.

Just as age-related changes in sensation have been noted, so also have age-related changes in perception. A decrease in fusion threshold for light flashes and auditory clicks is exhibited in later maturity. Age-related differences in ability to understand speech as a function of pacing also have been noted. Studies concerned with age-related effects upon susceptibility to illusions have produced contradictory results and are far from conclusive.

Progress Check

1. List and discuss two of the visual changes that often accompany old age. (pp. 96–99)

2. List three ways in which the older person might compensate for losses in visual functioning.   (pp. 96–99)

3. Describe two hearing losses that often occur in conjunction with advanced age.   (pp. 99–100)

4. List three ways in which we might attempt to compensate for hearing losses that occur in later maturity.   (pp. 100–102)

5. Discuss three possible consequences of declines in taste sensitivity occurring in old age.   (pp. 104–105)

6. What functions are performed by the sense of touch?   (pp. 105–107)

7. What are three possible consequences of sensory decline in old age? (pp. 107–108)

8. What is the difference between sensation and perception? (pp. 108–109)

9. Discuss age-related perceptual differences observed in fusion experiments.   (pp. 109–110)

10. What age-related differences in perception have been noted? (pp. 111–113)

11. Give three reasons why sensory acuity is so important to each human being.

Recommended Readings

Corso, J. F. Sensory processes and age effects in normal adults. *Journal of Gerontology,* 1971, 26, 90–105.
Offers an excellent discussion of age-related physiological changes in the five senses and accompanying declines in sensory functioning.

McFarland, R. A. The sensory and perceptual processes in aging. In K. W. Schaie, ed., *Theory and Methods of Research on Aging.* Morgantown, W. Va.: West Virginia University Press, 1968.
A well-integrated presentation of relationships between sensory acuity and perceptual experience. Age-related changes in sensory input and perceptual processing are discussed.

6

Aging and Personality

Preview ∾ *In this chapter personality will be defined, a distinction will be made between core personality and behavioral facade, and the uniqueness of each person's personality structure will be emphasized. Psychological techniques used to assess personality will be presented and various factors that may distort assessments of personality will be considered. We will identify and discuss four major personality types observed in later maturity, discuss "successful" aging from a practical and theoretical perspective, and present various research findings concerned with personality change in later maturity. We will stress the importance of differentiating the "process of aging" from other factors that might produce personality change in old age.*

The concept of personality refers to the psychological composition and characteristic behaviors of the individual as a whole. Personality encompasses those distinguishing mental, emotional, and social traits that contribute to each person's individuality and account for each person's unique adjust-

ments to the total environment. Personality may also be conceptualized as an internal predisposition to respond to various intrinsic and extrinsic conditions in predictable ways. For example, when faced with the prospect of illness or pain, one individual might maintain a stoic or courageous facade, another might become depressed or apathetic, and yet another might become visibly shaken and highly emotional. Underlying each reaction is the unique personality structure of the individual.

Personality: What We Are and What We Seem to Be

In the course of our daily social interactions, we usually observe, and present to others, only those aspects of self or personality that we choose to be made public. Although such public presentations of behavior may accurately reflect an individual's underlying, "true," or **core personality** structure, such is not always the case. For limited periods of time, it is possible for the individual to present a behavioral pattern that in no way validly portrays fundamental character traits. For this reason, we are often unable to accurately assess or understand another person's true personality. Such understanding usually results as a function of prolonged and close contact with a specific individual. Our inability to assess the personality structure of another person may result in disillusionment, surprise, and feelings of dismay or betrayal. It is not uncommon to hear a person say, "I never realized what he was really like until this happened," or "I can't believe how much she has changed since we got married . . . had children . . . graduated from college." In most cases the personality of the individuals about whom such statements are made has not changed as a result of the passage of time. Although they are basically the same, internal and external conditions have operated to modify the behavioral facade successfully maintained for a period of time. In some instances behavior becomes an increasingly accurate reflection of core personality as a result of time and change. In other instances time and change operate to promote manifestations of behavioral patterns that are artificial or "put on." Although we are quick to attach personality labels to other individuals, it is usually a mistake to believe that our understanding of the underlying dynamics (core personality) of another person's behavior and orientation will ever be totally accurate. The extreme complexity of each human being operates against this possibility.

When the subject of personality is discussed, it is generally with the implicit understanding that the total personality structure of the individual can never be fully assessed and that predictions of future behavior made on the basis of knowledge concerning personality traits can never be expected to be perfect.

When we increase our understanding of another person's personality, we gain information concerning accustomed social, emotional, and mental orientation and, as a result of this increased knowledge, make predictions regarding future behavior that are based upon probability. There is always the chance that such predictions will prove to be incorrect.

Personality traits.   When people are placed in a certain personality category or given a particular trait or character label, they are grouped with other individuals with whom certain psychological characteristics are shared. These shared characteristics or traits are deemed important underlying determinants of behavior and adjustment. However, although important psychological traits are shared by members of a group that are placed within a particular personality classification, each individual within that group possesses many characteristics that effectively differentiate him or her from all other members. Regardless of personality classification, each person tends to be highly individualistic. Uniqueness cannot and should not be erased as a result of externally imposed labels. In our discussion of personality and old age, certain personality categories and modes of adjustment common to later maturity will be examined. During the course of this discussion, you should keep in mind that personality categories into which individuals are placed are intended to be suggestive of overall patterns of adjustment and generalized social, emotional, and mental orientation. You should also remember that regardless of personality classification, the uniqueness of each individual persists and is likely to influence behavior in a number of unpredictable ways.

How Is Personality Assessed?

Personality traits or characteristics are most commonly assessed through the use of (1) questionnaires or inventories, (2) projective techniques, and (3) rating scales. When **questionnaires** are employed, the individual provides a self-description by responding to a number of statements pertaining to personal feelings, attitudes, perceptions, and behaviors, for example, "I feel happy most of the time"—True or False. Using **projective techniques** personality characteristics are imposed upon a neutral stimulus. The individual is presented with a picture, design, or configuration and asked, in some manner, to relate what is seen. The theory underlying projective techniques is that people will, in the course of viewing and discussing a particular stimulus, "project" or impose their own personality characteristics onto that stimulus. The joke involving the punch line, ". . . but they're your dirty pictures, Doctor," is based upon the use of projective instruments to assess personality. Finally, when **rating scales** are used, another person evaluates the individual's personality traits either on the basis of prior knowledge or direct observations of behavior. For example, after observing you for a day, I might be asked to rate you on a scale ranging from talkative to silent, sociable to unsociable, or nervous to relaxed.

Personality questionnaires

Three commonly used personality questionnaires are the *MMPI* (Minnesota Multiphasic Personality Inventory), the *CPI* (California Psychological Inventory), and the *16 PF* (The Sixteen Factor Personality Questionnaire). Probably the best known, and most frequently used questionnaire is the MMPI. When given the MMPI, an individual is asked to respond to statements using "true," "false," or "cannot say." Following completion of this instrument, responses are scored and a personality profile is charted. Assessment of personality is based upon the overall configuration of this chart or profile. A major advantage of questionnaires is the ease with which they may be administered. Individuals may read the statements (or listen to a tape recording of the questionnaire) and respond by themselves. The time and attention demanded of professional personnel is minimized. A second advantage is that questionnaires permit self-pacing of responses—a person is allowed to use as much time as needed to complete the instrument. This self-paced quality may be particularly advantageous when evaluations of elderly individuals are being made. Finally, questionnaires are useful when employed as initial screening devices from which information concerning the presence of potential psychological problems or difficulties may be obtained.

Problems and disadvantages.   Although useful in a number of settings, certain problems and disadvantages are noted in conjunction with the use of questionnaires to assess personality. Probably the greatest disadvantage posed by such instruments is their dependence upon the individual's honesty or motivation to respond in a truthful, straightforward manner. Although certain safeguards are built in, when questionnaires or inventories are used, successful faking is possible. Likewise, in the absence of any conscious attempt to fake or lie, some individuals may respond to statements according to how they would like to be or how they think they should be. The ability to respond honestly to statements posed by certain personality inventories is not possessed by all people. To some extent, personality inventories are vulnerable to temporary personal and situational factors that may operate to distort the individual's personality profile, for example, a person may feel depressed on the day of testing or may feel intimidated or anxious within the evaluation setting. Another potential disadvantage is that statements posed may be personally repugnant, offensive, or unacceptable to the individual. Statements pertaining to sexual activities, defecation, and urination are particularly offensive to some people. When confronted with statements that are personally offensive, a negative orientation toward the testing situation may develop and responses may be influenced. Finally, the length of some personality inventories may be a potential source of trouble. For example, when required to respond to 550 statements, a task that may become progressively tedious, some people may—after responding to half the items—begin to respond quickly and with little thought in order to complete the task. Fatigue and tedium may constitute intervening variables that affect assessment of personality when inventories or questionnaires are used.

Projective techniques

Perhaps the best known projective instruments are the *Rorschach* (ink-blots) and the *TAT* (Thematic Apperception Test). When the Rorschach is used, individuals are asked to describe what they see in each stimulus card or to tell what they are reminded of by it. Using standardized scoring procedures, responses are evaluated in terms of factors such as attention to details, descriptions of overall configurations, number of reactions, perceived movement, reaction time, and symbolic content. During administration of the Rorschach, the examiner is permitted to ask questions in an attempt to clarify responses and encourage elaboration. The TAT consists of 30 stimulus cards (pictures) in which various scenes, people, and situations are depicted and one stimulus card that is blank. When the TAT is administered, it is often presented as a test of imagination. Individuals are instructed to view each card and tell a story about what they see. Those taking the TAT are encouraged to relate what feelings, emotions, motivations, and thoughts they may perceive as characteristic of figures portrayed in each picture. Following administration of the TAT and Rorschach, it is recommended that the examiner conduct a follow-up interview for purposes of elaboration, clarification, and confirmation or negation of conclusions based upon the responses.

Advantages.   Projective instruments are invaluable to the clinician whose goal is to gain in-depth information regarding the personality characteristics of a particular individual. During the course of administering a projective instrument, opportunities to observe reactions, emotions, and various behavioral patterns are provided, with the aim of getting to know the person better. Likewise, during administration of a projective instrument, the examiner has an opportunity to establish a positive, productive relationship with the person being examined. In some cases observations and interactions incidental to the actual testing may prove to be more important than specific data derived from the instrument itself.

Disadvantages.   Although projective instruments generally promote better understanding of the individual than do questionnaires, professional time required for administration and scoring of such instruments is significant. It is not unusual for an examiner to devote several hours to one person in the course of administering, scoring, and following-up on a projective instrument. In many instances, this time requirement makes the use of projective instruments impractical. It should be noted that projective instruments should never be placed in the hands of an amateur. A high degree of professional training and sophistication is required of any individual intending to use projective techniques. In the absence of proper training and adequate sophistication, the examiner may actually do harm to the person being evaluated.

Rating scales

In an attempt to assess various personality and character traits, rating scales are used in many situations and by diverse facets of society. When compared with questionnaires and projective instruments, rating scales generally constitute a less formal method of trait assessment. For example, within the classroom, an instructor may give students a scale composed of various characteristics deemed relevant to effective teaching—for example, poise, organization, self-confidence, sensitivity—and ask students to rate the instructor's behavior on a five-point scale ranging from "very low to very high" or "never to always." Likewise, persons given as employment references may receive a scale upon which they are asked to rate an applicant on the basis of certain qualities considered important to success on the job. In both instances an individual's traits are being assessed by an outside observer. Although rating scales have the potential for providing worthwhile information, unless certain conditions are met, information derived from using them is not likely to be meaningful. In the first place, the rater must be sufficiently familiar with the person being rated so that evaluations accurately reflect characteristics under consideration. In many cases, this imperative is not met. The rater either may not remember the individual who is to be evaluated or may have had relatively little contact with that person. Secondly, it is important that the rater understand the particular scale being used, that is, the meaning conveyed by the scale should be precise and opportunities for misinterpretation should be minimized. Finally, maintenance of rater objectivity is basic to the collection of meaningful data from rating scales. If the rater is prejudiced in a favorable or unfavorable direction toward the person being assessed, ratings are not likely to provide much worthwhile information. For example, if an individual has just had a pleasant conversation with the subject who is to be rated, favorable evaluations might result. Loss of rater objectivity is referred to as the **halo effect.**

Personality Assessment in Old Age: Some Cautions

Regardless of what particular assessment technique is used to measure personality characteristics of the elderly, a number of factors may operate to distort our observations and findings. It is not unusual for repeated assessments of the same individual to produce varied results. Such variations arise because evaluators are human (and fallible), because those being assessed are human (and complex), and because personality assessment is not an exact science.

A crude art

Initially, it should be recognized that personality assessment is, at best, a crude art. It is based upon the assumption that underlying mental traits can be identified on the basis of observed behavior and that our behavior provides a valid representation of fundamental attitudinal, cognitive, and emotional predispositions. Our commonsense knowledge of human beings and their behavior tells us that this is not always true. Drawing upon everyday observations, we know that each person tends to behave differently within various situations (manifest different personality traits) and, within similar situations, may exhibit diverse reactions according to various personal determinants of behavior, for example, recent history, temporary emotional state, self-image, and physical condition. Although personality may be characterized by a relatively high degree of stability or constancy, behavior tends to fluctuate and cannot always be considered a highly valid reflection of personality. This is particularly true when short-term observations of behavior are used for assessment purposes.

Honest self-disclosure

In many situations valid assessments of personality depend upon the individual's willingness to engage in honest self-disclosure, that is, to expose certain aspects of self to the scrutiny of others in an undefended or open manner. Such willingness is frequently a function of variables such as sex, intelligence, and age. When comparisons are made between personality characteristics of young and old people, the subject of willingness to engage in open self-disclosure becomes a critical concern. Could willingness to engage in open self-disclosure account for observed personality differences between different generations? To what extent does experiential background influence our propensity to "tell all"? Considering these questions, it must be noted that although much of the present younger generation has been reared within environments that encourage unsuppressed expressions of emotions and attitudes and the talking out of problems, much of the present older generation are products of environments that encouraged keeping personal problems private, placed a premium upon maintenance of a stoic, impervious facade regardless of provocation, and drew a definite line between what one did or did not talk about outside the immediate family. In essence, many older individuals are products of environments in which self-disclosure was unacceptable or discouraged, but presently, honest exposure of self is valued by a large segment of the younger population. It is logical to suppose that this generational difference could account for some observed personality differences between young and old.

Generational attitudes toward psychology

Although not empirically substantiated, age-related differences in personality might be the product of generational differences in orientation toward, and perception of, the discipline of psychology. Although members of the younger generation may possess a generally positive attitude toward the psychological professional and view psychological intervention in a positive light, members of the older generation may be more inclined to question the worth of various psychological techniques, more reticent to become involved with psychologists and psychiatrists, and more likely to view many psychological practices rather negatively. If generational differences in orientation toward psychology do exist, there is reason to believe that elderly and young individuals would respond differently within a psychological evaluation situation. It may be suggested that the relationship between age-related differences in personality and generational differences in orientation toward the discipline of psychology would constitute a fruitful project for a researcher attempting to identify potential factors affecting personality measures in later maturity.

Negative stereotypes

Finally, attitudinal differences toward the young and old may function to distort measures of personality. We know that various negative stereotypes toward the elderly are held by large segments of our society. Individuals involved in the assessment of personality traits among the elderly are not always immune to such stereotypic attitudes. Although psychological examiners are trained to maintain objectivity within the assessment situation, as members of a society in which individuals have been instilled in prejudicial beliefs concerning old people, there is always the possibility that personality assessment of the elderly may be colored, consciously or unconsciously, by preconceived notions and misconceptions. We often see what we expect—or want—to see. Likewise, we often reject that which does not coincide with our previously established ideas and expectations.

What Personality Types Are Observed Among the Elderly?

As a result of intensive, long-term studies conducted by researchers at the University of Chicago (Neugarten and Associates, 1964), our knowledge of adjustment and related personality dynamics manifested in later maturity has greatly increased. These investigators initially sought to establish a relationship between activity level, adjustment, and personality. However, during the course of their research, it was observed that most of the older individuals included in the sample fell into four basic personality patterns. These basic personality patterns or types were given the labels (1) *integrated*, (2) *armoured or defended*, (3) *passive-dependent*, and (4) *unintegrated or disorganized*.

The integrated personality

The majority of individuals, and those showing the most satisfactory adjustment in old age, fell into the integrated personality pattern. These people enjoyed life, and satisfaction with past and present events and experiences tended to be high. The integrated personality had established and maintained affectionate, harmonious social relationships with other individuals, tended to display a good sense of humor, was tolerant of the actions of others, and generally exhibited behavioral and attitudinal flexibility. Although generally open to new experiences and ideas, the integrated personality was not likely to respond to internal or external stimuli in an impulsive, unthinking manner. Such people were likely to weigh the consequences of actions before responding. Critical characteristics of the integrated personality was ability to perceive self in a realistic light, to accurately evaluate past failures and successes, and to rationally assess future prospects. Although the integrated personality may have had some regrets regarding past omissions or actions, such regrets were accepted philosophically and did not pose a threat to positive functioning and adjustment in the present or future. Self-assertiveness was a behavioral characteristic frequently exhibited by the integrated personality. However, self-assertive behavior was free from aggressive feelings or actions. Although integrated individuals were likely to stand up for their rights or to speak out when injustice was perceived, reason rather than emotion was most likely to direct behavior. The integrated personality continued to maintain a balanced future orientation into later maturity, made constructive plans and executed duties in a responsible manner, and was successful in delaying personal gratification when circumstances demanded. A superior ability to tolerate frustrations, handle problems, and constructively cope with personal losses and setbacks was also noted. Feelings of resentment and hostility toward people who may have imposed personal injury in the past tended to have been overcome and no longer constituted a significant factor influencing positive adjustment and adaptation. The integrated personality tended to think well of self, was characterized by relatively high self-esteem, and was generally free from personally destructive self-recriminations. Regardless of how much time the integrated personality had left to live, death was anticipated without fear. A philosophical acceptance and approval of the inevitability of death as a consequence of life was frequently encountered.

The armoured or defended personality

The integrated personality was considered a manifestation of successful or psychologically satisfactory aging. The other three personality types—armoured or defended, passive-dependent, and disorganized—were considered indicative of less successful psychological adjustment in old age.

The armoured or defended personality type was characterized by a high degree of achievement-orientation, a persistent struggle to "stay young," and a compulsive preoccupation with remaining constantly active and involved in a number of undertakings. Such personalities were generally striving, ambitious, status-conscious individuals during most of their lives and continued to maintain this orientation into old age. The armoured or defended personality tried to maintain social position and status as long as possible by holding on to work and refusing to relinquish power and control until forced to do so. People of this personality type often exhibited a strong fear of growing old and would deny that they were aging by making frequent allusions to their own undiminished physical and mental abilities. Such allusions were often made in conjunction with detrimental remarks concerning the comparative deterioration of other members of the same age group—for example, "No one would believe that Jack and I are the same age. He really looks old." In an attempt to deny the reality of their own advanced age, armoured personality types would sometimes become frantically involved in a number of activities regardless of the enjoyment, or lack of enjoyment, derived from such undertakings. The conscious or unconscious philosophy of the armoured personality seemed to be, "If I keep terribly busy, I won't have time to contemplate the fact that I'm old and that my remaining years are relatively limited." Based upon this philosophic orientation, it follows that one of the greatest fears of this personality type was having "nothing to do." Likewise, an equally powerful fear was that of becoming dependent upon others or losing their independence in the eyes of others. This fear of "appearing not to be independent" underlay the common refusal of the armoured personality type to accept aid or help from any person or any agency. The focus of this personality tended to be external and such types were most comfortable dealing with problems, goals, and challenges arising from the environment. Little or no energy tended to be expended upon introspection, the better understanding of personal motives, emotions, and needs, or coming to terms with life and death. As a consequence, the armoured personality generally lacked insight into self, did not recognize the dynamics underlying personal behavior, and would probably continue to operate in a highly defensive manner throughout old age.

The passive-dependent personality

The third personality type identified in old age was designated passive-dependent. Within this particular category were found two distinct adjustment patterns, *succorance-seeking* and *apathetic.* Those individuals described as succorance-seekers exhibited a pronounced need to be dependent upon other people. Although the armoured personality would strongly resist the attempts of others to assume his or her responsibilities or to provide assistance, the succorance-seeker would gladly place all responsibilities and personal obligations upon the shoulders of others. Such individuals might be reluctant to perform even the most ordinary functions if another person could be persuaded or forced to execute that function. For example, although an individual was quite able to do grocery shopping, the help of a family member or friend would be enlisted for this purpose. As the succorance-seeker grew older, advanced age would be used as an excuse to relegate duties that were still within his or her physical and mental ability to perform. Such individuals were likely to engage in relatively few social activities, have a limited circle of friends, have few or no hobbies and interests, and be involved in few entertainment pursuits. The succorance-seeking type tended to derive gratification from food and drink and might at times overindulge. These individuals were generally not psychologically self-sufficient and would frequently need the emotional support and encouragement of others. When a helping hand was extended to the succorance-seeker, it was likely to be accepted without question and additional aid might subsequently be expected and sought.

Individuals described as apathetic were characterized by passivity rather than activity. These people tended to conform to the "rocking chair" stereotype of later maturity. Usually quite content to be involved in virtually no activities, the apathetic type looked forward to retirement, was quite content in having been released from the pressures and responsibilities of employment, and welcomed the opportunity to do little or nothing with personal time and resources. In relationships with others, the apathetic type was likely to maintain distance, exhibit a passive social orientation, and generally was reluctant to become involved in any interpersonal relationships that might pose a potential threat to his or her secure and comfortable life-style. Such individuals frequently acceded to the demands and wishes of the more dominant persons with whom they interacted and often coped with frustrations and problems by turning inward or withdrawing. The apathetic type tended to have a fairly realistic perception of his or her situation and possessed insight into the underlying personality dynamics that influence behavior. Life for this personality type was fairly satisfying and there was a pervasive lack of bitterness and hostility toward other people and the world in general. Individuals who manifested an adjustment pattern characterized by apathy in later maturity were generally those who had exhibited patterns of withdrawal, passivity, and apathy through their adult life. In old age this accustomed pattern of adjustment merely continued and sometimes became accentuated.

The unintegrated personality

The fourth major personality category encompassed a small number of aged people. Within this category were those individuals who were completely unintegrated, suffered from major psychological deficits, often had difficulty coping with everyday demands and responsibilities, and sometimes exhibited highly irrational and erratic behavioral patterns. In some situations the unintegrated type found it impossible to control his or her emotions, was subject to periods of marked depression, anger, and hostility, and exhibited emotion that was objectively inappropriate—laughing at something sad or becoming angry within an apparently pleasant situation. Deterioration of mental abilities popularly associated with old age was commonly noted in the unintegrated personality type. Such individuals sometimes had trouble concentrating, were unable to retain information in long-term memory, showed pronounced declines in measured intelligence, and experienced periods of disorientation and obvious confusion. The disorganized type tended to obtain no satisfaction from living, was generally unhappy, and derived little or no gratification from activities or interpersonal relationships. Although many disorganized personalities managed to maintain themselves independently within the community, their adjustment was considered marginal at best. In many instances, the needs of the unintegrated personality type were such that special outside care was warranted and provisions had to be made to assure the relatively effective functioning of these individuals.

It should be noted that older individuals manifesting unintegrated or disorganized personalities or patterns of adjustment make up only a small percentage of the aged population. The vast majority of those persons who have entered later maturity exhibit more positive and relatively successful patterns of adjustment.

What Is Successful Adjustment in Old Age?

We have previously discussed several behavioral manifestations that are used as bases for separating one pattern of adjustment or personality from another, for example, activity level, degree of dependence, and extent of social isolation or involvement. At this point, it is important to recognize that such overt behavioral patterns are not, in themselves, indicative of positive or negative psychological adjustment in old age. From a psychological perspective, successful or unsuccessful adjustment in later maturity is concerned with *why* a person exhibits certain behavioral patterns rather than specifically *what* a person does. Likewise, assessments of positive or negative adjustment in old age must be concerned with subjective factors such as happiness and contentment derived by the individuals as a result of their behavior, for example, their activities and interests, quantity and quality of interactions, and general social orientation. In the absence of information concerning why an individual behaves in a certain manner, the probability of making erroneous interpretations concerning the degree of successful or unsuccessful adjustment is relatively high.

Activity versus nonactivity

We are likely to look at the older individual who is engaged in a number of activities and believe this person to be well-adjusted and successful. Also there is a tendency to view the older individual who spends a great deal of time alone in apparent idleness as less well-adjusted psychologically than the socially active individual. However, such evaluations, based upon observations of overt behavior, may be quite incorrect. It is a mistake to believe that individuals who are actively engaged in a number of activities are better adjusted than those individuals who choose to spend much of their time alone and to remain generally idle. Unless we examine the psychological dynamics underlying the specific overt behaviors of such individuals, it is impossible to make an accurate evaluative judgment concerning their relative adjustment. In an attempt to ascertain the degree of positive or negative adjustment, it is necessary to ask a number of questions. Why does a person engage in a great number of activities? Does he or she pursue many activities out of a need to escape and deny the reality of old age? Does he or she enjoy the activities or are they merely a temporary diversion from an unacceptable reality or situation? Does a person choose to be alone because he or she enjoys social isolation or because a fear of social contact exists? Is pleasure obtained from social interaction or are such contacts simply endured because a person is afraid of being alone?

Research suggests that neither activity nor inactivity is indicative of successful or unsuccessful adjustment in later maturity (Havighurst et al., 1968; Neugarten et al., 1964). Both can be indicative of either positive or negative adjustment. If either behavioral pattern has developed from healthy needs and brings to the individual feelings of happiness and gratification, it is fairly safe to assume that successful psychological adjustment in old age has been achieved. If behavioral patterns develop from unhealthy or defensive needs and do not produce feelings of happiness and gratification, then successful psychological adjustment in old age has not been realized. In an attempt to better understand adjustment in later maturity, we must examine motivational factors and needs that underlie specific behaviors. It is not sufficient to look only at objective behavioral patterns exhibited by the older individual and, on the basis of such overt actions, make judgments concerning the degree of successful or unsuccessful adjustment.

Some cautions. Because adjustment cannot be determined solely on the basis of overt behavior, those who interact with the elderly should exercise extreme caution before attempting to bring about any changes in the behavior of the older person. In the absence of knowledge concerning the relative psychological adjustment represented by demonstrated actions, we may inadvertently attempt to modify behaviors that are, in actuality, indicative of positive or successful adjustment. For example, there may be a tendency to encourage all elderly persons to engage in social activities, to pursue hobbies, and to become actively involved in community, educational, and religious undertakings. Frequently, there is a tendency not to recognize that some older people are quite content to spend much of their time in relative isolation, enjoy rocking on the front porch for extended periods of time, and have neither the desire nor inclination to change their mode of existence. If we attempt to change the behavior of such individuals, the personal adjustment of these elderly people may suffer and little of a positive nature is likely to result from such well-meaning intervention. To assume that any person knows what is best for all other persons is an unpardonable error. To believe that one behavioral pattern is superior to all others in terms of personal adjustment and satisfaction is naive and, perhaps, can be potentially dangerous. Depending upon the unique personality characteristics of each individual, personal happiness and gratification can be derived from a variety of behavioral patterns and styles of life. Although we may be tempted to evaluate certain behaviors as negative or indicative of unsatisfactory adjustment, it is important to remember that each person is extremely unique and that contentment and happiness are achieved by different individuals in a great number of different ways.

Erikson's integrity versus despair

Erikson (1963), who proposed that human beings progress through eight stages of ego (self) development from infancy through old age (pp. 38–39), differentiated between successful and unsuccessful adjustment in later maturity in terms of feelings of integrity versus feelings of despair. Integrity, as a psychological designation of successful adjustment in old age, connotes acceptance of the life cycle, including death, acceptance of the past, and acceptance of self. Persons who have achieved integrity will perceive their lives as meaningful, will effectively integrate the past into the present, and will operate essentially on the basis of what "is" rather than what "might have been." To a great extent, individuals who have achieved feelings of integrity in later maturity manifest personality characteristics similar to those observed among the integrated personality types identified by the University of Chicago researchers (see pp. 124–125).

Conversely, individuals characterized by feelings of despair exhibit psychological orientations similar to those observed among armoured, passive-dependent, and unintegrated personality types. According to Erikson, feelings of despair are shown by persons who can see no meaning in life, who are not able to come to terms with the realities of the past, who want a second chance to live life, who are bitter, and who have not come to terms with the prospect of impending death. Central to feelings of despair are feelings of regret and hopelessness.

It is worth noting that no specific overt behaviors are associated with feelings of integrity or despair. Both psychological labels are concerned with varying degrees of personal adjustment that may possibly exhibit themselves in observable action. Furthermore, feelings of integrity or despair in old age are the product of numerous situational and personal factors that interact in various ways, for example, economic need, condition of health, relationships with family and friends, and intellectual functioning. Because of the critical nature of such interactions, successful adjustment in later maturity cannot be guaranteed on the basis of successful patterns of adjustment in earlier years.

Havighurst's developmental tasks

Robert Havighurst's (1972) developmental stages (see pp. 4, 6) offer another perspective from which successful and unsuccessful adjustment in old age can be viewed. Havighurst divided the human life span into six stages, each loosely associated with a particular chronological age and each characterized by a number of specific **developmental tasks.** Defining "later maturity" as 60 years and over, Havighurst listed the following tasks as appropriate to this final stage of human development.

> Adjusting to decreasing physical strength and health.
> Adjusting to retirement and reduced income.
> Adjusting to death of spouse.
> Establishing an explicit affiliation with one's age group.
> Meeting social and civic obligations.
> Establishing satisfactory physical living arrangements.

Employing this frame of reference, adjustment in later maturity may be conceptualized in terms of success or failure in mastering a number of specific tasks or problems. Although implicit in Havighurst's developmental tasks is the assumption that certain behaviors must be emitted if successful adjustment is to be achieved, emphasis is placed upon internal processes of adjust-ment rather than well-defined external performance standards. Six tasks are listed, but no attempt is made to operationally define what is entailed in the successful execution of each, to specifically delineate performance standards, or to recommend definite behavioral responses. Specifics concerning suc-cessful or unsuccessful handling of developmental tasks in later maturity are left to the discretion of the individual. For example, is the "establishing of satisfactory physical living arrangements" a matter of psychological percep-tion? What is satisfactory to one person may not be satisfactory to another. During later maturity, the major focus of Havighurst's developmental tasks is personal adjustment rather than external manifestations of behavior.

Maslow's self-actualization theory

Although Abraham Maslow (1954) did not specifically concentrate upon the subject of successful or unsuccessful adjustment in old age, his holistic-dynamic theory of personality suggests that a critical factor influencing re-alization of one's full potential is maturation. In his view, **self-actualization,** the epitome of the fully developed or successful personality structure, cannot be achieved by the very young. Based upon investigations involving various historical and contemporary individuals, Maslow identified certain qualities believed to be characteristic of the self-actualized person. Depending upon one's theoretical orientation, these characteristics may be used as a basis for distinguishing between successful and unsuccessful personality development in old age.

Self-actualized people tend to:

1.   perceive reality realistically and to tolerate uncertainty well.

2.   accept themselves, others, and the environment for what they are rather than for what one might wish them to be.

3.   be spontaneous and natural in behavior.

4.   be problem-centered rather than self-centered.

5.   have a good sense of humor that is not founded in cruelty.

6.   be independent and self-sufficient.

7.   have relatively few deep and intimate interpersonal relationships.

8.   have a tremendous capacity for creativity and the ability to view things in a novel way.

9.   concern themselves with the welfare of mankind.

10.   resist culturally imposed pressures toward conformity.

11.   be strongly democratic and able to relate well to individuals drawn from different social, economic, and cultural backgrounds.

12.   be open to new experiences.

13. differentiate effectively between means and ends while demonstrating a strong ethical-moral orientation.

14. derive great satisfaction from the most simple and ordinary experiences in life.

15. be capable of profound inner experiences and may, at times, appear detached from the world.

It may be observed that several characteristics attributed to the self-actualized individual are similar to these noted among integrated personality types identified among older individuals, for example, realistic perception of self, others, and circumstances; acceptance of self and others; democratic, flexible, and tolerant attitudes; openness to new experiences; and direction by moral-ethical considerations. Likewise, similarities between Erikson's feelings of integrity and Maslow's self-actualization are apparent. On the basis of such observations, a relationship between realization of our full potential and successful adjustment in later maturity may be hypothesized. By the same token, unsuccessful adjustment in old age might be a product of thwarted or frustrated attempts to realize our potential during the course of maturation. However, at this time, such hypotheses are purely conjecture.

Conclusions: Adjustment and personality

On the basis of our discussion regarding successful or unsuccessful adjustment in later maturity, the extremely close relationship between the concepts of adjustment and personality has probably become apparent. **Adjustment** is the process by which the individual person (personality) attempts to deal effectively with environmental demands and internal stresses. Personality may be defined as "the **gestalt** [wholeness] of the individual's attitudes, emotions, motivations, and activity patterns—the impression a man makes on others and the impression he makes on himself" (Chown, 1968, p. 134). In essence, personality may be conceptualized as an adjustment pattern used by individuals to deal with internal and external demands imposed during the course of their life. For this reason, the terms have been, and will continue to be, used interchangeably for purposes of considering psychological dynamics in old age. When an individual investigates adjustment patterns in later maturity, personality characteristics are being studied. Likewise, when questions concerning personality are posed, implicit considerations of psychological and behavioral patterns of adjustment are involved.

Does Personality Change As We Age?

Before we can attempt to answer this question, we need to address ourselves to two factors that stand in the way: (1) lack of a comprehensive personality theory, and (2) lack of research data.

Lack of a comprehensive personality theory

Initially, it must be emphasized that the study of personality in later maturity is handicapped by the lack of a comprehensive personality theory that encompasses the entire life span of the individual. Most personality theorists, with the exception of Erikson, have concentrated upon personality as a function of environmental and personal interactions occurring during infancy, early childhood, and perhaps, adolescence. Little serious consideration has been given to the possibility that personality continues to evolve and develop throughout adulthood and later maturity. According to many theorists, the major elements constituting our personality are firmly established during childhood and are rarely amenable to change. Such an orientation denies the possibility of growth during adulthood and ignores the critical influence of many environmental and personal determinants of personality that occur in later maturity. According to Kuhlen:

> Age is *time* in which other things of importance happen. Among the important "other things" are: biological changes; changes in cognitive abilities; changes in habit strengths (flexibilities and rigidities); changes in patterns of reward, threat, punishment, opportunity, deprivation, training schedules, the latter tending to be culturally age-graded; and changes in motivation. (1964, p. 554)

It would seem illogical to suggest that changes—such as physical, social, and cognitive—that impinge upon the older adult do not influence attitudes, emotions, motivations, and activity patterns making up the personality of the individual. Likewise, it is not logical to presume that an individual's personality remains static through a significant portion of his or her life.

Lack of research data

In conjunction with a lack of theoretical foundations upon which studies of personality in old age may be based, there is also a lack of research data concerned with modifications in the adult personality. Most research dealing with changes in personality has focused upon childhood and the study of characteristics and topics generally regarded irrelevant to our understanding of changes that might occur within the adult personality structure, for example, aggressive tendencies among children, how the Oedipal/Electra complex is resolved, the impact of sibling rivalry upon personality traits, and so forth. Although a great deal of information about personality development in early childhood has been amassed, very little information is available concerning the dynamics of personality growth and change in later maturity. With this in mind, the subject of personality and personality change in old age must be approached with appropriate trepidation.

The evidence

Does personality change in old age? According to Allport (1955), "Personality is less a finished product than a transitive process. While it has some stable features, it is at the same time continually undergoing change" (p. 19). In other words, personality is characterized by change and stability, by consistency and transformation. This observation concerning the inherent nature of personality is equally valid when applied to individuals drawn from various age groups, from different socioeconomic levels, and from diverse ethnic backgrounds. Although differences in degree of change may be observed as a function of various factors, personality, like the human body, changes constantly while remaining unchanged in many ways.

Although modifications in the personality of the normal aged adult will occur, in the absence of pathology or dramatic situational change, there is little reason to anticipate radical deviations from previously established patterns of adaptation. This basic conclusion has been reached by a number of investigators concerned with the dynamics of personality in adulthood and old age (Woodruff and Birren, 1972; Kelly, 1955; Havighurst, Neugarten, and Tobin, 1964; Neugarten, 1972). In the study conducted by Woodruff and Birren, the California Test of Personality was administered to a group of subjects whose average (mean) age was 19. The same test was administered to these same individuals 25 years later and concurrently administered to a new sample of teenage subjects. Results indicated little change in the two sets of personality scores obtained from the same group which was retested following a 25-year interim. Measures of personality did not appear to be significantly influenced by the passage of time or by aging. However, significant differences were found between personality scores obtained from the new sample of teenage subjects and personality scores obtained from the older sample of retested subjects. Data derived from this study suggested that although personality differences between generations are probable, the basic personality structure of the individual remains relatively stable or is not significantly affected by the passage of time.

Neugarten, Havighurst, and Tobin (1961) investigated the relationship between five factors constituting "life satisfaction" and age. Subjects ranging from 50 to 80 years were assessed according to the extent each individual (1) took pleasure from whatever activities constituted his or her everyday life; (2) regarded life as meaningful and accepted resolutely that which life had been; (3) held a positive image of self; (4) felt major goals had been successfully achieved; and (5) maintained happy and optimistic attitudes and moods. Data obtained from this study showed no overall age-related trends in personality when defined in terms of life satisfaction. However, changes were noted among individuals who had reached and passed their seventieth birthday. Lieberman (1965) also observed systematic modifications in the personality characteristics of individuals who were approximately 70 years and older.

Perhaps the most significant information available concerning personality change in later maturity has been derived from a series of studies known collectively as "The Kansas City Studies" (Neugarten & Associates, 1964). Studying the relationship between personal orientation toward the environment and age, investigators found that 60-year-olds were more likely than 40-year-olds to perceive the environment as complex, threatening, and potentially dangerous. In conjunction with this observed difference in personal orientation, it was noted that older subjects tended to be more conforming and cautious than were their younger counterparts. This study suggested a possible age-related progression from active to passive mastery of the environment. However, it is possible that observed differences could be a reflection of generational characteristics rather than a function of aging. In the same study, differences in sensitivity to the reactions of others and degree of interpersonal empathy were noted between younger and older samples. Younger subjects tended to be more sensitive and empathetic than were older subjects. Again, it is impossible to know whether such differences are the product of aging or generational factors.

Schaie and Marquette (1971) conducted research which supported the finding that older individuals exhibit lower levels of responsiveness (sensitivity and empathy) and higher levels of caution than do younger individuals. These investigators also found evidence to suggest that as individuals grow older, they tend to become increasingly introverted, increasingly serious, and manifest lower achievement needs. Several studies (Gutman, 1966; Sealy and Cattell, 1965; Heron and Chown, 1967) have noted a similar relationship between increased age and growing tendencies toward introversion. However, whether changes in responsiveness, caution, achievement orientation, seriousness, and introversion are the result of externally imposed environmental variables or the aging process is not clear. For example, might not a person's need for achievement diminish within a society that provides few rewards or opportunities for achievement among the elderly? Likewise, if opportunities for social interactions are significantly reduced, might not the aged individual become increasingly introverted? On the basis of data presently available, no definitive relationship can be established between personality changes in later maturity and the aging process. Although personality changes may be observed among the aged, it is impossible to state categorically that such changes are the product of increased chronological age.

What Factors Might Change Our Personality in Old Age?

A major problem involved in the study of personality change in old age centers upon the subject of causation—the successful establishing of a cause and effect relationship between age-related personality change and one or more variables. The extreme difficulty inherent in establishing such a relationship becomes apparent upon consideration of the fact that personality changes in later maturity could be a function of such factors as income, marital status, trauma, sex, education, physical disability, social isolation, mobility, employment, and family. It is obvious that the preceding list of potential causative factors could be continued indefinitely and that each factor could constitute a potent force contributing to changes in each person's personality. Unless research can effectively eliminate the possibility that such factors might influence personality characteristics in later maturity, observed changes in social, emotional, and mental traits (personality) cannot be attributed to the aging process. Presently, no researcher has successfully isolated aging from all other factors that might produce personality change in old age. For this reason, consideration must be given to factors, other than the aging process, that might cause modifications in the personality of the elderly.

Motivation or achievement needs

As previously mentioned, various studies have noted a relationship between advanced age and differences in **motivation** or achievement needs. Upon examination of changes in motivation that are exhibited throughout the entire life span of any individual, it is possible to trace such changes directly to three sources: (1) differences in what the individual wants at a particular point in time, (2) differences in the amount of energy the individual is willing or able to expend in an attempt to acquire whatever is wanted, and (3) differences in the availability of rewards, goals, or incentives presented to individuals during various periods of their lives. In many instances, changes in motivational patterns that occur in conjunction with old age may be traced to a combination of these three variables. For example, although an elderly individual may wish to maintain his or her position as a corporate executive, he or she may lack the energy necessary for such a demanding position or may not be given the option of continued executive functioning by a society that traditionally has imposed mandatory retirement upon its citizens. In this case, the motivational pattern of the individual is influenced by two factors: personal inability to expend requisite energy and the actual absence of available desired rewards or **incentives.** Acquisition of what the individual wants or desires is made impossible by the reality of physical limitations and the presence of externally imposed social barriers that preclude goal acquisition. When such discrepancies exist between personal desires and the ability to realize ambitions, desires, or wishes, there is a relatively high probability that personality will be affected. However, in such instances, possible changes in personality may be traced to factors extraneous to the actual aging process.

Introversion

What factors might promote increased introversion among the elderly? Introversion, a term used by Carl Jung, refers to the tendency to withdraw, to turn inward, to value thoughts and feelings over actions and objects, and to avoid social interaction. Upon consideration of this definition, a person would not be hard pressed to enumerate various factors encouraging a propensity toward introversion among the aged population. Initially, before aged individuals begin to withdraw from society, society has already begun to withdraw from them. As a person approaches later maturity, factors such as retirement, death of spouse and friends, lack of transportation, changes in living situation, lack of social organizations, and loss of previously enjoyed economic resources and social status may operate to segregate the individual from the social mainstream and to promote the turning inward of self. If a person becomes deprived of accustomed interests, pleasures, interpersonal relationships, and activities, adjustment will, in all probability, become increasingly characterized by introversion. However, tendencies toward introversion are not inherent to the aging process. Therefore, it might be reasonable to suggest that within different social milieus, age-related changes in introversion may assume different characteristics or disappear.

Conclusion

In essence, all personality changes observed among elderly individuals can, at this time, be explained in terms of causative factors extraneous to the actual process of aging. Although observed changes are noted in the personality structure of the aged, we do not know the source of such changes or the extent to which changes are developmental in nature. Upon examination of research concerned with the assessment of personality characteristics in later maturity, the "state of the art" is probably best summarized as follows.

> Psychologists agree that there are observable changes as well as observable consistencies in adult personality. The problems are how to delineate those personality processes that are most salient to successive periods in adulthood, how to describe those processes in terms that are appropriate, and how to isolate those changes that are development from those that are not. Only after solving these problems can we assess the utility of various conceptual frameworks for explanation and prediction. (Neugarten, 1973, p. 312)

Summary

Personality is a hypothetical concept that refers to the psychological composition and characteristic behaviors of the individual as a whole. Although personality characteristics are inferred from observations of behavior, to some extent behavior may or may not validly reflect the true personality structure. Because of the extreme complexity of each human being, no one can expect to completely understand the underlying dynamics of another person's behavior or personality. Although individuals are characterized in terms of certain personality traits, all human beings are unique.

Personality is usually assessed using questionnaires or inventories, projective techniques, or rating scales. Questionnaires and projective techniques depend upon responses emitted by the individual in reference to a specific stimulus. Rating scales depend upon evaluations of the individual's characteristics made by an outside observer. All assessment techniques have certain advantages and disadvantages. It would appear that generational factors may influence measures of personality regardless of procedure used.

Four basic personality types have been identified among the elderly: the integrated type, the armoured or defended type, the passive-dependent type, and the unintegrated or disorganized type. Associated with each personality type are various patterns of adjustment and characteristic modes of response. The majority of elderly individuals fall into the integrated category. What constitutes successful adjustment in later maturity is generally not defined in terms of specific behavioral patterns or activities. Degree of positive or negative adjustment rather than overt behavior appears to constitute the most useful gauge of successful aging. Erikson, Havighurst, and Maslow have contributed to our conceptual understanding of successful adjustment in old age and have suggested various criteria to be used as a basis for determining adjustment.

Based upon our present knowledge, it is not clear whether personality changes in old age, whether personality change is a function of the aging process, or whether observed personality differences between younger and older generations are the result of various causative factors separate from the actual aging process. Establishing causation is the important challenge confronted by individuals concerned with the investigation of relationships between personality changes and aging.

Progress Check

1. Why might a person's behavior not accurately reflect underlying (core) personality structure?   (pp. 118–119)

2. List and define three methods used to assess personality. Give consideration to potential disadvantages and advantages inherent in each. (pp. 119–122)

3. What three factors might account for assessed differences in personality between old and young persons?   (pp. 122–124)

4. List four major personality types identified among the elderly and give two characteristics of each.   (pp. 124–128)

5. Discuss why behavior is frequently a poor indicator of successful adjustment in old age.   (pp. 128–130)

6. What similarities may be noted between the integrated personality type and Erikson's personality who has achieved integrity?   (pp. 129–130)

7. List four developmental tasks proposed by Robert Havighurst as appropriate to later maturity.   (pp. 130–131)

8. List six characteristics of the self-actualized person.   (pp. 131–132)

9. Discuss five possible relationships between the integrated personality type and the self-actualized person.   (pp. 131–132)

10. What personality differences have been noted between young and old persons?   (pp. 134–135)

11. List and discuss four factors, other than aging, that might cause personality to change in later maturity.   (pp. 135–137)

Recommended Readings

Kuhlen, R. G. Personality change with age. In P. Worchel and D. Byrne, eds., *Personality Change.* New York: John Wiley, 1964.
Examines possible psychological and behavioral orientations that may change as a function of increased age. Variables affecting changes in personality that occur with age are considered.

Neugarten, B. L. Personality change in later life: a developmental perspective. In C. Eisdorfer and M. P. Lawton, eds., *The Psychology of Adult Development and Aging.* Washington, D.C.: American Psychological Association, 1973.
Presents a discussion of successful aging as a function of different life-styles and patterns of adaptation. An excellent theoretical discussion of personality that gives consideration to Maslow, Erikson, and Jung is offered in this selection.

7

Aging and Stress

Preview ∾ *In this chapter we will introduce the concept of stress, distinguish between sources of stress, and discuss various reactions to stress and stress-provoking situations. The importance of expending stress-related energy will be emphasized. Consideration will be given to the quantity and quality of stress encountered in old age, to potential age-related outlets for the expression of stress-related energy, and to the cumulative nature and effects of stress. Stress will be viewed from the perspective of life change units, the general adaptation syndrome, and the frustration-aggression hypothesis. We will also examine the relationship between stress and disease, differentiate between destructive and constructive ways of coping with stress, and consider the relationship between personality and reactions to stress. Finally, we will look at certain steps that may be taken to facilitate successful coping behavior when stress is encountered.*

Stress is an integral part of living with which every human being must contend. Some individuals are generally successful in their attempts to handle and cope with stress. Others are less successful and may adopt self-defeating and destruc-

*tive modes of coping. From a psychological perspective, indi-
viduals who cope successfully with stress are considered to
be well adjusted. Those who persistently manifest ineffective
coping strategies are considered to be maladjusted.*

How Can We Define Stress?

We can define **stress** as a state of physical or psychological strain resulting
from the actual or perceived presence of threat. The distinction made between actual and perceived threat is important in that a great deal of stress
experienced by individuals within our society is the product of fears and
apprehensions that have no objective base in reality. For example, a person
may experience a great deal of stress within a social situation that is, as
perceived by all outside observers, characterized by a total absence of threat
to that individual. Likewise, a very rich person who has previously experienced poverty may experience stress in relation to money concerns. It is a
common misconception that threats that are "all in a person's mind" or are
non-reality based do not exert stress comparable to that exerted by objective
or "real" environmental threats. Non-reality based sources of stress often
exert strains upon the individual that equal or exceed those exerted by
stresses that are grounded in objective reality.

Non-reality based or idiosyncratically perceived stresses may prove particularly devastating to the individual for the following reasons: (1) The individual may not fully understand or appreciate the source of such stress; (2)
Direct action designed to eliminate the source of stress may not be possible;
(3) Help in alleviation of stress may not be forthcoming from family or friends
who discount its importance; (4) The perceived source of stress may or may
not be indicative of that which is actually threatening to the individual; (5) The
non-reality based source of stress may have constituted a threat to the individual for many years and may evoke well-established or habitual patterns of
response that are extremely difficult to modify. A person who experiences
stress in conjunction with a non-reality based threat will, in all probability,
gain no relief from assurances that discount the importance of such a
threat—for example, "There is nothing to worry about" or "Nothing's going
to hurt you." In most cases, the threatened individual has already recognized
the irrationality of the stress reaction and needs no one to point it out.
However, the ability to intellectually grasp the irrationality of an emotional
response may in no way change the caliber or intensity of that response.

How Do We React to Stress?

Stress is considered to be any condition that functions to mobilize an individual's physiological resources and causes an increase in energy expenditure.
In our evolutionary past, this increase in energy expenditure was exhibited in

the "fight or flight" reaction. In the face of threat the individual could either withdraw or directly attack the source of threat. For better or worse, conditions are no longer quite so simple for human beings. In many stress situations, neither fight nor flight represents feasible behavioral options. For example, when a person is rejected by a loved one, fails an important exam, or loses a job, resulting stress may not be eased through dynamics involving either fight or flight. However, the energy that has been mobilized in each situation must be dealt with in some fashion. When such energy is expended in a constructive manner specifically designed to alleviate stress or eliminate sources of strain, it can be highly instrumental in assuring an individual's physical and psychological well-being and survival. However, when such energy is not expended constructively, becomes "bottled-up" in the person, or is turned destructively toward self or others, it may prove to be a force capable of inflicting great physical and psychological damage. When energy resulting from stress is given no outlet, it becomes anxiety and may manifest itself in a number of unpleasant ways, for example, discomfort, real and imagined illnesses, depression, fear, and suicide. Energy which is given no outlet becomes anxiety, and anxiety is the foundation of a large group of emotional and mental disturbances collectively referred to as neuroses.

Does Increased Age Affect Stress and Our Reaction to It?

All human beings are subject to stress. As people enter later maturity, however, the quality and quantity of stress to which they are subjected changes. The specific stresses to which we become increasingly vulnerable gradually assume a different character with advanced age. As we enter later maturity, specific outlets available for the discharge of energy resulting from stress also change significantly. During our younger years, most stress results from pressures to behave effectively, to achieve, to earn social and financial status, to compete and gain recognition, and to successfully meet a variety of socially imposed demands and expectations. The younger person is placed under constant stress to "be somebody" and "do something." During earlier stages of development, the character of much stress encountered by the individual encourages and rewards direct action and aggressive behavior. A person is constantly provided with many and varied outlets for energy resulting from stress. We can work hard to succeed in a job, expend great amounts of energy in the pursuit of an education, and actively strive to achieve a vast number of personal goals. During this period of life, a person is encouraged to expend energy in a constructive manner, is provided with outlets for the expenditure of such energy, and is expected to assume an active role in the alleviation and elimination of stress.

Activity versus passivity

In old age the relationship between stress and behavior undergoes a drastic change. No longer are we expected or encouraged to achieve; no longer are outlets readily available for the constructive venting of stress-related energy; no longer is direct action or aggressive behavior equally effective or feasible in the handling of stress-provoking situations. The relationship between stress and behavior gradually changes from one characterized by activity to one characterized by passivity as we grow old. Although a variety of social forces may promote and reinforce an attitude of passivity in old age, the inherent nature of stress encountered in later maturity is, in part, responsible for the increasingly passive orientation adopted by many individuals. Much stress encountered in later maturity simply cannot be eliminated through the use of direct action or aggressive behavior. Such behavior may be futile since much stress in old age results from various personal losses that are often permanent or irrevocable. No amount of direct action or aggressive behavior will restore a friend or mate who has died, will return us to more pleasant times, or will banish the reality of spent youth, reduced physical vigor, and perceptible decline. As we age, stress becomes increasingly related to loss of family, friends, status, work, independence, health, and a number of cherished, valued, and accustomed experiences and circumstances.

Coping with stress

When losses are permanent or irrevocable, the problem of adjusting to related stress may be extremely great. To some extent, the seriousness of this problem is compounded by the lack of preparation provided by our society for **coping** with such losses. That is, we do not learn to cope or to deal with such problems and difficulties by adopting specific behaviors and orientations. Within our society, most people devote a great deal of their lives to learning how to get what they want, how to achieve their goals, and how to overcome obstacles that may lie in their paths. Relatively few people devote time to learning how to tolerate stressful situations in which goal attainment is impossible, in which irrevocable loss must be faced, and in which no amount of action will result in a desired external change. Very few people learn how to effectively cope with situations in which alleviation of stress is totally dependent upon their ability to expend energy upon the constructive restoration of self. Throughout our lives, we are taught that willingness to work and perseverance will make all things possible. When our experiences prove this not to be the case and we are suddenly faced with a stressful situation that is impossible to change, the result may be personally shattering. Although some people learn this difficult lesson early in life, most individuals are confronted with this unpleasant reality only upon reaching middle or old age. To some extent, our ability to cope with permanent loss will be a major factor influencing psychological and physical well-being throughout later maturity.

Quality and Quantity of Stress: Is There a Relationship?

The work of Thomas Holmes, a psychiatrist, has done much to increase understanding of specific sources of stress and the intensity of psychological strain imposed upon the individual by each. Holmes and Rahe (1967) have isolated and identified 43 crises or events that most human beings may expect to face and have to cope with during the course of life.

Life change units

The name **life change units** has been given to the numerical stress ratings assigned to each separate stressful situation. These life change units provide a general gauge of the severity of stress that might be expected to result from each isolated event. The greater the numerical rating, the greater the intensity of stress. As you read the list of 43 events that provoke stress, it will become readily apparent that most individuals are susceptible to more than one stressful situation at any time. Furthermore, it is highly unlikely that any single stressful event will occur in total isolation from all other crises or that our life will progress for any significant period of time in the total absence of stressful events. According to Holmes, if people compute the total life change units to which they are subjected at one particular time and derive a numerical total of 200 or more, there is possible cause for concern. Such people are operating under an extremely high level of stress or pressure and their ability to cope successfully may be severely taxed. If they have a stress rating of 200 or more it may be necessary to stop, reevaluate their situation, and perhaps implement significant modifications in their life.

Upon reading the list of stress-provoking events and their accompanying life change units (see Table 7.1), it may be useful to concentrate upon the possible interrelationships that exist among many of the separate categories. In so doing, you may better appreciate the potentially cumulative nature of psychological strain. For example, what stressful events are likely to accompany retirement? What additional crises may occur in conjunction with Christmas?

As an exercise in totaling life change units in a hypothetical situation, consider for a moment that you have just been admitted to a nursing or convalescent home. On the basis of the 43 life events previously listed, how many life change units do you think would be operating upon you at that particular time or as a result of that specific change in residence? Although change in residence is specifically assigned the numerical designation of 20, changes resulting from such a move might bring your number of life change units to, and above, the 200 mark. For example, changes might be expected in eating habits, sleeping habits, recreation, personal habits, financial state, health, social activities, and so forth as a direct result of change in residence. Regardless of the absolute numerical designation given a central or major life event change, unless we give consideration to the side effects or changes

Table 7.1: Life Events and Their Impact in Life Change Units

Life Event	Life Change Units
1. Death of spouse	100
2. Divorce	73
3. Marital separation	65
4. Jail term	63
5. Death of close family member	63
6. Personal injury or illness	53
7. Marriage	50
8. Fired at work	47
9. Marital reconciliation	45
10. Retirement	45
11. Change in health of family member	44
12. Pregnancy	40
13. Sexual difficulties	39
14. Gain of new family member	39
15. Business readjustment	39
16. Change in financial state	38
17. Death of close friend	37
18. Change to different line of work	36
19. Change in number of arguments with spouse	35
20. Mortgage over $10,000	31
21. Foreclosure of mortgage or loan	30
22. Change in responsibilities at work	29
23. Son or daughter leaving home	29
24. Trouble with in-laws	29
25. Outstanding personal achievement	28
26. Wife begins or stops work	26
27. Begin or end school	26
28. Change in living conditions	25
29. Revision of personal habits	24
30. Trouble with boss	23
31. Change in work hours or conditions	20
32. Change in residence	20
33. Change in schools	20
34. Change in recreation	19
35. Change in church activities	19
36. Change in social activities	18
37. Mortgage or loan less than $10,000	17
38. Change in sleeping habits	16
39. Change in number of family get-togethers	15
40. Change in eating habits	13
41. Vacation	13
42. Christmas	12
43. Minor violations of the law	11

Source: Reprinted with permission from T. H. Holmes and R. H. Rahe, "The social readjustment rating scale," *Journal of Psychosomatic Research, 11,* pp. 213–218. Copyright 1967, Pergamon Press, Ltd.

accompanying that life event, it will be impossible to derive an accurate assessment of stress imposed upon any individual at any specific time. The cumulative nature of stress resulting from life changes may, in part, explain the difficulty each of us has in fully appreciating the position of others or in "putting ourselves in another person's shoes." Until we have personally experienced a particular situation or event, it may be virtually impossible to identify or understand all potential ramifications associated with that situation or event.

The relationship between life change units and illness

According to Holmes and Masuda (1973), a relationship exists between total number of life change units and the probability of developing physical or psychological illness. The greater the number of life change units, the greater the likelihood that illness will result. The extent to which changes are perceived as pleasant or unpleasant appears to have little effect upon this relationship. Both pleasant and unpleasant changes exert stress upon the individual, require adaptation, and result in some physiological or psychological strain (Levi, 1971). Change itself, rather than the subjective character of change, functions to influence our susceptibility to illness (Holmes and Rahe, 1967; Rahe and Arthur, 1968). When individuals are subjected to little change, are not required to make significant adjustments in life, and have little need to exercise adaptive behavior, the probability of illness tends to be significantly low (Rahe, 1969).

Although few would argue that changes demanding adaptation do not impose increased strain upon the individual, factors such as existing health, ability to cope, established patterns of adjustment, and degree of control over the situation appear to be related to susceptibility to illness (Nelson, 1974). Likewise, the extent to which changes can be anticipated and the extent to which the person is able to prepare for such changes seem to be related to likelihood of developing illness (Lowenthal and Chiriboga, 1973). Neugarten (1970) has hypothesized that life changes occurring in old age that are anticipated or expected are less likely to constitute a traumatic event than are life changes that occur unexpectedly. For example, an older person who, by virtue of advanced age, is more likely than the younger person to anticipate the death of a spouse, will probably experience less severe stress reactions than the younger individual who is not prepared for the eventuality of such a loss. However, the extent to which anticipation of dramatic life change operates to ease the impact of stress is debatable. Research indicates that persons whose spouses die following a prolonged illness are more likely to exhibit pronounced negative reactions than are persons whose spouses die suddenly or following a brief illness (Gerber et al., 1975). In such cases, it may be that the potential positive effect of anticipation may be overpowered by the potential negative effect of cumulative stress. Also, research indicates that illness and death among aged surviving spouses during the months following widowhood are significantly greater than among comparable aged individuals who have not suffered the loss of spouse (Parkes, Benjamin, Fritz-gerald, 1969; Gerber et al., 1975). It would appear that although loss of spouse may be intellectually anticipated in later maturity, this intellectual anticipation does little to reduce stress that occurs as an accompaniment of the actual loss.

In later maturity factors such as poor health, economic circumstances, loss of roles, and reduced control over our environment and circumstances may operate cumulatively to render us more susceptible to the negative effects of life changes. However, the relationship between life change among the aged and stress reactions has not been studied sufficiently to warrant any definitive conclusions regarding the subject.

Do We React in Similar Ways to Stress?

Most people inevitably face and must cope with stress during the course of their day-to-day existence. Generally, such stress is not particularly severe, is not characterized by sudden onset, and is not of a prolonged nature. Such daily stress is usually handled quite successfully by the majority of human beings regardless of age. However, as we enter later maturity, the probability increases that we will be confronted with intensely stressful situations that occur suddenly and must be endured for extended periods of time. Much stress encountered in old age is of a crisis nature—the death of a spouse, the loss of health, and drastic changes in work and living situations. In later maturity the initial reactions to acute stress may be shock. This initial shock reaction may be followed by a relatively brief period of immobilization and disorientation. When the initial shock reaction has passed, the elderly individual may then have to tolerate a stress-provoking situation that could conceivably continue to exert its influence during the entire remaining course of life. The prolonged character of many stress situations encountered by elderly individuals may be the critical factor underlying a variety of psychological and physical problems that occur in old age.

The relationship between prolonged stress and psychological or physical problems may be conceptualized in terms of Selye's theory of stress (1976). Hans Selye proposed that when the body is exposed to prolonged stress, it responds in three sequential phases referred to as the **general adaptation syndrome.**

General Adaptation Syndrome: Stage One

The first phase of the general adaptation syndrome is called the **alarm reaction** and is characterized by a general mobilization of physical or psychological resources. The individual becomes immediately prepared to attack, defend self, or to retreat from danger. As a result of increased hormonal activity, greater amounts of energy become available and an acceleration of bodily functioning, in heart rate, respiration, and perspiration, is experienced. At this time, the individual is physically ready for defense against the source of stress or danger. However, as previously noted, it is frequently impossible to take direct action in the face of many types of stress and the individual may perceive no effective outlet for increased energy. During this phase, if the stress-provoking event is sufficiently threatening, the individual may become totally immobilized or may discharge excess energy in an erratic or uncontrolled manner. Such unproductive reactions are particularly likely when we are faced with an intensely stressful situation that occurs suddenly and offers no truly constructive behavioral options. That is, when a person is suddenly faced with a crisis situation about which nothing can be done, immobilization or erratic behavior may result. For example, when people are told of the death of a close friend or family member, one person may react by sitting and staring into space; another person, upon hearing the same news, may begin to compulsively pace about the room and vigorously wring his hands. In both cases reactions are to a stressful event that provides no constructive behavioral options and no outlets for the effective expenditure of energy resulting from stress.

General Adaptation Syndrome: Stage Two

The second phase of the general adaptation syndrome is called the **stage of resistance.** During this phase, the body continues to function within circumstances characterized by elevated pressure or strain. All physical and psychological resources continue to be rallied in an attempt to ward off stress and to cope effectively with the stress-provoking situation. During this stage of resistance, psychological or physical problems may develop. As a result of prolonged stress, the individual may experience high blood pressure, become asthmatic, exhibit signs of acute depression or pronounced swings in mood, sleep erratically, and lose appetite. As a result of exposure to prolonged stress, the individual is likely to suffer a gradual, but constant, erosion of psychological and physical well-being. During the resistance stage, there is an increased probability that the individual will turn to **tranquilizers,** sedatives, alcohol, and other drugs in an attempt to alleviate the subjective feelings of discomfort associated with the stressful event. If pain or feelings of strain are successfully reduced through the use of drugs, psychological or physical dependence may soon develop. Once dependence is established, the individual may increasingly feel unable to cope with any stressful event without the aid of drugs and may take refuge in pills or drink at the slightest provocation. When established in later maturity, such dependence is likely to exert an influence upon us during the remaining course of our lives.

General Adaptation Syndrome: Stage Three

If people continue to be exposed to stress for a prolonged period of time, they will ultimately move to the third stage of the general adaptation syndrome, the **stage of exhaustion.** As the name suggests, during this phase, the person becomes totally worn-out and simply cannot tolerate further stress. In essence, the body is no longer able to maintain the increased level of energy required to handle the stress situation, attempts to cope are abandoned, and the ability to resist or fight is lost. As a result of continued long-term resistance to stress, physical and psychological resources gradually become depleted, our ability to withstand pressures and strains slowly diminishes, and a physical or mental breakdown becomes more probable. In extreme cases the prolonged stage of resistance may be followed by exhaustion accompanied by death.

If we hope to avert serious mental or physical problems resulting from prolonged stress, every effort should be made to provide care and assistance during the resistance phase (or before the exhaustion phase) of the general adaptation syndrome. By so doing, it is possible that stress will be sufficiently alleviated to permit avoidance of the final exhaustion phase. However, if the exhaustion phase is reached, massive intervention may be required if our former state of health and well-being is to be regained.

Does Frustration Cause Stress and Aggression?

Frustration resulting from loss is probably a major precipitant of maladaptive behavior or maladjustment in later maturity. **Frustration** occurs when a barrier or obstacle is placed between an individual and a desired goal. In stressful situations characterized by loss—particularly permanent loss—the degree of frustration we experience will probably be great because our desired goal can never be reached. For example, a person whose spouse has died (permanent loss barrier) wants the companionship, love, and support (goal) of the deceased mate. A person who has retired (permanent loss barrier) wants the status, power, and remuneration (goal) provided by former employment. In both situations the barrier to goal attainment is impermeable and the probability of experiencing frustration is extremely high.

The frustration-aggression hypothesis

The **frustration-aggression hypothesis** (Dollard, Doob, Miller, Mowrer, & Sears, 1939) considers aggression to be the most common reaction of human beings to frustration. Thus, within a frustrating situation, behavior that is hostile, assaulting, and fundamentally destructive in character is likely to be exhibited. Such aggression may manifest itself in a number of ways and may be directed inward or outward. Aggressive energy can be directed toward people or things outside the frustrated individual (outward) or upon the individual who is actually experiencing the frustration (inward).

Negative outward aggression.   When aggression is turned outward, the frustrated individual may become highly argumentative, direct verbal or physical abuse toward others, attempt to do physical or psychological harm, or generally behave in a manner that is socially destructive. Outward directed aggression may also show itself in more subtle but equally dangerous forms. The frustrated individual may do psychological harm to others by becoming overly protective, demanding, interfering, and extremely dependent. Some people might attempt to arbitrarily impose their will upon others, to direct and control when possible, and to provoke feelings of guilt and inadequacy in those with whom contact is made. By behaving in such ways, the frustrated individual is able to vent aggressive energy and may derive some satisfaction from the successful manipulation of the lives and emotions of others.

Negative inward aggression. When aggression is directed inward, the resulting psychological and physical damage done by the frustrated individual to self may be great. Manifestations of aggression that has been turned inward or directed toward self are feelings of acute guilt, remorse, apathy, and depression. The frustrated person who directs aggressive energy inward may do physical harm to self, be neglectful of personal requirements or needs, disregard health considerations, indulge excessively in alcohol, smoking, and other drugs, and, in extreme circumstances, commit suicide. Suicide is, after all, the ultimate expression of aggressive energy directed toward self.

Positive inward and outward aggression

Previously cited examples of aggressive energy expenditure have all been of a maladaptive or destructive nature. However, in the process of coping, energy resulting from frustration may also be directed inward or outward in a constructive, well-adjusted manner if appropriate energy outlets are available and if the individual's psychological orientation is conducive to positive adaptation.

When an individual directs aggressive energy outward in a constructive manner, large amounts of energy may be expended in the pursuit of pleasurable undertakings, physical exercise and exertion, community or social projects, helping others, engaging in various interpersonal activities, self-improvement through education, and effective management of personal affairs. When aggressive energy is turned constructively inward, the frustrated individual may concentrate upon developing a better understanding of self, actively working out psychological problems, maintaining an optimistic orientation, continuing to think well of self, and taking positive steps to preserve the perception of self as a valued, worthwhile human being.

In itself aggressive energy resulting from frustration is neither good nor bad, constructive nor destructive. How frustrated people use and vent such energy is the critical factor in determining their level of adjustment to stress and ability to cope.

Does Our Personality Make Us Vulnerable to Stress?

Although age is obviously an important factor influencing our reactions to stressful events, it is commonly recognized that similar aged individuals, old or young, react to stress in vastly different ways. To some extent, differences in reactions to stress may be traced to individual differences in perceptions of events (Neugarten, 1973). That which is important and holds great meaning for one person may be unimportant or insignificant to another. One person, for example, may perceive retirement as highly stressful. Another person may perceive this event as totally devoid of stress. In the face of diverse perceptions, diverse reactions must be expected. Stress is never inherent in an event. Rather, the manner in which the individual perceives an event determines the quality and quantity of stress involved. Unfortunately for researchers, no single event is equally stressful to all persons.

Differences in reactions to stress may be traced to differences in the personality structure of each human being. As discussed in the previous chapter, personality influences our tendency to respond to certain situations in certain ways. This influence is, of course, exerted in situations that are either stressful or unstressful.

Type A personality and heart disease

Friedman and Rosenman (1974) studied the relationship between personality type and the incidence of coronary disease among men. Two personality types, Type A and Type B, were identified. **Type A,** or the stressful personality type, tended to respond to everyday situations in such a way that stress became a chronic and characteristic aspect of normal functioning. Highly competitive, hard-driving, extremely impatient, and habitually rushed, the Type A personality generally strives to accomplish more than feasible, to execute more than time allows, and to function at an accelerated pace regardless of activity. Such individuals tend to be tempestuous, are often barely able to control fits of rage or hostility, and may expend great amounts of energy keeping anger in check. However, feelings of anger and hostility persist below the surface and may be exhibited in clenched fists, facial grimaces, grinding of teeth, facial tics, and tensing of muscles. The Type A personality may be engaged in many activities, but very few of these are recreational diversions or hobbies. Recreation usually involves aggressive competition (must win) and feelings of guilt are frequently experienced in situations requiring or allowing the individual to relax. Essentially, the Type A personality structure is such that everyday situations and circumstances, perceived as unimportant or unstressful to many persons, constantly impose strain. For such individuals, the actual source of stress is within themselves rather than within their environment. Therefore, attempts to modify stress and its effects must concentrate upon personal behavioral patterns and orientations rather than upon externally imposed factors that impinge upon the individual.

A significant relationship has been established between Type A behavior and coronary heart disease. Rosenman (1974) reported that Type A's were five times more likely than Type B's to suffer a second heart attack. In addition, fatal heart attacks actually occurred twice as frequently among Type A personalities than among Type B personalities. Age appeared to operate as a significant factor influencing the relationship between coronary heart disease and personality type. Personality type proved to be a statistically significant predictor of heart disease among subjects aged 39 to 49. Researchers, however, found that this statistically significant relationship did not persist among subjects aged 50 to 59 (Rosenman et al., 1970). Although heart disease, in the absence of Type A behavioral patterns, is practically nonexistent before age 70 (Friedman and Rosenman, 1974), personality type has proven to be a poor predictor of heart disease among older adults. The absence of a significant relationship between behavioral pattern and disease in later maturity might be traced to factors such as age-related physiological changes, modified role demands and expectations, or refocusing upon other aspects of personality. However, at this time, factors operating to confound the relationship between personality type and coronary heart disease in later maturity have not been identified.

Hypertensive personalities

Studying the relationship between reactions to stress and personality, a number of researchers have theorized the existence of a **hypertensive type** who reacts to stress with exaggerated elevations of blood pressure (Brod, 1971; Torgersen and Kringlen, 1971; Harris and Singer, 1967). According to researchers, the hypertensive personality is characterized by feelings of insecurity, anxiety, and lack of self-assertiveness, and is actively or passively aggressive. In childhood the hypertensive personality tended to be a "good child," was submissive, quiet, obedient, and frequently kept to himself. As adults, hypertensives were more likely to behave in a socially abrasive manner and engage in hostile interpersonal actions. Although there is little agreement among researchers regarding the specific personality traits underlying hypertension, it is probable that the roots of the hypertensive stress reaction may be found in childhood and that this characteristic pattern of response persists into later maturity. It is very likely that early experiences teach the individual to respond to stress in a hypertensive manner and that the cumulative effects of such responses become increasingly apparent as a person ages. As with most well-established patterns of behavior, there is little evidence to suggest that hypertensive reactions change significantly in old age. Although the quality and quantity of stress encountered in later maturity may greatly change, the fundamental response of the aged hypertensive is not likely to significantly deviate from that shown during earlier years. Likewise because personality traits tend to become increasingly stable or more fixed as a result of increased age, there is little reason to believe that any personality dynamics that may underlie hypertension should drastically change in old age. If the individual survives, it is probable that the middle-aged hypertensive will become the elderly hypertensive and that this accustomed pattern of response to stress will persist.

How Can Successful Coping Be Facilitated?

Although it must be emphasized that most aged individuals cope exceptionally well with whatever stress is encountered, successful coping may often be facilitated by friends, relatives, social institutions, and a variety of environmental factors. For the person who has suffered a dramatic loss or has been placed within an acutely frustrating situation, intervention on the part of an individual or an institution may provide the temporary support needed to aid positive adjustment. Although the following suggestions should not be considered to be all inclusive, they represent some basic guidelines for those concerned with promoting mental health and well-being among individuals who are within a crisis situation, are having difficulty adjusting, and are having unusual demands made upon their ability to cope.

Venting emotions

An individual who has experienced a dramatic change or permanent loss should be permitted and encouraged to vent emotions in an atmosphere of sympathy, understanding, and acceptance. Allowing people to cry, to talk about their feelings and problems, and to discuss what has been lost or changed in a free and open manner can do much to dispel pent-up energy. Because the expression of strong emotions, particularly those considered unpleasant, such as hate and anger, often proves personally embarrassing or disconcerting to many people, there is a tendency to discourage their open expression. Friends and relatives may attempt to divert conversation from the subject of loss, to withdraw when negative or unpleasant emotions are exhibited, and to encourage the frustrated or stress-ridden person to keep feelings inside. Overtly or covertly, those who come in contact with a person who has suffered a significant loss may encourage keeping a "stiff upper lip," displaying only "acceptable emotions," and continuing behavioral patterns that give the appearance that nothing has changed. By so doing, the probability is increased that stress-related energy will become bottled up inside and will subsequently discharge in a destructive fashion. Energy resulting from stress must be expended. To discourage or block its natural and spontaneous expression may prove psychologically and physically harmful to the person experiencing stress and potentially damaging to those persons or things with which such an individual may come in contact. If friends or family are unwilling or unable to encourage and permit the free and normal expression of negative emotions, the stressed individual would be well advised to seek out a therapeutic environment in which such energy discharge is acceptable and recognized as psychologically healthy. Such an environment may be provided by various mental health workers, psychologists, psychiatrists, ministers, and physicians. It is important to remember that a sympathetic, accepting attitude toward the stressed individual can do much to facilitate the discharge of stress-related energy, and as a result function to alleviate subjective feelings of strain and tension.

Providing new goals

The provision of substitute goals or objectives can be highly effective in facilitating the expenditure of energy resulting from stress. Although the availability of substitute goals should not be expected to eliminate all stress and frustration, a person who is provided with a number of pursuits and activities upon which energy may be spent in a constructive manner is less likely to exhibit patterns of maladjusted behavior than is the individual who is deprived of such outlets. Substitute goals may entail travel, interactions with various social groups, pursuing some achievement-oriented objective such as work or education, physical and mental self-improvement, and a number of assorted activities designed to refocus energy and attention in a constructive manner. Although it is important that such substitute goals be personally meaningful to the individual, it is a mistake to postpone or discourage active involvement in substitute activities until a strong interest or motivation is exhibited. Initial involvement in the pursuit of substitute goals may be quite halfhearted. A person under stress may be reluctant to try anything new and may be somewhat resistant to suggestions involving personal change. However, when a person's active participation in a new undertaking is encouraged and successfully obtained, personal interest, enthusiasm, and commitment to that undertaking may develop and grow. When this occurs, an important outlet for stress-related energy will have been established. In attempting to establish substitute goals for yourself or others, remember that it is generally more effective to concentrate upon changing behavior in reference to a particular goal rather than attempting to change attitudes toward that goal. If behavior can be effectively changed, changes in attitude frequently follow. Although no individuals should be forced to engage in any activity against their will, during times of frustration and stress, active encouragement of participation in various undertakings that may serve as substitute goals may prove to be psychologically beneficial.

It is unfortunate, and perhaps tragic, that many permanent or dramatic losses suffered during the course of our life span are accompanied by secondary losses that severely reduce the number of substitute goals or activities remaining available. That is to say, when substitute goals or objectives are most needed by the person, they are most likely to be withdrawn. For example, when a woman is widowed (dramatic loss stress situation), she is frequently deprived of accustomed activities and interests as a result of her loss. She is likely to be systematically excluded from a variety of social activities, deprived of the companionship of friends who are married, and may no longer feel welcome in homes and establishments she formerly frequented as a married woman. She may suddenly find that she no longer "fits in," is no longer an accepted and welcomed member of social circles she was previously part of as a married woman, and is treated quite differently by friends and acquaintances. Her change in marital status is likely to produce many painful and unexpected side effects. Essentially, the recently widowed individual must not only cope with the irrevocable death of a spouse. She must also face the additional loss of interests, activities, companionships, social status, and pursuits that had been an integral and crucial aspect of her marital existence. At a time when the provision of substitute goals or activities is most critical to the psychological and physical well-being of the stress-ridden individual, such goals and activities are suddenly withdrawn. In many situations, the loss of secondary or substitute goals and activities may be almost as devastating to the welfare of the individual as is the actual trauma imposed by the major loss.

Avoiding major changes

Although the pursuit of substitute goals and activities should be encouraged and supported during times of stress, major life changes should be avoided. Although radical changes in life-style, for example, buying a new house, moving in with a son or daughter, or turning control of finances over to another person, may seem to hold the promise of increased happiness or satisfaction, life changes during times of stress are more likely to aggravate rather than alleviate pressures and strains. A person who is under a great deal of stress should be advised to maintain status quo and to make no major changes that may be irreversible and later regretted. If a person is determined to bring about major life-style changes during periods of high stress, it is advisable that such changes be implemented on a trial basis. For example, if a person wants to move in with a son or daughter, he or she should consider moving in for a few months to see how things work out. If all isn't as anticipated, the individual will then have a home to which he or she can return and will have been spared the extreme stress commonly associated with such an ill-advised move. In times of stress, additional life changes should be avoided.

Quickly reassuming responsibilities

Although everything possible should be done to provide support and encouragement to the person who has suffered an acute loss, care should be taken to assure that such an individual is not totally divorced from personal duties and responsibilities for prolonged periods of time. Well-meaning attempts to remove all responsibility for management of personal affairs, duties, and obligations may be counterproductive, engender accentuated dependence, and intensify feelings of personal inadequacy. When responsibility for the management and direction of our life is assumed by another person, a disservice is ultimately done to those from whom control and direction is taken. A person who has experienced a dramatic loss or is in an acutely frustrating situation should be expected to assume responsibility for personal affairs and business matters as soon as possible. However, this expectation should be coupled with the certain knowledge that help and support is readily available if and when it is needed. It should be remembered that in the execution of our own duties and responsibilities, energy is being discharged and a constructive outlet for feelings of frustration utilized. When everything is done for another person, energy that might otherwise be channeled into constructive activity may be redirected toward self or others in a destructive manner.

Seeking professional help

If an individual is unsuccessful in attempts to cope with stress, remains depressed or withdrawn for extended periods of time, and shows little movement in the direction of recovery or positive adjustment, that person should be encouraged to seek professional help in dealing with problems and stress. However, the suggestion that professional help is needed may be met with defensiveness, hostility, and rejection. Such negative reactions can generally be traced to two major factors. First, many individuals who are experiencing intense stress, are emotionally upset, and are exhibiting maladaptive patterns of behavior fail to recognize the erratic or irrational nature of their own behavior. Such individuals may cling to the notion that they are responding in an effective manner, are coping successfully, and maintaining a rational orientation toward self, others, and the environment. Any suggestion to the contrary is likely to be received poorly. Second, within our society, psychological disorders and mental and emotional problems are stigmatized and surrounded by an aura of prejudice and ignorance. Such problems are often perceived as shameful, degrading, and a legitimate source of embarrassment to self and family. For this reason, it is commonly believed that mental and emotional problems should be concealed. Many people believe that inability to successfully work through their own problems without the aid of outside assistance is a sign of personal weakness and indicative of a basic character flaw. There is also a commonly held misconception that anyone who needs help in coping with mental or emotional problems is "crazy" or insane. Fear of having such frightening labels attached may prove to be a powerful deterrent to seeking psychological help. Finally, there is a pervasive belief that mental disorders can never be cured and that people requiring psychiatric assistance may be expected to function in a less than optimal manner during the remaining course of their lives. In terms of future employment opportunities, interpersonal relationships, and various situations requiring personal trust and confidence, this erroneous belief could prove to be a significant handicap to the individual who has undergone psychiatric treatment. In many cases, our fear of potential repercussions accruing from undergoing psychiatric treatment may overshadow our desire to obtain relief from mental strain. Unfortunately, we do not view psychological and physical problems in the same light. Although few people would hesitate to consult a physician in the event of physical injury or illness, many people are highly reluctant to seek professional help in the event of mental illness or psychological distress.

If a person can be convinced that a need for psychiatric or psychological assistance exists, several resources may be drawn upon in an attempt to obtain such help. The personal physician can be first consulted and a referral to a competent professional or institution be obtained. However, if a personal physician is not available, one of the following resources may be consulted for a referral: (1) local hospitals, (2) mental health clinics, (3) state or county department of mental health, (4) local chapter of the state mental health society. A person in need of help should be discouraged from choosing a therapist from the yellow pages of the telephone directory without the support of additional information. Likewise, those who promise miraculous cures and use highly unorthodox treatments should be avoided. The guidelines followed in choosing a mental health professional should be essentially the same as those followed in the choice of any medical specialist. Furthermore, if people are dissatisfied with their mental health professional, feel that no progress is being made, or that a positive interpersonal relationship has not been established, consideration should be given to changing therapists. Just as no rule binds a patient permanently to one medical doctor, there is no reason to assume that our choice of a mental health professional cannot be changed.

Summary

Although all people are subjected to stress, individuals cope in different ways and achieve varying levels of adjustment. Stress, whether reality or non-reality based, tends to be a pervasive characteristic of life and is defined as a state of physical or psychological strain resulting from the actual or perceived presence of threat. Since many types of stress cannot be handled using the "flight or fight" reaction, there is the possibility that stress-related energy may turn destructively upon self or others. At the same time, however, stress-related energy may be expended in a number of constructive ways. In terms of physical and psychological well-being, it is important that such energy be discharged and not become bottled up within the individual.

In later maturity, outlets for release of energy resulting from stress tend to change. Many stresses encountered during this period may not be amenable to direct action or active involvement. As we age, reactions to stress may assume a progressively passive quality and successful adjustment may become increasingly dependent upon our ability to constructively expend energy upon the restoration of self. Unfortunately, little in life may effectively prepare a person to deal with stressful events that cannot be changed through direct action.

Holmes and Rahe have devised a scale composed of 43 events that impose stress upon the individual. In this scale each event is rated according to the intensity of stress imposed. Their work has done much to increase awareness of stress resulting from change—pleasant or unpleasant—and the potentially devastating effects of cumulative stress associated with multiple life changes. This work has also increased awareness of difficulties involved in the accurate assessment of stress imposed upon any individual at any specific point in time. Research indicates that the probability of physical and psychological pathology increases as an accompaniment of prolonged exposure to stress associated with significant life changes.

According to Hans Selye, the body responds to stress in three sequential phases referred to as the general adaptation syndrome. The three phases are the alarm stage, the stage of resistance, and the stage of exhaustion. In the alarm stage an acceleration of bodily functioning (heart rate, respiration, perspiration) is experienced and the individual is poised to react. During the resistance stage, the body continues to function under elevated pressure and strain and a gradual depletion of physical and psychological resources results. Finally, when the exhaustion stage is reached, the individual's physical and mental resources have been spent and continued toleration of stress becomes impossible. At this point, physical or mental breakdown becomes increasingly probable.

Much stress may be related to frustration and that frustration leads to aggression. Frustration occurs when an obstacle is placed between a person and a desired goal. In stressful situations, particularly those involving permanent loss, the degree of frustration experienced by the individual will probably be great because the desired goal can never be reached. Aggressive energy resulting from frustration may be expended in constructive or destructive ways and may be directed inward or outward. The manner in which such energy is expended depends upon a number of factors such as personality, social demands and expectations, and general environmental characteristics.

A relationship appears to exist between our reactions to stress and our personality structure. A relationship has been established between a personality pattern, Type A, and increased probability of coronary disease in middle age. Yet, this relationship does not appear to continue into later maturity. However, personality dynamics associated with the hypertensive person appear to persist and exert an influence into old age.

Certain steps may be taken to help the person adjust successfully within acute stress situations. In an attempt to facilitate positive coping behavior, (1) free and open expression of emotions should be encouraged and accepted, (2) substitute goals should be provided, (3) major life changes should be delayed or avoided, (4) responsibility for self within a supportive atmosphere should be encouraged, and (5) finally, if needed, professional help should be sought.

Progress Check

1. What is stress?   (p. 142)

2. Why might non-reality based stress be more difficult to cope with than reality based stress?   (p. 142)

3. How do behavioral options in reference to stress tend to change as we grow older?   (pp. 143–144)

4. What is the relationship between life changes and stress? (pp. 145–148)

5. How might we attempt to determine the amount of stress to which we are exposed at a particular point in time?   (pp. 145–147)

6. What stages do we progress through when exposed to prolonged stress? What are some characteristics of each stage?   (pp. 148–150)

7. What are some examples of constructive and destructive behaviors that may be exhibited within a frustrating situation?   (pp. 150–151)

8. What is the theoretical relationship between frustration and aggression? (pp. 150–151)

9. What are some examples of inward and outward expressions of aggression?   (pp. 150–151)

10. What are three characteristics of the Type A personality?   (p. 152)

11. What is the relationship between age and heart attacks in Type A personalities?   (pp. 152–153)

12. What are four ways in which successful coping with stress might be promoted?   (pp. 153–158)

Recommended Readings

Friedman, M. & R. H. Rosenman. *Type A Behavior and Your Heart.* New York: Alfred A. Knopf, 1974.
This book explores the relationship between characteristic responses and orientations toward life and the development of heart disease. Of special interest are recommendations concerning how typical personality patterns can be modified.

Holmes, T. H. and M. Masuda. Life change and illness susceptibility. In J. P. Scott and E. C. Senay, eds., *Symposium on Separation and Depression,* 161–186. (Publication No. 94) Washington, D.C.: American Association for the Advancement of Science, 1973.
The authors discuss how the imposition of stress resulting from life changes can make the individual more vulnerable to disease and illness. Attention is given to life change units as qualitative indicators of stress intensity.

Selye, H. *The Stress of Life,* rev. ed. New York: McGraw-Hill, 1976.
A standard reading in stress. Investigates the relationships between stress, physiological change, and illness. Considers reactions to stress in terms of the general adaptation syndrome.

8

Aging and Psycho- pathology

Preview ∽ *In this chapter we will examine various types of psychopathology. Major categories used to group various psychopathic disorders will be introduced, and a differentiation will be made between organic and functional disorders. Specific types of mental disorders will be defined and symptoms associated with each will be discussed. Factors influencing maladaptive patterns of behavior in old age will be identified and consideration will be given to the relationship between aging and the incidence of psychopathology. Throughout this chapter, emphasis will be placed upon the fact that significant psychological disorders are not experienced by most elderly people.*

Psychopathology is a broad term used to denote mental and emotional disturbances and disorders that may afflict human beings. It is commonly believed that psychopathology may be traced to our failure to successfully adapt to various physical or psychological stresses. Such stresses may occur in the form of physical disease, mental or physical crises, *problems, and frustrations, and numerous losses that erode our feelings of security, satisfaction, and purpose. As change occurs, physical or psychological demands upon the individual to adapt are made. When successful adaptation does not occur, psychopathology is the result.*

How Are Psychopathological Disorders Categorized?

Psychopathology may be separated into two major categories, organic disorders and functional disorders. **Organic disorders** may be traced to some physiological change that operates to adversely affect the ability of the individual to adjust successfully and to behave in an effective manner. **Functional disorders** occur in the absence of any detectable physiological or organic cause and, presently, are not attributable to any disease, injury, or abnormal functioning of the body.

Organic disorders versus functional disorders

Organic disorders may be caused by a physiological change involving injury, disease, or some malfunctioning of the body, for example, the thyroid gland. Brain tumors, arteriosclerosis, neural injury resulting from disease or externally imposed **trauma,** and hormonal imbalance may underlie psychiatric disorders that are organic.

Unlike organic disorders, functional disorders cannot be directly linked to pathological or traumatic changes in the physical body. Functional disorders are considered to be adaptation failures arising from psychological causes.

Although a distinction is made between organic and functional disorders in terms of cause, behavioral characteristics associated with the two types of psychiatric disorders are sometimes quite similar. For example, acute depression, confusion, hallucinations, and memory and speech impairment may be organic or functional in origin. For this reason, accurate diagnosis may prove difficult and should be relegated to those individuals who understand both physical and psychological dynamics of human functioning. Because effective treatment depends upon accurate diagnosis, the possibility of organic or functional causes should be thoroughly investigated before establishing causation or initiating treatment. If a correct diagnosis is not made, the result may be catastrophic. A person, on the basis of a functional disorder diagnosis, may enter psychoanalysis and then die six months later from a brain tumor. When psychiatric disorders are considered, the critical importance of accurate diagnosis cannot be overemphasized.

Other categories of disorders

Although the fundamental distinction between organic and functional disorders is basic to any consideration of psychopathology, physical versus psychological causation represents but one division used to classify mental and behavioral disorders and, by itself, does not offer an adequate delineation or differentiation. Regardless of cause, various mental disturbances and disorders exhibit different symptoms, involve different dynamics, and respond to different types of treatment. On the basis of such differences, mental disorders are frequently grouped into one of the following broad categories: (1) *functional psychoses*, (2) *acute and chronic organic brain syndromes*, (3) *neuroses*, (4) *psychosomatic disorders*, and (5) *character disorders.*

What Are Functional Psychoses and Their Symptoms?

Psychoses are major psychological disturbances involving personality disorganization. **Functional psychoses** are mental disturbances that cannot be traced to physical causes and are characterized by possible loss of contact with reality, disturbed thought processes, pronounced swings of mood, and severely impaired interpersonal relationships. Inability to control ourselves and our life is often indicative of functional psychosis. Two principal categories classified beneath the heading functional psychoses are *affective psychoses* and *paranoia*.

Affective Psychoses: Depression

The term *affect* refers to emotions or feelings. Thus **affective psychoses** are mental disturbances characterized by pronounced swings or changes in moods or emotions. One type of affective psychosis is depression.

Although most individuals experience periodic bouts with depression— feel blue, listless, and less hopeful, energetic and enthusiastic than usual— the intensity, duration, and various physical symptoms of psychotic depression distinguishes it from normal depressive episodes (Beck, 1972; Pfeiffer, 1968). People suffering from **psychotic depression** often experience acute feelings of anxiety, are extremely sad, exhibit little or no interest in activities or the immediate environment, tend to become extremely withdrawn, and view life as hopeless. Such feelings, perceptions, and behaviors may persist for months. In despair, the depressed person may become exceedingly listless, experience a slowing of speech and thought processes, and perceive self as worthless, or even evil. More common physical manifestations of depression are pronounced fatigue (no energy to do anything), loss of appetite with accompanying weight loss, inability to sleep or erratic sleep patterns (early rising or inability to go back to sleep if awakened during the night), and digestive difficulties. Although depressed people may weep a great deal, some individuals may become so depressed that they can't even cry.

In old age the most frequently observed functional psychiatric disorder is depression (Tongas and Gibson, 1969; Peak, Polansky, and Altholz, 1971). In research executed by Butler (1963), it was reported that approximately one fifth of his healthy older subjects were diagnosed "mild reactive depressives" by psychiatrists and that depression was the largest single diagnostic category into which older people were placed. Likewise, Busse et al. (1955) noted that depressive episodes become increasingly frequent in old age. However, for the vast majority of elderly individuals, such depressive episodes are relatively mild and do not persist for prolonged periods of time.

When depression occurs in old age, it is usually in response to stresses resulting from psychological or physical losses (Post, 1965). Because such stressful losses—of friends, family, and health—become increasingly common in old age, it is logical to assume that the incidence and duration of depressive reactions will increase as an accompaniment of advanced chronological age. To a great extent, depressive reactions noted among the elderly appear to be responses to "normal" changes accompanying old age rather than the result of the aging process itself. In old age there is usually a lot more to become depressed about than in youth. While recognizing that we become less resistant or more vulnerable to stress in old age, the relationship between advanced age and depression may, to some extent then, be one of increased provocation rather than increased susceptibility.

Possibility of suicide.   Among severely depressed individuals (particularly the aged), the possibility of suicide is ever present. Frequent accompaniments of depression are suicidal thoughts that may take the form of passive "death wishes" or may involve definite plans to end one's life. In some instances, individuals who have such wishes or plans may openly relate them to others. Yet, the real possibility of suicide is not taken seriously in many cases and indications of impending self-destruction are often ignored or go unheeded. Although many people feel that a person who talks about suicide is unlikely to commit such an act, this is an extremely incorrect and highly dangerous belief. All indications of potential suicide should be taken very seriously and treated accordingly. When persons contemplating suicide make their morbid intentions clear to others, they may be asking for help and still may be accessible or open to outside intervention. Any indication of potential suicide should be perceived as an opportunity to help.

Unfortunately, we know that elderly people are less likely than young people to share suicidal thoughts and plans with others. Thus opportunities to help the potential suicide victim are less likely to arise from the elderly population. The elderly are also less likely than the young to meet with failure when attempting to take their own life. When an elderly person attempts to commit suicide, the probability of succeeding is relatively high.

On the basis of information derived from research, a strong relationship appears to exist between depression in old age and suicide (Gardner, Bahn, and Mach, 1963; Robins et al., 1959). According to these studies, most suicides occurring in old age have been preceded by depressive reactions of either long or short duration. This relationship between depression and suicide in old age underscores the importance of accurately identifying and effectively dealing with depressive reactions that occur in later maturity.

Affective Psychoses: **Mania**

A second type of affective psychosis, often involving feelings of marked enthusiasm, euphoria, and optimism, is labeled **mania,** or manic reactions. To a large extent, the characteristics of mania are opposite those of depression. The depressed person is extremely low while the manic individual is extremely high. Persons experiencing manic reactions are likely to feel very happy, to view themselves and the world in a highly optimistic light, to believe that nothing can't be accomplished or overcome, and to give little consideration to practical matters or constraints. Manic individuals may speak at an accelerated pace and exhibit behaviors characterized by increased and more rapid activity. Great energy, great enthusiasm, and great elation are significant parts of manic behavior. During episodes of mania, the individual may become involved in business deals, make interpersonal commitments, undertake unrealistic projects, and make various purchases (for example, a car) that are later regretted.

Although the major characteristic of mania is euphoria or elation, episodes of depression, irritability, and hostility are often an integral part of the manic reaction. Although such low periods may be relatively short-lived, they may occur unpredictably and present a startling contrast of behaviors. As with depressive reactions, there is always the possibility that the elderly person on the "low side" of mania may pose a threat to self and engage in suicidal behavior. Such individuals often require relatively close supervision and guidance if problems are to be averted and optimal functioning promoted.

Paranoia

Besides the affective disorders, a second major group listed under the heading of functional psychoses is paranoia or paranoid reactions. Paranoid reactions are the second most common psychiatric disorder encountered in old age following depressive reactions. **Paranoia,** or paranoid reactions are characterized mainly by the presence of some persistent delusion or delusional system. **Delusions** are thoughts or beliefs that are false or contrary to reality. They tend to occupy some important place in the individual's life and may influence behavior in reference to particular persons, places, things, or situations. For example, within social situations, people suffering from paranoia may believe that others are secretly plotting against them. They may believe that their food is being poisoned or that their housekeeper is trying to steal prized possessions. Apart from the specific focus of the individual's delusions, other aspects of the paranoid person's life frequently remain untouched by this psychiatric disturbance. Everyday functioning may be quite normal until something happens to trigger the delusional beliefs.

Paranoia and sensory deficits. Some investigators have noted a relationship between increased incidence of paranoid thoughts and decreased sensory acuity (Eisdorfer, 1960; Bromley, 1974). Paranoid reactions that accompany functional loss may be disruptive but are frequently not of a psychotic nature. It has been theorized that as less sensory information becomes available to elderly persons, they become increasingly apt to "fill in" missing material in an idiosyncratic manner. For example, a person who has experienced a significant auditory decline may believe that others are turning down the television volume to prevent news from being heard, are conversing in a whisper in order to keep secrets, or are planning some unknown event. Because the person is actually unable to hear what transpires, interpretations and explanations increasingly evolve from self rather than from the environment. In an attempt to better understand the relationship between paranoid beliefs and changes in sensory input, pretend for a moment that you are standing in a room with a number of people. At the far end of the room, three of your friends are standing close together, giggling, and occasionally glancing in your direction. In such a situation do you impose your own interpretation upon the behavior of others? In the absence of sufficient sensory input, do you simply "fill in" what's missing? If you are like most other human beings, you will begin to fill in or personally interpret what is happening almost immediately. If information to the contrary is not forthcoming, it is probable that your personal interpretation of the situation will remain unchanged. By the same token, serious doubts concerning your personal perceptions may never arise.

To a significant degree, paranoid reactions that occur in old age may be successfully treated using measures designed to correct sensory deficits. As sensory deficits are corrected or compensatory measures are employed, increased reality-based information is input, and demands upon individuals to impose their own personal interpretations upon persons, things, or situations are reduced. Fewer gaps are present in the individual's cognitive or mental structure and fewer opportunities and necessities for developing paranoid delusions exist. In later maturity the prognosis for paranoid reactions tends to be quite good and intervention procedures frequently produce positive results. However, initial attempts to overcome paranoid beliefs (particularly suspicion) may be resisted and persistent attention may be required.

What Are Organic Brain Syndromes and Their Symptoms?

Organic brain syndromes or diseases **(OBS)** are specific types of mental disorders resulting from neural impairment or brain damage. It must be emphasized that OBS are disease entities that in no way reflect the normal aging process. Because the characteristics of OBS are those that have become popularly associated with the concept of senility (see page 10), a widespread belief is held that mental impairment is a natural accompaniment of old age. This, of course, is not the case. Although all human beings experience a progressive loss or dying of brain cells with increased chronological age, such losses do not typically disrupt behavior to any significant extent or result in pathological symptoms associated with OBS. What we refer to as *senility* is not a normal product of aging.

According to current statistics, about 50 percent of all mental disturbances encountered in later maturity may be attributed to OBS (Kramer, Taube, and Redick, 1973). However, although OBS account for a significant proportion of mental disturbances encountered in old age, it should be remembered that only 2 to 3 percent of the 65-and-over population are afflicted with such disorders (Busse and Pfeiffer, 1973). That is, the actual prevalence of OBS is quite restricted and the odds against experiencing this disorder are extremely good.

Acute and chronic OBS

Organic brain syndromes are divided into two groups of disorders—acute and chronic. The onset of acute OBS tends to be relatively sudden. Chronic OBS, however, are long-standing and have usually progressed over an extended period of time. The distinction between chronic and acute OBS is most important in terms of prognosis. In many cases the effects of acute OBS are reversible and the prognosis for recovery is very good (Butler and Lewis, 1977). However, chronic brain syndromes are not reversible and attempts to treat this disorder or to significantly alter its effects have proven to be unsuccessful.

Acute brain syndromes may result from factors causing permanent brain damage or may be precipitated by factors provoking temporary change. Strokes, brain tumors, and externally imposed injury to the brain are possible causes of permanent brain damage. Temporary conditions provoking acute brain syndromes are malnutrition, drug intoxication, metabolic malfunctioning, psychological trauma or stress, and bodily infections (Butler and Lewis, 1977; Engel and Romano, 1959). When such temporary conditions or causes of acute brain syndromes are removed, the previously afflicted individual will, in many cases, return to normal functioning. When acute brain syndromes are caused by factors resulting in permanent brain damage, the prognosis continues to be relatively good. Although organic dysfunction associated with brain damage, for example, partial paralysis or slurred speech, may persist, the specific behavioral and psychological characteristics associated with acute brain syndromes may be successfully treated.

Chronic brain syndromes are *progressive*—characterized by continued deterioration; causal factors include cerebral arteriosclerosis, cardiovascular diseases, epilepsy, syphilis, and brain injuries (Bromley, 1974; Zarit, 1977). Chronic brain syndromes progress over an extended period of time as symptoms become increasingly pronounced. By the time many individuals are diagnosed as having a chronic brain syndrome, the pathological condition has reached a point requiring close supervision or institutionalization.

Chronic brain syndromes are reflections of *extensive* brain damage and continued neural deterioration. At the present time, such neural deterioration cannot be halted and there is little hope of improving the mental condition of persons with chronic brain syndromes (Thompson et al., 1976). However, some disturbances (for example, depression, anxiety, withdrawal) associated with this pathological condition may be mitigated through the provision of a therapeutic or caring environment (Butler, 1960). Although researchers are currently investigating procedures designed to improve the functioning of individuals with chronic brain syndromes, breakthroughs have not been forthcoming (Zarit, 1977; Goldfarb et al., 1972; Thompson et al., 1976). At this point, prevention rather than cure appears to be the more realistic goal in reference to chronic brain syndromes.

Symptoms of OBS

There are a number of behavioral characteristics or symptoms commonly associated with organic brain syndromes. However, although such symptoms may be indicative of organic brain syndromes, they may also occur in the absence of these pathological conditions. Because variables such as personality, extent of neural damage, and environmental conditions affect behavioral manifestations, these symptoms may or may not be accurate indicators of organic impairment (Kahn et al., 1961; Zarit and Kahn, 1975; Blessed et al., 1968). Likewise, symptoms do not adequately differentiate chronic from acute brain syndromes. This differentiation is usually based upon an individual's history of impairment including rapidity of pathological onset.

Changes in behavior found in conjunction with organic brain syndromes may be intellectual and emotional. Individuals may experience impairments in short and long-term memory, ability to absorb new information, visual-motor coordination, ability to handle abstractions, and ability to concentrate or maintain attention. The mind may wander, reality orientation toward the environment may be severely impaired, for example, "Where am I?" "Why am I here?" "What's happening around me?" and interpersonal relationships may greatly suffer. Persons may experience high levels of anxiety, become violent, exhibit emotional extremes subject to rapid change, and become quite withdrawn. Moodiness, aggression, and depression are aspects of organic brain syndromes. **Hallucinations,** both visual and auditory, and delusions are experienced. As might be expected, individuals with such organic impairments suffer disturbances in established sleep and dietary habits. In extreme cases all communicative skills may become severely diminished—speech may become so distorted that understanding is impossible—and the individual may lose motor skills needed for personal care—dressing, washing, and feeding.

Diagnosis: The Mental Status Questionnaire

Because many symptoms characteristic of organic brain syndromes are shared with other psychiatric disorders, the possibility of incorrect diagnosis

Table 8.1: Mental Status Questionnaire

---

1. Where are you now? (What place is this? What is it called?)

2. Where is it located? (What is the address?)

3. What is the date today? Day?

4. What month is it?

5. What year is it?

6. How old are you?

7. When were you born? Month?

8. Year of birth?

9. Who is the president of the United States?

10. Who was the president before him?

What is your main trouble? (Why did you come here?)

Have you ever been in another (place with the same name)?

Have you ever seen me before?

What do I do? (What is my job called?)

Where were you last night?

Source: *The American Journal of Psychiatry*, vol. 117, pp. 326–328, 1960. Copyright 1960, The American Psychiatric Association.

is ever present. At this time, an important toc' in the diagnosis and assessment of organic brain syndromes is the Mental Status Questionnaire. The rationale underlying this instrument is that certain intellectual or cognitive deficits occur in association with organic brain syndromes that are not usually found in conjunction with other psychiatric disturbances. Such intellectual deficits adversely influence the ability to maintain reality orientation within the environment and to recall basic information. When results derived from the Mental Status Questionnaire are compared with results obtained from various direct physical measures of brain damage, the correlation (degree of agreement) is high.

The Mental Status Questionnaire (see Table 8.1) is used for purposes of diagnosing organic brain syndromes and for purposes of continuing assessment. According to Kahn and Associates (1961), the presence of three or more errors on the Mental Status Questionnaire is highly suggestive of organic brain syndrome.

What Are Neuroses: What Neuroses Are Most Common Among the Aged?

Neuroses are emotional or behavioral disturbances involving excessive and potentially disabling amounts of **anxiety,** a persistent fear arising from sources that may or may not be known to the individual, but associated with conflict, threat, or frustration. It is the critical factor underlying neuroses. Essentially, neuroses are patterns of response that are designed to control subjective feelings of discomfort and pain arising from anxiety. Such patterns of response tend to be exaggerations or intensifications of normal everyday behavior and are generally not recognized as abnormal until they significantly disrupt or interfere with ordinary functioning. Although neuroses are generally not incapacitating and do not require hospitalization, people who suffer from them usually operate at a diminished level of efficiency, derive little pleasure or gratification from life, and constantly expend great amounts of energy on the nonproductive control of anxiety. Neurotics are not happy people.

Certain types of neuroses are more common among the older population. Such neuroses are usually exhibited by individuals who have previously exhibited similar patterns of neurotic behavior in early adulthood or middle age. When faced with additional stresses that usually accompany old age, neurotic responses become intensified as people strive to cope with increased levels of anxiety. However, in times of acute stress, neuroses having no historic antecedents may arise. In later maturity the following neuroses are exhibited with increased frequency: (1) *anxiety reactions,* (2) *hypochondriasis,* and (3) *obsessive reactions* (Bromley, 1974; Pfeiffer, 1977; Simon, 1973). Also, with advanced age, irrational fears or *phobias* may develop.

Anxiety reactions

Anxiety reactions involve the subjective experiencing of severe and disabling levels of anxiety accompanied by physical changes that may include heart palpitations, sweating, dizziness, faintness, cold hands and feet, diarrhea, inability to catch the breath, and nausea. Anxiety reactions, the manifestations of anxiety neuroses, usually occur without warning (for example, the individual may be sitting calmly having a cup of coffee) and tend to be quite frightening. Individuals who experience anxiety reactions often believe they are having a heart attack or stroke and that death is imminent. It may be difficult to convince such persons that the problem is psychological rather than physical. When anxiety reactions occur for the first time in old age, they are frequently precipitated by dramatic loss associated with acute stress, for example, death in the family. However, such reactions may appear some time later. A widow, for example, may experience an anxiety reaction days following the funeral of her husband. In most instances anxiety attacks do not recur over extended periods of time and, in the absence of therapeutic intervention, anxiety neuroses often evolve into neurotic behavior patterns that are more complicated but less painful and disabling to the individual.

Hypochondriasis

Hypochondriasis involves excessive preoccupation with one's health or bodily functions. The belief that one is diseased or ill, regardless of evidence to the contrary, may be tenaciously held by the individual who is hypochon-driacal. Assurances from a physician that no pathology exists are usually rejected, additional opinions are sought, and medical treatment demanded. On the other hand, a physician who is not alert to the possibility of hypo-chondriasis may fail to accurately diagnose this psychological disturbance and may undertake a variety of physical treatments. The treatment of phys-ical symptoms will, of course, do little to alleviate underlying causes of pathol-ogy. Finally, the psychological bases for the elderly persons' complaints may be ignored by a physician who perceives disease and illness as natural ac-companiments of old age—someone who thinks, "What do you expect at your age?" When hypochondriacal reactions are involved, the probability of misdiagnosis is relatively high.

As hypochondriacal persons keep close watch upon their bodies, physical symptoms and complaints are carefully noted and duly reported. In some instances preoccupation with health and body become so pronounced that interpersonal relationships become strained or are destroyed. People may withdraw from individuals who complain constantly, or hypochondriacal per-sons may withdraw from those who do not sympathize with their condition. In either case difficulties may arise. Hypochondriacal individuals tend to resist any suggestions that their problems may be emotional or psychological in origin and continue to fixate upon physical symptoms and causes to the exclusion of all else. For this reason, attempts to involve the hypochondriacal person in any type of psychotherapy usually prove futile. Although the dy-namics of hypochondriasis are not fully known, it is proposed that the uncon-sciously motivated belief that we are ill or physically incapacitated permits acceptable withdrawal from situations and responsibilities that are anxiety-provoking. Viewed from this perspective, we can better understand the great reluctance and refusal of hypochondriacal persons to relinquish their symp-toms or to consider the possibility of psychological cause. In old age, the proportion of people with hypochondriacal complaints increases. Likewise, with advanced age, the proportion of psychiatric disorders diagnosed as hy-pochondriasis becomes larger. The incidence of this disorder increases among both sexes in later maturity, but women appear to be significantly more likely to exhibit hypochondriacal behavior patterns than are men (Earley and von Mering, 1969).

Obsessive reactions

Obsessive reactions represent unconscious attempts to control anxiety with the intrusion of persistent ideas, thoughts, or images that cannot be voluntarily dismissed. Such obsessive thoughts serve to control anxiety and concern the specific obsession to the exclusion of whatever the actual causes of anxiety are. For example, if it is possible to occupy your mind by repeat-edly counting to 100 throughout the course of the day, anxiety-causing thoughts will be given no opportunity to enter your awareness. In old age much of the content of obsessive thoughts tends to be of a morbid nature and is frequently irrational. Individuals may constantly think that their doors or windows are unlocked, that some physical harm may be done to them or to others, that they will be unable to control some undesirable behavior, or that their telephone conversations or mail is being monitored. It is not uncommon for paranoid content to become involved in obsessive ideation. Although people experiencing obsessive reactions usually recognize the irrational nature of their thoughts, this recognition does little to diminish the impact of such ideas or to assist in their removal. As long as the person is unable to cope with underlying causes of anxiety which obsessive thoughts operate to control, such persistent thoughts or images are likely to persist.

Phobias

Phobias are intense, irrational fears that occur in association with stimuli—people, places, events, situations or things—that hold relatively little possibility of danger or harm, such as the color green, shaking hands, elevators and closets, open spaces, and water. Although certain phobias relate to objects that could prove harmful to the individual (germs, dirt, disease), the fear reactions elicited by such stimuli are much greater than the threat involved. Whether or not a phobia is incapacitating depends more upon the prevalence of the feared stimulus than upon the intensity or characteristics of the individual's reactions. If the object of our fear is something that must be repeatedly faced and is an integral aspect of our daily interactions, the phobia is likely to be incapacitating. For example, if you experience a phobic reaction to people, streets, cars, or trees, you may be completely unable to cope successfully. However, when the object of the phobic reaction is rarely encountered, relatively few negative effects may be experienced.

Phobias that occur in old age may be triggered by highly stressful situations in which a person's ability to cope becomes overtaxed and previously effective defenses against long-standing anxiety fail. In such cases previously controlled or repressed anxiety is permitted to surface and may be exhibited as a phobic reaction. It is believed that phobias may be symbolic representations of the individual's real source of anxiety yet may be clearly indicative of that which is feared. For example, a person who is extremely anxious about the prospect of death may develop a phobia in reference to enclosures, darkness, cemeteries, and funeral homes. Although phobic reactions can be very painful and distressing to a person, such neurotic patterns permit "compartmentalization" of anxiety and may allow extended periods of functioning that are relatively free from subjective feelings of stress.

Although certain types of neurotic patterns are noted with increased frequency in old age, such neuroses are not often antecedents of more severe psychological disorders. When neurotic patterns of adjustment are exhibited, such patterns usually reflect well-established and characteristic modes of coping rather than transitory states.

What Defense Mechanisms Are Common Among the Aged?

Defense mechanisms represent attempts by the individual to avoid, reduce, or defend oneself from the disabling effects of anxiety. Anxiety is an unpleasant feeling that may range from mild discomfort to severe pain. No one wants to feel anxious. For this reason, each of us employs—to a greater or lesser extent—various strategies designed to guard ourselves from anxiety. Such strategies are called defense mechanisms and are characteristic of neurosis only when used extensively or overused. **Defense mechanisms** are unconscious psychological processes and the individual's understanding of his or her strategies for dealing with anxiety may be marginal at best. The development of defense mechanisms may be traced to early childhood. Depending upon personality, each individual will employ different mechanisms during periods of stress or anxiety.

There is no indication that defense mechanisms are more extensively used in old age than in early adulthood or middle age. However, among the elderly population, certain types of strategies used to handle anxiety become increasingly prevalent and characteristic of adjustment to stress. In later maturity the most common defense mechanisms used are: *denial, projection, rationalization,* and *overcompensation* (Simon, 1973; Simon, 1976; Bromley, 1974; Pfeiffer, 1977).

Denial

Denial involves refusal to admit or accept the existence of information or material that is anxiety provoking. For example, elderly persons may deny that they have reached old age. Although denial may seemingly be a harmless and at times beneficial defense against anxiety, refusal to recognize or accept reality may have devastating consequences. In cases involving physical illness or disease, denial may prevent a person from seeking needed medical attention. Likewise, denial of losses in sensory acuity may prevent a person from obtaining corrective aids and devices. When denial of loss occurs, adjustment to loss must be postponed until recognition and acceptance is achieved. In such situations denial may provide a person with time in which physical and mental resources may be rallied for purposes of coping with the loss. Such temporary denial may have positive consequences in terms of overall adjustment.

Projection

When our own characteristics or behaviors are attributed to another, **projection** is involved. In many instances projected characteristics are unacceptable to the individual and would prove anxiety-provoking if recognized in oneself. When people use projection extensively, they may blame others for everything that goes wrong and refuse to assume responsibility for other than positive outcomes. When projection occurs, an older person may accuse other people of operating on the basis of motives and needs that presently direct or directed their own behavior in earlier years. For example, a mother who is stingy and conservative may be unable to perceive these characteristics in herself and may incorrectly attribute them to her daughter. A man who has been irresponsible and selfish during most of his life may project these characteristics onto male members of the younger generation. Although projection tends to be quite effective in guarding a person against anxiety, those who use projection extensively frequently have problems involving interpersonal relationships and may learn little from their personal mistakes that are blamed upon others.

Rationalization

Rationalization refers to logical, rational, and acceptable explanations or justifications for behavior that are formulated "after the fact" and conceal actual motives. For example, a man may explain that he never visited his mother because business matters kept him too busy. In reality, he had plenty of time to visit but chose not to do so. In later maturity rationalization may be used to maintain feelings of independence ("I only moved in with my daughter because she needed help with the house"), to guard against disturbances provoked by the actions of others ("My son can't visit me because he's too busy at the office"), and to allay guilt feelings associated with past actions ("I only drank so much because she keeps nagging me"). Rationalization is the most common defense mechanism used by adults and represents a generally innocuous strategy for dealing with anxiety.

Overcompensation

Overcompensation is a person's overreactions to potential sources of threatened anxiety. If a person grew up in poverty, he or she may devote all waking hours to the pursuit of money. A person who was frail as a child may strive to become an Olympic athlete.

In later maturity overcompensation usually centers upon maintenance and restoration of youth. Overcompensating people begin to dress in youthful fashions, attempt to copy the fads of youth, and try to identify with the younger generation. In pursuit of youth—or fleeing from old age—organic diets, unrealistic exercise regimes, and radical changes in life-styles may be adopted. Through the vigorous pursuit of youth, some may be able to retard the effects of aging. For others, overcompensation may entail the futile dissipation of energies and resources that ultimately result in an acceleration of the aging process.

In themselves, denial, projection, rationalization, and overcompensation are neither good nor bad. If they are not used to excess, pose no impediment to successful functioning, and effectively control anxiety, such defense mechanisms may be viewed as positive coping strategies. However, if such defenses are overused, result in adjustment difficulties, or do not adequately control anxiety, they must be viewed as neurotic.

What Are Psychosomatic Disorders?

When identifiable physical disease, illness, or damage results from psychological rather than physical causes, we are referring to **psychosomatic disorders.** Although hypochondriacal reactions center upon "imagined" physical problems, "real" physical problems result from psychosomatic disorders. Peptic ulcers, migraine headaches, colitis, high blood pressure (to some extent), asthma, and certain skin eruptions or rashes are believed to be physical expressions of psychological stress. Current research also suggests that various cardiovascular diseases and possibly cancer may be attributed, in part, to psychological causes and may thus be linked to psychosomatic disorders.

Any person who has been placed in a stressful situation, has experienced a sudden psychological shock, or has been mildly nervous understands that certain discernible physical changes accompany such periods of emotional disturbance. Muscles tense, heartbeat accelerates, perspiration increases, and the stomach may begin to feel queasy. During this period, increased amounts of adrenalin are being deposited into the bloodstream and the body is operating under conditions of increased strain. When the human body is forced to continue operating under conditions of increased strain for an extended period of time (perhaps months or years), pathological organic change may ultimately result.

Many psychosomatic illnesses observed among the elderly population have roots in early adulthood or middle age. Such illnesses were present in younger days and have continued to follow an established pattern into old age. On the basis of medical histories and time of onset, such disorders are recognized as having psychosomatic foundations and are likely to receive both physical and psychological treatment. However, prolonged periods of frustration and conflict frequently encountered in old age may be instrumental in precipitating the initial onset of psychosomatic malfunctions.

Because old age is a time associated with increased disease and illness, it is highly probable that such psychosomatic reactions will be mistakenly viewed as the inevitable results of physical aging and will be treated without consideration of psychological causation. When this occurs, attention will be focused upon such a person's physical symptoms rather than the underlying causes. Thus, physical deterioration is likely to continue. In cases involving psychosomatic illness, treatment designed to help the individual deal more effectively with anxiety is in order. Likewise, strategies designed to alleviate stress or remove the source of anxiety, such as intervention designed to combat social isolation, to allay feelings of insecurity through the provision of a secure, dependable, and healthful environment, or to provide support services in times of need, may prove effective in the treatment of psychosomatic disorders. Without treatment geared to deal with psychological causes as well as physical symptoms, the probability is low that significant positive results will be achieved with individuals suffering from psychosomatic disorders.

What Are Some Character Disorders?

Character disorders, also referred to as **behavior disorders,** are abnormal patterns of adjustment characterized by actions that are contrary to established and accepted social values, morals, and norms. Although there are many types of character disorders, our discussion will be restricted to crime **(antisocial behavior)** and alcoholism (and alcohol abuse).

Crime

Rather than increasing, the incidence of crime decreases as old age is approached and reached. After age 65, there is a marked decrease in number and proportion of crimes committed. Most crimes committed by the adult population occur within the 15-to-40 age group. The 65-and-over population has the lowest crime rate of any age group. Crimes involving physical assault and violence are practically nonexistent among the elderly. The absence of such crimes cannot be explained in terms of physical changes that make older people incapable of executing such violent acts. Our ability to shoot another person, for example, probably doesn't decline with advanced age. Rather, it is likely that crimes involving violence and assault decline for a number of complex reasons, including age-related changes in personality and motivation. Rather than being the perpetrators of violent crimes, the elderly are more likely to be the targets.

Crimes that increase in old age are often indicative of mental illness, and there is some question whether these acts should be considered *criminal.* Such crimes include vagrancy, public or chronic drunkenness, disorderly conduct, violation of public decency, and gambling (Riley et al., 1968). Such crimes are most frequently committed by men. Although the crime rate is higher for men than for women across all age categories, women commit practically no crimes in old age. Violations of the law, with the possible exception of infrequent petty theft or shoplifting, are not attributed to older women. However, whether committed by men or women, most criminal activities noted among the elderly population are associated with mental deterioration or some identifiable psychopathological disorder.

Alcoholism

Alcoholism, the chronic and excessive use of alcohol and resulting addiction to it, is a significant problem for many elderly people (Simon, Epstein, and Reynolds, 1968; Redick, Kramer, and Taube, 1973). Most of these people have been chronic and excessive users of alcohol during much of their lives. Others turn to alcohol in old age as a means of relieving stress resulting from factors such as loneliness, psychological trauma, and physical pain. As a person becomes less able to cope successfully with various problems and conflicts associated with aging, drinking may be turned to as an effective and readily accessible means of temporary relief. What had previously been "social drinking" may develop rapidly into alcohol abuse. In old age, alcoholism may be superimposed upon various psychological disturbances that represent maladaptive ways of dealing with anxiety. For example, an elderly person who becomes acutely depressed may turn to alcohol in an attempt to escape from the painful and distressing sensations accompanying this disorder. Alcohol (although a depressant) is frequently used by people to alleviate feelings of sadness, despair, and helplessness. When alcoholism is superimposed upon underlying problems, the real cause of difficulty may be overlooked and "cure" may be equated with abstinence. However, if underlying psychological disturbances are ignored, the probability that the individual will return to drink is great.

In most cases elderly people who have long histories of alcohol abuse have incurred permanent damage which is frequently reflected in various physical and psychological pathologies, such as liver damage and organic brain syndromes. Typically, such problems and disorders will continue to plague elderly individuals throughout the remaining course of their lives. The actual drinking behavior may cease, but its effects will never be completely eradicated.

Although alcoholism or alcohol abuse constitutes a significant problem for many aged individuals, the extent of this problem is really unknown. Elderly individuals who use alcohol excessively may never come to the attention of medical or psychological agencies or personnel unless acute disturbances occur (**delirium tremens**) or problems arise with the law (public drunkenness and disorderly conduct). Likewise, physicians may be reluctant to diagnose individuals as alcoholic and, if diagnosed, the records of such persons are not open to public scrutiny. At this time most statistics concerning the incidence of alcoholism among the aged population are drawn from state-supported hospitals, mental institutions, and mental health clinics. The degree to which such statistics accurately portray patterns within the general population of elderly individuals can only be conjectured.

Does Increased Age Affect Our Mental Health?

The prevalence of psychopathology in later maturity is very poorly documented. No one knows exactly how many older people suffer from psychological disturbances or disorders. However, most researchers agree that higher incidences of psychopathology are associated with old age and that mental and emotional disturbances become increasingly pronounced in advanced old age—beyond age 75 (Pfeiffer, 1973; Srole & Fisher, 1978; Whanger, 1973). Likewise, there is general agreement that state of physical health is highly related to incidence of psychopathology (Anderson and Davidson, 1975; Busse, 1968). People who are physically ill are more likely to exhibit maladaptive behavior patterns than are people who enjoy good health. Finally, it is generally agreed that personality is an extremely critical factor influencing whether or not psychopathic reactions will develop in old age (Kahn et al., 1961; Zarit & Kahn, 1975).

In old age, patterns of adjustment, whether successful or unsuccessful, are frequently extensions of previously developed and incorporated coping strategies. In most instances psychopathic behaviors exhibited in old age are intensifications of patterns that were present in earlier years and have become more pronounced in conjunction with increased stress. The probability is high that a person who is well adjusted and effectively copes with stress during early adulthood and middle age will continue to maintain a level of successful adjustment in later maturity. Likewise, when maladaptive patterns of behavior have been learned and practiced during a significant portion of a person's life, such patterns are likely to be exhibited in old age.

It should be noted that although the incidence of psychopathology increases in old age, most elderly people cope successfully during this period of life and show no signs of significant mental or emotional disturbance. This fact is particularly important in that the majority of elderly people are subjected to a variety of mental and physical stresses that should operate to greatly increase the probability of psychological dysfunction. When consideration is given to the numerous crises and traumas encountered in later maturity, the ability of most older individuals to effectively adjust to change, loss, and pressure is exeptionally good.

Summary

Psychopathology refers to mental and emotional disturbances and disorders. Such disturbances and disorders are indicative of a person's failure to successfully adjust to stress and may be traced to physical (organic) and psychological (functional) causes. Correct diagnosis of organic and functional causation is critical in determining treatment. However, it is often difficult to distinguish between the two.

Mental disorders are frequently grouped as follows: (1) functional psychoses, (2) acute and chronic organic brain syndromes, (3) neuroses, (4) psychosomatic disorders, and (5) character disorders.

Functional psychoses are mental disturbances that cannot be traced to physical causes and may be characterized by symptoms such as loss of contact with reality, disturbed thought processes, swings of mood, and severely impaired interpersonal relationships. They include the affective psychoses, depression and mania, and paranoia.

Organic brain syndromes are types of mental disorders resulting from neural impairment or brain damage. Though the onset of acute organic brain syndromes is sudden, chronic organic brain syndromes are long-standing and progressive. Although the symptoms of chronic and acute organic brain syndromes may be similar, prognoses differ significantly. The effects of acute OBS may be reversible, but those of chronic OBS are not reversible and attempts to alter pathological effects have been unsuccessful.

Neuroses are emotional or behavioral disturbances characterized by anxiety. Among the common neuroses in old age are anxiety reactions, hypochondriasis, and obsessive reactions. To some extent, phobic reactions also increase as an accompaniment to aging. In an attempt to control anxiety, defense mechanisms of denial, projection, rationalization, and overcompensation are commonly employed in later maturity.

When identifiable physical disease, illness, or damage results from psychological causes, psychosomatic disorders are involved. Examples of such disorders are ulcers, migraines, colitis, and skin rashes. In cases involving psychosomatic disorders, both physical and mental treatment are required.

Character disorders are abnormal patterns of adjustment characterized by actions that are contrary to established and accepted social values, morals, and norms. Two examples are crime, which is antisocial behavior, and alcoholism. Whereas relatively few crimes are committed by the elderly population, alcoholism constitutes a significant problem for many older adults.

The prevalence of psychopathology in later maturity is very poorly documented. However, it is generally recognized that the incidence of mental and emotional disturbance increases as a function of advanced age. Factors affecting the occurrence of mental pathology in old age include physical health and personality. In old age established adjustment patterns tend to continue and may become exaggerated. Positive adjustment in early life is a good predictor of positive adjustment in later life. Considering the increased number and types of stresses encountered in old age, the fact that most elderly people are able to cope successfully may be viewed as quite remarkable.

Progress Check

1. What is psychopathology?   (pp. 163–164)

2. What is the difference between organic and functional disorders?
   (p. 164)

3. What are three major categories of mental disorders?   (p. 165)

4. What are the two principal categories included within the functional
   psychoses heading? What are some characteristics of each?
   (pp. 165–168)

5. What is paranoia and how might sensory decline promote this disorder?
   (pp. 167–168)

6. How do chronic and acute organic brain syndromes differ in cause,
   damage incurred, and prognosis?   (pp. 169–170)

7. What are five possible causes of organic brain syndromes?
   (pp. 169–170)

8. What are five behavioral symptoms that might occur in association with
   organic brain syndromes?   (p. 170)

9. What are neuroses?   (pp. 171–172)

10. What neuroses are most common among the aged?   (pp. 172–174)

11. What are three defense mechanisms commonly used in old age? How
    might each be defined?   (pp. 175–177)

12. What is the difference between hypochondriasis and psychosomatic
    illness?   (pp. 172–173; pp. 177–178)

13. What is a character disorder? Give two examples.   (pp. 178–179)

14. Why might alcohol easily become a problem in old age?
    (pp. 178–179)

15. What are two factors influencing psychopathological manifestations in old
    age?

Recommended Readings

Redick, R. W., M. Kramer, and C. A. Taube. Epidemiology of mental illness
and utilization of psychiatric facilities among older persons. In E. W. Busse
and E. Pfeiffer, eds., *Mental Illness in Later Life.* Washington, D.C.:
American Psychiatric Association, 1973.
Discusses the incidence and distribution of mental illness among the elderly
population. Concerned with the types of psychiatric facilities used by older
persons and the reasons for use of such facilities.

Simon, A. Psychological changes that influence patient care. In *The
Psychosocial Needs of the Aged: Selected Papers.* Los Angeles: The Ethel
Percy Andrus Gerontology Center, University of Southern California, 1976.
Presents various research studies concerned with psychopathological
reactions in old age. Looks at common defense mechanisms used in later
maturity and offers suggestions regarding care of mentally disturbed older
persons.

9

Aging and Sexual Behavior

Preview ∽ *In this chapter we will attempt to dispel the myth of sexless old age. We will distinguish between sexuality and sexual behavior and examine relationships between these two concepts. A number of facts concerning sexual activity in old age will be presented and factors influencing such activities will be examined. We will then look at physiological and functional sexual changes in the aged female and the aged male. Finally, the subject of sexual adjustment in later maturity will be discussed.*

To understand sexual behavior in old age, we need first to consider what sexual behavior is and how it is related to our sexuality—our gender. Sexuality and sexual behavior are separate but related entities that influence each other during most of each person's life.

Sexuality and Sexual Behavior: They're Not the Same

Sexuality refers to "who you are" and sexual behavior refers to "what you do." The two are separated but interdependent. **Sexuality** is an important dimension of each individual's personality structure that forms a basis for self-identity. **Sexual behavior** involves specific actions usually designed to obtain sexual gratification. Although sexual behavior does not have to be indicative of underlying sexuality, there is usually a corresponding relationship between actions and personality orientation, that is, sexual objects and activities are generally determined—or strongly influenced—by our sexuality.

Where Does Our Sexuality Come From?

Sexuality is learned early in life and becomes a fairly well-established part of our personality by age two or three. As a result of socially imposed demands and expectations concerning sex-appropriate behavior ("Boys don't cry," "Girls don't get dirty"), individuals quickly learn to view themselves as masculine or feminine and to respond accordingly. Although norms or social definitions of appropriate masculine or feminine behavior may vary from one society to another and reflect different standards of maleness or femaleness, it is important to recognize that such standards are incorporated early and will continue to affect adjustment and behavior during the remaining course of our life.

Not from our sex organs

Our sexuality is not determined by our sex organs. Rather, sexuality is the product of social forces that are set in motion the moment infants are born. Beginning in the cradle, little boys and little girls are treated differently in a number of subtle but critical ways. Such differences in treatment influence personality development. In most cases differential treatment effectively produces "feminine" girls and "masculine" boys.

However, if the sex of the child is incorrectly identified, if parents opt to rear the child as though he or she were a member of the opposite sex, or if society responds to the child as it would to members of the opposite sex, "masculine" girls and "feminine" boys may result. Sexuality, determined by social rather than anatomical factors, may not coincide with one's physical sex. Although such cases are relatively rare, they have been mentioned for purposes of emphasizing the socially determined characteristic of sexuality. Determined by social forces, sexuality will remain vulnerable to the influence of social factors throughout the course of the individual's life.

Not from our sexual behavior

Just as sexuality is not determined by our sex organs, it is likewise not determined by our sexual behavior. When people abstain from sexual activities, they do not become less masculine or less feminine. Likewise, increased sexual involvement does not make a person more male or more female.

Sexual behavior reflects but one specific aspect of the individual's sexuality. In the absence of such behavior, sexuality does not disappear. According to Simone de Beauvoir:

> In childhood, sexuality is polymorphous: it is not centered upon the genital organs. . . . From this we may draw the conclusion that a person whose genital functions have diminished or become nonexistent is not therefore sexless: he is a sexed being—even eunuchs and impotent men remain sexed—and one who must work out his sexuality in spite of a given mutilation. (de Beauvoir, 1972)

What Negative Role Can Sexuality Play?

Although our sexuality is not determined by sexual behaviors, feelings of masculinity and femininity are often influenced by our involvement in sexual activities. For example, a man who is sexually impotent may begin to view himself as less aggressive, dominant, forceful, and worthwhile. He begins to consider himself less of a man in terms of his criteria of masculinity. Likewise, a woman who has had no opportunities to engage in sexual activities may begin to view herself as unattractive, undesirable, and somehow less than feminine. Extent of involvement in sexual activities may be closely related to feelings of personal esteem and worth. At the same time, feelings of personal esteem and worth will influence involvement in sexual activities.

Sexual dysfunction

When sexual behavior and sexuality are confused (consciously or unconsciously), the probability is relatively high that a cyclical pattern of sexual dysfunction will develop. An older person who is unable to engage in sexual activities may develop feelings of insecurity, inadequacy, and inferiority. In turn, such negative feelings toward self may adversely affect subsequent attempts to engage in sexual behaviors, and intensified feelings of inadequacy may result. Because very few of us are able to successfully segregate "who we are" from "what we do," sexual dysfunction or the absence of sexual activities often trigger self-deprecatory feelings that impose increased stress and tax our ability to cope effectively.

Anatomical loss

For some people, the inability to distinguish between sexuality and the specific sexual parts of the body is pronounced. Parts of the anatomy become symbolic of who the person is. If such parts are removed, fail to function properly, or are damaged, the person feels that masculinity or femininity has been greatly diminished or lost. A woman who must have a **hysterectomy** or **mastectomy** may feel that she is "no longer a woman." With the surgical removal of the uterus or breast, a significant symbol of femininity is taken away and the woman may react as though a critical aspect of her identity and personality has been destroyed. When a man is not able to control or effectively use the major symbol of his masculinity, his penis, he may believe he is "no longer a man," may develop problems centered upon personal identity, and experience generalized feelings of inadequacy, powerlessness, and incompetence in day-to-day interactions. Although such reactions are irrational, they may be significant obstacles to successful coping in times of physical change. In many instances ability to cope may depend upon whether or not those who interact with such individuals share their confused perception of sexuality and anatomy. For example, if a husband believes his wife to be less feminine as a result of breast surgery, this attitude will be transmitted to her and will probably make adjustment much more difficult. On the other hand, if a husband continues to perceive his wife as feminine, attractive, and desirable, this attitude will be conveyed and will make it easier to adjust.

Decreased self-identity and self-esteem

Sexuality is the basis for self-identity ("I am a woman/I am a man"), humanness (in the absence of sexuality, we must be less than human), and self-esteem ("I am a female/I am a male and I am therefore valued and worthwhile"). Once incorporated as a dimension of personality, our sexual orientation toward self and others is, for all practical purposes, not amenable to significant change. However, feelings and behaviors related to our sexuality may be greatly influenced by various factors.

If we are treated as though we are sexless, attitudes toward ourselves may gradually change. If it is communicated that behaviors that were previously appropriate to our sex are no longer acceptable, new behaviors and perceptions of self are likely to evolve. If previously rewarded manifestations of sexuality are now punished or ignored, we will begin to behave and feel differently. The attitudes and behaviors of others toward a person's sexuality will greatly influence orientation toward, and expressions of, this particular dimension of personality.

What Do We Know About Sexual Activity in Old Age?

Although our present knowledge of sexual activities in old age is far from complete, virtually nothing was known about this subject until recent years. Most information regarding sexual behavior in old age has been compiled during the past three decades.

Stumbling blocks to research

There continues to be a dearth of facts related to the subject of old age and sexual behavior. For the most part, this lack of information can be traced to three factors.

First, when elderly individuals constituted a significantly smaller portion of the general population, few researchers exhibited interest in aging or the relationship between advanced age and sexual behaviors. However, as the number and proportion of elderly persons has grown, research interest has also grown. Second, many researchers have found it difficult (if not impossible) to inquire into the sexual lives and activities of older adults (Pfeiffer, 1977). Such researchers feel embarrassed or uncomfortable and are unable to maintain an attitude of detached objectivity in reference to such investigations. Third, most of today's elderly individuals were not reared in environments that promoted or tolerated the open discussion of sexual matters. Such individuals may be unaccustomed, unwilling, or unable to frankly address such matters.

Twelve generalizations

On the basis of what research has been done, a number of generalizations or commonly agreed upon "truths" concerning sexual behavior among the aged population have been accepted by most researchers. Among the more commonly accepted generalizations concerning sexual activity in old age are the following statements.

1. The capability to engage in sexual activities, including intercourse, is not lost when old age is reached. This capability is found among some 70, 80, and 90-year-old individuals (Pfeiffer, 1974).

2. In old age, sexual activities are engaged in less frequently by both men and women (Christenson and Gagnon, 1965).

3. The age at which significant drops occur in frequency of sexual activities is different for women than men—late sixties for women and late seventies for men (Verwoerdt, Pfeiffer, and Wang, 1969a). The sexual capabilities of elderly men, however, exhibit more rapid and greater age-related declines than do the sexual capacities of elderly women.

4. The sequential pattern of physiological stages associated with sexual excitation and orgasm does not change in association with advanced age (Masters and Johnson, 1966). These sequential phases of sexual response are the excitement phase, the plateau phase, the orgasmic phase, and the resolution phase.

5. Changes in temporal patterns of sexual response change in association with advanced age. Increased time is required for arousal and orgasm (Masters and Johnson, 1966).

6. Increased incidences of illness (psychological or physical) function to limit (temporarily or permanently) the amount of sexual activities engaged in during old age (Pfeiffer, 1974).

7. Marital status is highly related to continued participation in sexual activities (Swartz, 1966; Newman and Nichols, 1960).

8. Sexual activities and patterns in old age are frequently reflective of patterns and activities established in previous years (Christenson and Gagnon, 1965; Pfeiffer and Davis, 1972).

9. There is a sexual waning or progressive decline in sexual performance with advanced age (Kaplan, 1974).

10. In old age, great variations in sexual capacity and performance are noted between individuals. Likewise, marked variations may be noted within the individual over time.

11. Various psychological and physical factors influence patterns of sexual activity in old age. To a significant extent, changes in sexual behavior that occur in old age may be traced to psychological rather than physiological factors.

12. The stereotype of sexless old age is false.

However scarce, such available information has done much to remove the myth of sexless old age. It is now recognized that sexual dysfunction and old age are not synonymous, that sexual capabilities and interests do not suddenly and mysteriously disappear in later maturity, and that sexual satisfaction and enjoyment in old age should be viewed as healthy and normal.

What Factors Affect Sexual Behavior As We Age?

A number of factors may work alone or in combination to change patterns of sexual behavior in old age. Such factors may be extremely subtle and operate below the level of conscious awareness or may be readily discernible. Likewise, factors resulting in change may be mental, physical, or social. The extent to which such factors will influence sexual behavior will vary from individual to individual and from time to time. There are no hard-and-fast rules concerning the relationship between sexual activities in old age and the presence or absence of specific change factors. In the face of such potentially influential forces, great variations in sexual behaviors are exhibited.

Social attitudes and beliefs

Social attitudes and beliefs that regard sexual behavior as inappropriate, abnormal, repugnant, or impossible in old age may function to effectively curtail sexual activities in later maturity. Within our society, there is a pervasive belief that sexual activities are somehow appropriate to youth and inappropriate to old age. This belief is held by many older, as well as younger, persons. Those older individuals who view sex as inappropriate to their age may gradually renounce sexual activities and interests. Others may continue to engage in sexual activities but experience feelings of guilt as a result. According to Pfeiffer (1977), strong negative attitudes held by society in reference to sex in old age are extensions of the incest taboo. In many children, a great deal of anxiety is generated by the thought that their parents engage in sexual activities. Because the elderly represent the parent generation, ideas of sexual activities among this group evoke similar unpleasant feelings of anxiety or discomfort. The relationship between attitudes toward sex in old age and attitudes toward sexual activities on the part of our parents is succinctly stated by Claman (1966) in the following passage.

> Our aversion to serious discussion about sex in older people may be based on the fact that we identify old people with our parents, and are therefore made uncomfortable when we think of our parents in this connection. Sam Levenson, the schoolteacher-homespun philosopher of television fame, once said: "When I first found out how babies were born, I couldn't believe it! To think that my mother and father would do such a thing! . . . ." Then, after reflection, he added: "My father— maybe, but my mother—never!" (p. 207)

Although the extent to which attitudes and beliefs influence sexual behavior in old age is unknown, it is generally recognized that social expectations effectively control actions in many situations. People usually conform to society's expectations concerning appropriate behaviors. If society expects the elderly to be asexual, it becomes more likely that sexual activities in old age will become increasingly irregular. Also, if society expects sexual capacity and interest to vanish in old age, such expectations may be reflected in the sexual performance and orientation of the elderly individual. In many cases social expectation (beliefs and attitudes) become self-fulfilling prophecies, and behavior will be determined by these expectations.

Marital status

Marital status is an important factor affecting sexual activities in old age. Partner availability or opportunities for sexual intercourse are critical factors determining sexual continuation. Swartz (1966) found that seven out of ten married couples who were physically healthy continued to be sexually active beyond sixty and many continued into their eighties. It was also found that 70 percent of married males aged 70 had sexual intercourse approximately once per week (Newman and Nichols, 1960) and that 70 percent of married females aged 60 continued to engage in coitus (Christenson and Gagnon, 1965). On the other hand, only 7 percent of those individuals who were divorced, single, or widowed in the 60-and-over group were found to be sexually active (Newman and Nichols, 1960).

Because females tend to marry males who are older than themselves and because the life expectancy for males is approximately seven years less than for females, a significant portion of women within our society live for a number of years in the absence of sexual outlets afforded by a male partner. For many of these women, widowhood rather than age is the major reason for discontinuation of accustomed sexual activities (Verwoerdt, Pfeiffer, and Wang, 1969b). In old age many women find that opportunities to remain sexually active are practically nil. In the absence of male companionship,

masturbation (self-stimulation) may be employed as the only available sexual outlet. According to Rubin,

> A strategy for living in the older years must take into account those who are single or widowed and who have no other opportunities for sexual release than masturbation. (1976, p. 223)

Christenson and Gagnon (1965) found that incidence of masturbation was higher among unmarried females than among married females with approximately 25 percent of unmarried females aged 70 continuing masturbation. Because of longevity factors and the tendency of men to marry younger women, the prospect of being without a sexual partner must be faced less frequently by men than by women. For every 135 females at age 65, there are approximately 100 males. With increased age, the proportion of females in the aged population continues to grow as opportunities to find a male sexual partner continue to diminish.

Quality of marital relationship

Butler (1967) suggests that a major factor associated with discontinued or reduced sexual activities in old age is marital deterioration. During old age, physical, social, and psychological forces may exert stresses that are qualitatively different from those encountered during earlier years of marriage. In the presence of such stress, marital relationship may begin to break down. If feelings of hostility, anger, and resentment accompany old age, such feelings are likely to be vented upon our spouse. Frustrations resulting from various losses (social status, economic resources, physical strength) may be shown in hostile or aggressive interactions within the marriage. Likewise, because married couples who are elderly tend to spend greater amounts of time with each other than do younger couples, opportunities for conflict and discord increase. In many instances constant exposure to our marital partner exerts a tremendous strain upon the relationship. This is particularly true when patterns of contact or exposure change suddenly and radically, such as with retirement.

Consistency of sexual expression

A very important factor influencing sexual activities in old age is consistency of active sexual expression (Masters and Johnson, 1966). Maintenance of effective sexual behavior appears to be related to continued and regular sexual performance. In most instances, patterns of sexual expression are established earlier in life and continue into old age. High rates of sexual activity in old age have usually been preceded by high rates of sexual activity in early adulthood and middle-age (Newman and Nichols, 1960). Rather than depleting the individual sexually, sexual responsiveness, interest, and activity tends to be increased or maintained as a result of regular performance.

Personal attitudes

In addition to performance, personal attitudes toward sex and the function it plays are influential in determining sexual activities. Individuals who perceive sex as enjoyable, fun, personally gratifying and worthwhile for its own sake are likely to continue active involvement during later maturity. Conversely, if sexual activities have not been enjoyed, are regarded as fundamentally evil, or have imposed a hardship or strain upon the individual during earlier years, old age may be grasped as an excuse to stop them completely. If procreation is considered to be the only function rightfully performed by sex, sexual activities may cease following **menopause,** or the change of life. However, for those couples who enjoy sex but fear the possibility of pregnancy, the period following menopause can be a time of increased sexual activity and gratification. Because sexual activities are strongly affected by attitudes, personal orientation toward sex and sexual relations may be critical in determining incidence of performance in old age.

Specifications affecting the aged male

Studying the aged male, Masters and Johnson identified the following six factors that function to limit sexual activities and responsiveness in old age: (1) monotony of a repetitious sexual relationship (boredom with partner); (2) preoccupation with career or economic pursuits; (3) mental or physical fatigue; (4) overindulgence in food or drink; (5) physical infirmities of the individual (or the spouse); (6) fear of failure or inability to perform. The more important factors will be examined in detail.

Monotony.   It is believed that loss of interest as a result of monotony is probably the most frequent cause of reduced sexual activity in the aged male. However, it is unlikely that sexual relations with the same partner would first become boring with the onset of old age. In all probability, monotony has characterized such relationships for a number of years and, as higher levels of stimulation are required to produce arousal, this lack of excitation becomes more critical in old age. However, Masters and Johnson reported that many women who were interviewed showed little interest in sex or in the sexual concerns of their husbands. Such attitudes would, of course, promote boredom within any interpersonal relationship. Likewise, it is possible that age-related changes in physical attractiveness may render the sexual partner less stimulating and exciting. However, the degree to which changes in physical appearance adversely affect sexual functioning in old age is not known. Beauty is, after all, in the eyes of the beholder.

Overindulgence.   Excessive eating and drinking (particularly drinking) tend to diminish sexual performance. Because alcohol is a depressant, its use may render the individual less able to successfully engage in sexual activities. Increased time may be required for arousal, temporary **impotence,** or inability to attain erection, may result, and **orgasm,** or climax, if achieved, is likely to be less pleasurable, satisfying, and intense than usual. Unfortunately, the relationship between temporary impotence and the use of alcohol may not be recognized by the individual and intake may increase in an attempt to overcome feelings of inadequacy and fear. Of course, instead of improving the situation, alcohol will probably make it worse.

Fear of failure. In reference to "fear of failure," Masters and Johnson write the following:

> There is no way to overemphasize the importance that the factor "fear of failure" plays in the aging male's withdrawal from sexual performance . . . many males withdraw voluntarily from any coital activity rather than face the ego-shattering experience of repeated episodes of sexual inadequacy. (1966, pp. 269–270)

To the extent that sexual potency is symbolic of the individual's masculinity (adequacy, independence, strength, dominance, and so forth), adjustment problems are likely to arise in association with sexual decline or dysfunction. Although some older men may withdraw from sexual activities in the face of possible failure, others may attempt to reinforce feelings of masculinity by "proving" themselves with new sex partners. Because new partners add new dimensions of excitement and interest to sexual relationships, the sexual performance of the male is likely to improve. However, individuals who hope to regain levels of sexual potency characteristic of youth are likely to be disillusioned.

Physical infirmity. Physical infirmity, as a factor affecting sexual activities, becomes more important in old age than in any other time during a person's life. Illness and disease does increase in association with advanced age. After age 70, health problems are likely to be present and may constitute a significant obstacle to effective sexual functioning. However, fear that sexual activities will produce adverse physical results may influence sexual behavior to an equal or greater extent than physical infirmities themselves. Because sexual excitation produces blood pressure and heart rate increases and imposes additional stress upon the cardiovascular system, individuals who have suffered heart attacks or strokes may feel that continued sexual activities pose a threat to their physical well-being (Butler, 1967). The extent to which such activities may be dangerous depends, of course, upon the particular characteristics of each person's illness and the degree of exertion involved in sexual interactions. Whether or not sexual activities pose a threat to the individual must be determined by a physician. However, in the majority of cases, diseases involving the cardiovascular system do not impose a permanent ban upon sexual activities.

Conclusion

On the subject of sexual behavior in old age, it cannot be overemphasized that a significant portion of changes in sexual activities that occur in later maturity do not result from the aging process. Rather, various factors may occur in conjunction with old age and differentially affect sexual interest, capacity, and performance.

Most factors influencing sexual behavior among the elderly influence sexual behavior during the entire course of each individual's adult life. Regardless of age, if a person is ill, has an unhappy marriage, is worried about work, or is bored with a relationship, sexual behavior will be adversely affected. Likewise, good health, marital happiness, freedom from stressful cares, and stimulating interpersonal relationships are positive factors that may contribute to effective and satisfying sexual behavior at any age. Although changes in sexual activities and behaviors occur in association with advanced age, the extent to which such changes may be attributed to increased chronological age has not been ascertained.

How Do Age-Related Changes Affect Sexual Behavior in Women?

As a result of intensive research, various age-related changes in the female body have been identified and described by Masters and Johnson (1966). Based upon studies involving 61 women whose ages ranged from 41 to 78 years, the following physical changes, with associated changes in sexual functioning or response, were found to occur within the aged female.

Physical changes

1. The wall of the vaginal barrel becomes tissue-paper thin and takes on a light pinkish color. In young women, the vaginal wall appears corrugated, thick, and reddish.

2. There is a shortening of both the vaginal length and width.

3. The Bartholin gland secretion is slowed. Although vaginal lubrication occurs very promptly in response to sexual arousal in young women, lubrication is delayed in the aged female. In the absence of proper lubrication, sexual intercourse may be painful or difficult.

4. The cervix and uterus shrink in size.

5. The vagina loses some of its ability to expand and some of its elasticity.

6. Uterine cramping or contractions may cause painful intercourse.

7. Thinning of the vaginal wall, insufficient lubrication, and uterine cramping may result from lack of hormones. However, sexual responsiveness (capacity, interest, desire) appears to be largely independent of **estrogen** (a female sex hormone).

8. Women who have experienced no discomfort or unpleasant sensations in association with sexual activities during earlier years may experience vaginal burning or irritation and aches and pains centered around the pelvis during later maturity. Likewise, urination may occasionally be experienced as burning or irritating.

9. Combinations of estrogen and progesterone may prove effective in relieving pain or discomfort associated with intercourse.

10. Immediately following coition, older women frequently experience increased urgency to urinate.

11. Although the intensity of the reaction diminishes in old age, the pattern of nipple erection exhibited by younger women during **coitus** (sexual intercourse) continues to be manifested by elderly women.

12. Demonstrated patterns of clitoral response during coition do not change as a result of aging.

13. Changes in occurrence of the sex flush over the skin develop in association with advanced age.

14. Vaginal contractions during orgasm do not change qualitatively as a function of increased age. However, in older women such contractions last for a shorter period of time.

15. In old age, sexual stimulation and gratification occur more slowly than in youth. Increased time is required to achieve orgasm.

16. Elderly women "suffering from all the vaginal stigmas of sex-steroid starvation still will retain a far higher capacity for sexual performance" if "opportunity for regularity of coital exposure is created and maintained."

17. The older woman's desire for sex is influenced as much by personality as by changes in hormone levels. It is possible that psychological factors are more important than physiological factors in determining **sex drive.**

Social and psychological factors

For many women, Masters and Johnson observed, the postmenopausal years are characterized by significant sexual capacity and effective sexual performance. However, maintenance of significant sexual capacity and effective sexual performance is dependent upon regular sexual expression. Elderly females who have opportunities for regular intercourse will retain a higher level of sexual capacity, interest, and performance than will those elderly women to whom such opportunities are not available.

Our desire and capacity for sex in old age is directly related to sexual patterns or habits established during earlier years. Dramatic changes in sexual orientation or performance are not likely to be shown by women who have enjoyed sex for many years, have a satisfying marriage, and a stimulating partner. Marked declines in sexual activities are most often noted among older women who have failed to establish satisfactory sexual relations at an earlier age.

Because women's sexual capability declines more slowly than men's, and because women usually marry men who are older than themselves, women are often capable of more active sexual lives than they lead. Studying women who were married to younger, older, and same-age husbands, Christenson and Gagnon (1965) found that the sex lives of those women with younger husbands were most active and the sex lives of women married to older men were least active. It would appear that male capability is a very important determinant of female sexual expression in old age. For many elderly women, male capability rather than advanced age is the limiting factor imposed upon sexual relations. Because it is not unusual for a woman's desire for sexual intercourse to exceed her husband's ability to perform, frequency of sexual performance among older women may not be a valid indicator of sexual ability or responsiveness among elderly females.

In their chapter on the aging female, Masters and Johnson (1966) summarized some findings and ideas in their concluding statements.

> There seems to be no physiologic reason why the frequency of sexual expression found satisfactory for the younger woman should not carry over into the postmenopausal years. . . . There is no reason why the milestone of the menopause should be expected to blunt the human female's sexual capacity, performance, or drive. The healthy aging woman normally has sex drives that demand resolution. The depths of her sexual capacity and the effectiveness of her sexual performance, as well as her personal eroticism, are influenced indirectly by all of the psycho- and sociophysiologic problems of her aging process. *In short, there is no time limit drawn by the advancing years to female sexuality.*

How Do Age-Related Changes Affect Sexual Behavior in Men?

Studying 39 men whose ages ranged from 51 to 89, Masters and Johnson (1966) investigated sexual changes in the aging male. The following are their major findings.

Physical changes

1. The male's sexual responsiveness wanes or declines with increased age. Criteria for sexual responsiveness included existing levels of sexual excitement; ability to successfully make coital connection; ability to end coition with ejaculation; and incidence of masturbation, **nocturnal emissions,** and coitus.

2. The mean frequency of orgasm declines as the male ages.

3. Penile erection usually takes longer to achieve as the male grows older.

4. Although penile erection takes longer in old age, it may be maintained for extended periods of time without **ejaculation.**

5. Among elderly men, full penile erection is frequently not reached until just before ejaculation.

6. Immediately following ejaculation, the penis of the elderly man may return to a flaccid condition. Among younger men, erection following ejaculation may be maintained for a number of minutes.

7. Following orgasm, increased time is required before erection and ejaculation is again possible. After age 60, an interim of 12 to 24 hours may be required before penile erection can again be achieved.

8. The vasocongestion and muscle tensions that accompany sexual intercourse exhibit patterns of decreased intensity and duration in association with increased age.

9. Pleasure associated with ejaculation may diminish. ". . . the aging male, particularly if his erection has been long maintained, may have the experience of seepage rather than of seminal fluid expulsion." (p. 259)

10. "The younger male can expel the seminal fluid the full length of the penile urethra under such pressure as to deposit initial portions of the seminal plasma 12 to 24 inches from the unencumbered urethral meatus. The man over 50 years of age exhibits markedly reduced ejaculatory prowess, 6 to 12 inches being the average distance that the seminal plasma can be expelled." (ibid)

11. Whereas younger males experience a two-stage ejaculatory process, a single-stage ejaculatory reaction is common among elderly men.

12. Sexual decline or dysfunction among elderly men can frequently be traced to infirmity, preoccupation, fatigue, overindulgence, boredom, or fear of failure.

13. **Secondary impotence** (inability to attain erection because of psychological causes) increases significantly after age 50.

14. When the aging male is not stimulated over long periods of time, his responsiveness may be lost.

15. Active sexual involvement or expression is the most important factor in maintaining the elderly man's ability to engage effectively in sexual activities. Sustained sexual functioning in old age is promoted by repeated and regular stimulation.

16. In old age, a man's sexual capacity doesn't suddenly decline. The rate of sexual decline (begun in one's twenties) among males remains relatively constant throughout the life span and "slowing up" is gradual.

Social and psychological factors

The sexual capabilities of elderly men exhibit greater age-related declines than do the sexual capabilities of elderly females. Yet, men retain higher levels of sexual interest and activity than women throughout old age (Newman and Nichols, 1960; Cameron and Biber, 1973). As previously discussed, lower levels of sexual activity among older women may be explained in terms of opportunity or partner availability. Because men tend to marry women somewhat younger than themselves; because men frequently die before their wives; and because opportunities for remarriage or sexual contact are often more readily available to the widower, it is less likely that sexual activities of older men would be significantly impeded by lack of partner availability. However, whereas the relationship between opportunity and activity seems to be fairly clear, it is less apparent why older men maintain higher levels of sexual interest than do older women. Pfeiffer and Davis (1972) suggest that declines in sexual interest may be defensive and part of the individual's pattern of adjustment. That is, if a person can't have sex, an effective means of coping with this deprivation is to repress, inhibit, or deny sexual interests and desires. Because sex is likely to be more available to the aged male than to the aged female, it would be logical to assume that higher levels of sexual interest would be maintained by men throughout later maturity. However, this relationship between adaptation and sexual interest is purely speculative. We might also speculate that differences in expressed sexual interest between males and females may be a product of cultural conditioning. It is possible that men feel their masculine image is maintained or enhanced through the expression of continued high-level interest in sex. With the object of projecting a culturally accepted masculine image or with the object of "looking like a man," males may report more interest in sex than they actually experience. Therefore it is possible that some men lie about sexual interest in order to "look good." Again, the relationship between reported levels of interest in sex and feelings about one's masculinity is only speculative.

Although important qualitative changes in sexual response are noted among elderly men, quantitative changes tend to be more pronounced— changes in frequency of sexual activity, changes in number of orgasms experienced, changes in time required to achieve erection and ejaculation, and changes in remission time. Such quantitative changes occur in association with increased age and gradually modify characteristic sexual performance as men grow older. However, although age-related changes do impose certain restrictions upon the sexual activities of elderly men, they do not render older males incapable of effective sexual performance. In many cases, a man's perception of such age-related sexual changes will influence sexual functioning to a greater extent than will actual or real changes. It is likely that increased incidence of secondary impotence occurring in middle age is related to feelings of inadequacy and fear arising from recognition of one's own changing sexual capacity and performance. Worry and concern focused upon declining sexual ability and the threat of impending dysfunction can precipitate secondary impotence. A number of factors, other than age, can result in significant disruptions of male sexual behavior.

> It is presumed that only physical defect or the depletion of the aging process will interfere with the male's innate erotic interest and his ability to respond to sexual stimuli. Two conceptual errors defeat these basic presumptions: First, any fear of performance, displeasing sensation, or sense of rejection affects male eroticism as much as it does the physiologic effectiveness of his response; and second, age does not necessarily deplete the male's physiologic ability or psychologic interest in sexual performance. (Masters and Johnson, 1966, p. 259)

How Might We Adjust to Sexual Change in Old Age?

When age-related changes in sexual ability occur, adjustment problems may stem from feelings of threat to our sexuality, the concept of our masculinity or femininity. As a result of sexual decline, negative perceptions of self may develop as feelings of positive worth and self-esteem erode. In such instances changes in ability to perform sexually hold symbolic connotations that transcend involvement in any specific sexual activities. A man who finds his sexual capability waning may feel that he is becoming "less of a man"—less adequate, competent, and worthwhile as a person. Sexual impotence (or decline) may spawn diffuse feelings of powerlessness or loss of control that may produce anxiety and may tax the individual's ability to cope. In a similar manner, the woman who has no opportunity to engage in sexual intercourse may begin to feel less attractive, valued, and secure. Inability to attract a man may prove to be very ego-deflating.

Adjusting to physical changes

When an individual's sexuality is threatened by normal age-related physical changes in sexual behavior, therapy designed to improve sexual performance is, of course, not in order. In such cases attempts to promote positive adjustment must involve helping the individuals to distinguish between who they are as persons and what they can or can't do as sexual partners. Self-identity and sexual behavior need to be segregated.

However, the process of helping the individual separate self-identity from sexual behavior may be extremely lengthy and difficult. In many instances, the best that can be anticipated is limited success. Some elderly individuals may be helped to adjust to waning sexual ability by the provision of factual information concerning normal aging and sexual behavior. When people better understand that sexual changes observed in themselves are normal and shared by other people their age, changes in ability or opportunity to perform sexually may become less personally threatening to the individual.

Handling psychological and social problems

When sexual decline or dysfunction in later maturity is traced to psychological causes rather than age-related physical changes, fear of failure is found to be the overriding problem. Although many older men are able to accept the fact that their ability to play tennis, basketball, or football has declined over the years, the idea of accepting changes that have occurred in their ability to perform sexually may be practically nonexistent. When sexual ability is concerned, significantly more than physical capacity may be on the line. Any indication of sexual decline may be met with anxiety and fear. Because sexual performance is acutely sensitive to attitudes and feelings, in the presence of anxiety and fear, our ability to function sexually in an effective manner will suffer. The harder a person tries, the worse performance may become.

Types of therapy

A number of different types of therapy specifically designed to enhance sexual performance and promote sexual enjoyment and satisfaction are currently available. Such therapeutic procedures usually incorporate three dimensions; information provision, psychological counseling, and opportunities to practice specific sexual behaviors.

Factual information is presented to aid the individual in better understanding age-related changes in sexual functioning and to teach specific sexual techniques or behaviors. Counseling may involve helping the individual work through depression, fear, and anxiety associated with confrontation of age-related limitations in sexual performance. Acceptance of age-related changes in sexual capabilities may be the major objective of psychological counseling. Finally, opportunities to practice specific sexual techniques within a controlled environment may be provided. Within such controlled situations, individuals may be directed to engage in certain sexual activities under the guidance of trained sex therapists. Sexual behaviors are practiced slowly as potential sources of stress are guarded against. Strategies encourage the gradual progression of sexual activities without fear, guilt, revulsion, anxiety, or other negative emotional responses. Individuals are encouraged to relax and enjoy. Sexual enjoyment, accompanied by elevated feelings of self-esteem, is most important. In effective sex therapy specific sexual behaviors, the "whole" person, and interpersonal relationships are treated.

If sex therapy is to be successful, certain conditions must usually be met. The most important condition is that individuals enter therapy of their own volition and willingly participate. Little of a positive nature is likely to be accomplished in the face of strong resistance to change. Secondly, when individuals are married, it is critical that both partners participate in therapy. According to Masters and Johnson (1970), "there is no such thing as an uninvolved partner in any marriage in which there is some form of sexual inadequacy." The marital relationship must be treated. Finally, success depends upon therapist expertise—a great deal of training, experience, and skill is required—and specific strategies employed. Depending upon problem and personality, certain types of therapy will prove more effective than others. Care taken in choosing a sex therapist should equal that taken in choosing a surgeon, lawyer, or psychiatrist. With the provision of proper therapy, the prognosis for most cases involving sexual inadequacy is quite good. Many cases of secondary impotence and loss of sexual responsiveness in later maturity can be treated successfully.

Summary

Sexual behavior refers to specific actions usually designed to obtain sexual gratification. Sexuality is an important dimension of personality involving self-identity and personal esteem. Sexuality and sexual behavior are related but independent. Sexuality is learned within the social environment and is not determined by our sex organs or specific sexual parts of our body. Problems may arise when individuals are unable to distinguish between their sexuality and their physical body. Because our feelings of masculinity or femininity may be closely tied to sexual performance and activities, age-related changes in sexual capability may affect the manner in which individuals perceive and value themselves. Such changes in self-identity and self-esteem may prove anxiety-provoking and may pose adjustment problems.

The following generalizations concerning sexual activity in old age are widely accepted by researchers. In old age (1) sexual capability is not lost; (2) sexual activities decrease in frequency; (3) differences in frequency of sexual activities are noted between men and women; (4) the sequential pattern of physiological response doesn't change; (5) temporal patterns of sexual response change; (6) illness often limits sexual activities; (7) a strong relationship exists between marital status and sexual activities; (8) earlier established sexual patterns tend to continue; (9) sexual performance wanes; (10) individual variations in sexual performance may be great; (11) psychological and physical factors influence sexual activity; (12) the stereotype of sexlessness is false.

Psychological, physical, and social factors affect sexual behavior in old age. Potentially influential factors include social attitudes and beliefs, taboos, marital status, partner availability, consistent sexual expression, history of sexual enjoyment, monotony, preoccupation, fatigue, overindulgence, physical infirmity, fear of failure, and marital deterioration.

A number of age-related changes in both the female and male bodies with associated changes in sexual functioning or response have been identified and described. On the basis of research, it is believed that physiological changes that accompany increased age should not deprive a person of sexual satisfaction and enjoyment. Among healthy, well-adjusted people, the potential for sexual activity has no time limit.

In later maturity adjustment difficulties may arise from threats to our sexuality. In such cases therapy designed to aid adjustment may concentrate upon segregation of "self" from "sexual behavior." When sexual decline or dysfunction is prompted by fear of failure, sex therapy involving education, counseling, and practice may be required. The success of such therapy will depend upon the participant's willingness, involvement of both sex partners, therapist expertise, and specific therapeutic strategies used. In cases of sexual dysfunction arising from psychological causes, the prognosis tends to be quite good.

Progress Check

1. What is the difference between sexuality and sexual behavior? (pp. 186–187)

2. How does our sexuality affect our sexual behavior?   (pp. 187–188)

3. What are four widely accepted generalizations concerning sexual activity in old age?   (pp. 189–190)

4. What are seven factors other than chronological age that might affect sexual behavior in old age?   (pp. 190–193)

5. Why do you think society has a negative attitude toward sexual activities in old age?   (pp. 190–191)

6. What are five sex-related changes that occur in the female body in association with increased age?   (pp. 195–196)

7. What factors might cause the female's sexual activities to decline in old age?   (pp. 196–197)

8. What are five sex-related changes that occur in the male in association with increased age?   (pp. 197–198)

9. What factors might result in sexual dysfunction among males in later maturity?   (pp. 199–200)

10. What might cause secondary impotence in later maturity? (pp. 199–200)

11. How might the elderly person be helped to adjust to changes in sexual capability and behavior?   (pp. 200–201)

12. What three factors do you think are most important in determining effective sexual functioning in old age?

Recommended Readings

Masters, W. H. & V. E. Johnson. *Human Sexual Response*. Boston: Little, Brown & Co., 1966.
This is a highly interesting and informative discussion of physiological changes that accompany the sex act and various sex-associated characteristics of males and females. A standard work in the field of sexual behavior.

Rubin, I. *Sexual Life After Sixty*. New York: Basic Books, 1976.
This book provides a fascinating and clear discussion of sexual behavior in later maturity. Sexual practices and factors affecting sexual practices in later maturity are examined. Very readable and entertaining.

10

Social Aspects of Aging

Preview ∽ *A number of basic social concepts will be introduced in this chapter. We will look at the impact of society upon the individual, discuss the normative nature of social functioning, and consider age-related social forces. Common myths and stereotypes concerning old age and the family will be presented and factors affecting adjustment to retirement will be discussed. We will focus upon age-related patterns of leisure activity, economic conditions among the elderly, and variables influencing housing in old age. Throughout this chapter, suggestions designed to make effective social functioning easier in later maturity will be offered.*

Each person is a social being. We interact with other human beings; we exert influence upon the attitudes, emotions, and behaviors of others; in turn, we are influenced by them.

How Does Society Influence Us As We Age?

When consideration is given to the social aspects of aging, attention is focused upon how older people interact within the social structure and are affected by the society in which they live. Concern is with the manner in which age affects social roles and statuses and how social expectations change in conjunction with increased age. Concern is also with patterns of interpersonal relationships in old age and patterns of interaction between the elderly and social institutions.

Norms—society's guidelines for acceptable behavior

Functioning within a defined organization of people and institutions referred to as **society,** people are molded, to a great extent, by the rules and regulations of the particular society in which they live. Within each society, **norms,** established guidelines for acceptable or normal behavior, are present. Each society expects and demands that its members conform to established norms. If a member of society does not conform to accepted behavioral norms, **social norms** designed to bring the person into line will be imposed. For example, a social norm might dictate that elderly women should not wear shorts or halters in public. If the elderly woman does not accede to this standard of appropriate behavior, society will react in a way that encourages or promotes **conformity,** or behavior that is in accordance with established social norms. People may stare, friends may refuse to talk to her or be seen with her in public, and she may become the butt of unkind jokes. By employing such strategies, society may be successful in its attempts to get individuals to behave as they are "supposed to."

Age-related changes in norms, social roles, and social status

In later maturity social norms, expectations, and pressures that dictate, guide, and control behavior will be different from those encountered at an earlier age. What is expected and demanded of the elderly individual is likely to differ significantly from what is expected and demanded of the middle-aged person. To a great extent, adjustment in later maturity means adjustment to changes in age-related social norms. If a person's personality is such that important needs, emotions, and desires do not conflict with established social norms, the probability of marked adjustment problems appearing in old age is significantly reduced. However, when personality and social norms collide, increased strain may be placed upon the individual's ability to cope and successful adjustment may prove to be more difficult. For example, if the needs of an elderly woman prompt her to marry a young man, she will be exposed to various social pressures and stresses that stem from her violation of acceptable behavior. Social norms are very difficult to defy. When individuals operate in defiance of social norms, they usually must pay for their actions in some way. Likewise, those individuals who conform to social norms while sacrificing personal needs, emotions, and desires must also pay. When behavior is not congruent with personality or when behavior is in defiance of social norms, increased stress will be placed upon the individual's ability to adjust and a physical or psychological toll will be exacted.

Changes in social roles. In old age a number social roles change or are lost. **Social roles** are patterns of activity and customary functions intrinsic to a particular position. The student role, for example, might involve such activities as studying, taking tests, dating, and living in a dorm. Social role changes or losses will always be accompanied by changes in status. **Social status** is the relative position within the social structure entailing certain rights, privileges, duties, and responsibilities. Relative power held by the individual within the social structure is indicative of status. Because role and status are inseparable, role change or loss will always produce status change or loss. For example, when people retire (role change), their ability to command respect or wield power may be restricted (status change). Likewise, with widowhood (role change), responsibilities, privileges, and prerogatives associated with marriage will be withdrawn (status change).

Because social roles are basic to **self-concept** or **self-identity** (who I am) and status is basic to feelings of **self-esteem** (what I'm worth or how I'm valued), role and status changes that occur in later maturity may pose threats to the individual's psychological well-being. Such changes may force the individual to modify perceptions of self, others, and society, and to adapt accordingly. During later maturity, most role changes result in the diminishing or loss of status; however, in rare instances, role change in old age may produce increased status. In some families, for example, the grandmother role has more status than the mother role. Although increased status may accompany role change in later maturity, this is not usually the case. In old age, role restriction and status reduction rather than role expansion and status elevation is the rule.

Many social expectations, pressures, roles, and statuses are age-related. They change as a function of increased chronological age. Throughout our lives, such social variables effectively influence behavior and affect adjustment. The extent to which various social factors operate to the detriment or advantage of the individual will vary from situation to situation and from person to person. All elderly people do not share identical roles or equal statuses. Likewise, depending upon factors such as role and status, social expectations and pressures will exert varying degrees of influence upon each elderly person. For example, roles, statuses, and pressures to conform will vary according to the amount of wealth possessed by the older individual. When attention is given to various social aspects of aging, normative or average patterns rather than individual differences are stressed. Within the aged population certain patterns of social interaction are more common than others. In addition, certain roles and statuses become increasingly common with advanced age. However, although focus is upon that which is "normal" or average, it should be remembered that great differences exist within the aged population and that which is "normal" or average for this age group may not be characteristic of every elderly person. Although certain similarities predominate, significant differences exist.

What Happens in the Family?

In the present context, **family** is used to denote pairs or groups of persons who are related by virtue of blood or marriage. Within this definition are included the nuclear family (parents and dependent children), multigenerational families (more than two generations), extended families (including aunts, uncles, grandparents, and other relatives), and the single couple, composed only of husband and wife. Within our society, families are the most fundamental social unit. The family is the source of intense and personal social relationships, companionship, psychological support, and security. In time of need or stress, the family is also the most important source of relief, protection, and help. For most people, family is extremely important.

Misconceptions about old age and the family

The relationships between old age and the family is beset by a number of stereotypic beliefs that are supported by a majority of the population. Such stereotypic beliefs or myths are often generated on the basis of a single observation and subsequently generalized to the entire population. If an elderly neighbor never sees her children, for example, we might conclude that all older people are neglected or ignored by their sons and daughters. Likewise, stereotypic beliefs may be based upon non-reality based perceptions of the past. It is not unusual for a person to decry the passing of "good old days" when the elderly were respected, venerated for their wisdom, and functioned as integral and contributing members of the multigenerational family. However, such nostalgia ignores the fact that multigenerational families have never been the norm in the United States, that relatively few people survived to advanced age in the past, and that little evidence supports the notion that older individuals are happier, more well-adjusted, or better-off financially or physically when included within the multigenerational household. Finally, myths concerning old age and the family are given credence by media coverage. Elderly people who have been placed in nursing homes, have been forgotten and neglected by their family, and have lived solitary and isolated lives may be the subject of a news report. But older people who interact happily with family members and maintain relatively close family ties are not considered newsworthy. In essence, that which is atypical, abnormal, or unusual is "news." Unfortunately, it is easy to believe that the media accurately portrays the entire elderly population. Such, of course, is generally not the truth.

Six common myths

Some of the more common stereotypic beliefs concerning old age and the family are the following:

1. If elderly persons are not institutionalized (placed in a nursing home), they will ultimately end up moving in with family members, usually their children.

2. In most instances elderly people are neglected or abandoned by their childrem.

3. Most elderly people are a source of financial drain and are dependent upon the resources of various family members.

4. Grandparents "spoil" their grandchildren.

5. Grandparenting is universally enjoyed.

6. Most elderly people feel that is their children's responsibility to care for them in old age.

As will all stereotypes or myths, those concerned with old age and the family have some bases in truth. It cannot be denied that some older people are financial drains upon the family, do move in with their children, and do view their children as responsible for their care. However, although the behavior and attitudes of many older people do conform to stereotypes, deviations from stereotypic norms are more common. For this reason, it is unfair that stereotypes and myths concerning old age and the family be imposed upon the entire elderly segment of society. We will now examine each of these myths in more detail.

Myth One: Living arrangements

According to the most recent national census, only 3 percent of households in the United States contain a parent or parent-in-law of the head of the house. Three-generation families living together are highly atypical. Although most elderly people live within families, such families are usually composed of only the older husband and the older wife. Figures obtained from the Administration on Aging (see Table 10.1) indicate that the majority

Table 10.1: Percent of Elderly Men and Women in Various Living Arrangements, 1970

Living Arrangement	Men	Women
Family	79	59
Head of household	71	10
Wife is head of household	x	33
Other relative is head of household	8	16
Alone or with nonrelatives	17	37
Head of Household	14	35
Living with a nonrelative	3	2
Institution	4	4

Source: Population Reference Bureau, Inc., 1975, p. 16: Administration on Aging. *Facts and Figures on Older Persons,* No. 5. Washington, D.C.: Department of Health, Education, and Welfare, Pub. (OHD) 74-20005, pp. 4–6.

of elderly individuals maintain head of household status throughout later maturity.

When elderly people move in with their children it is frequently because of illness or economic need. Likewise, if individuals are very old or unmarried, the probability increases that they will become part of their children's household. However, most older people (approximately 90 percent), feel that living with their children is not desirable.

Myth Two: Neglect and abandonment

Although most older individuals manage to maintain separate and independent households, they also maintain involvement with their children. In a survey conducted by Shanas et al. (1968), 90 percent of elderly respondents reported having seen at least one of their children during the preceding month. In the same study, it was found that 75 percent of the elderly sample has at least one child who lived less than thirty minutes away. According to Hill et al. (1970), closest ties are usually maintained by adjacent generations, that is, interactions between parents and children are usually quantitatively more significant than interactions between grandparents and grandchildren. Generally speaking, daughters give more attention to parents than do sons, and unmarried children maintain closer ties than do married ones. Likewise, sons and daughters usually maintain contact to a greater degree than do sons-in-law and daughters-in-law. In most instances degree of attention and contact are highly related to proximity. Children who live far away from parents are less likely to keep in touch than are children who live nearby. Within our society, it is normal or common for parent-child interactions to continue throughout old age.

Myth Three: A financial drain

There is very little support for the notion that elderly people impose financial burdens upon family members. Rather than being a financial burden, most elderly persons are financial and resource assets to their families. Older people commonly contribute money or services to kin, usually to sons and daughters. In most cases sons receive monetary aid and daughters are given services such as cooking and baby-sitting. Even when the older individual is not well-off financially, continued contributions to the children are the rule rather than the exception. Rather than being passive recipients of the family wealth and resources, elderly people are frequently active contributors.

Myth Four: "Spoiling" grandchildren

No single relationship or behavior pattern exists between all grandparents and all grandchildren. Just as mothers and fathers differ greatly in their handling and interacting with children, so also do grandparents differ. In research executed by Neugarten and Weinstein (1964), five styles of grandparenting were distinguished.

1. *Formal*—Do not interfere with the parenting of the mother and fa-
    ther; behave in a concerned manner but do not offer unsolicited ad-
    vice.

2. *Funseeker*—Really enjoy grandchildren and tend to indulge (spoil)
    them. Playful relationships predominate.

3. *Surrogate*—Parental duties and responsibilities are, in part, as-
    sumed. This role is more commonly assumed by the grandmother
    who may be helping the working daughter.

4. *Reservoir*—Maintain authority over grandchildren. An authoritarian
    role is maintained with emphasis upon power and control.

5. *Distant*—Contact with grandchildren is fleeting. Grandparents may
    participate in special events (as birthdays and weddings) but, for the
    most part, will have no particular involvement in the grandchildren's
    lives.

According to the researchers, the surrogate or substitute parent role and
the reservoir role are least common. The funseekers are most commonly
middle-aged. For many grandparents, periodic and short-lived contacts with
grandchildren are the most desirable and satisfactory.

Myth Five: Enjoying grandparenting

Although most of us would prefer to believe that all older people enjoy the
role of grandparent, such is not always true. In the previously cited study
conducted by Neugarten and Weinstein, it was concluded that one third of
the grandparents surveyed found the grandparent role to be uncomfortable,
unpleasant, disappointing, and unrewarding. Not only did older persons differ in terms of enjoyment derived from the grandparent role, differences in
terms of significance attached to that role were pronounced. For the most
part, grandparents looked upon grandchildren as a source of continuity or
biological renewal, emotional self-fulfillment, and vicarious achievement.
However, many grandparents perceived themselves as a resource person to
the grandchildren or perceived the grandchildren as having little or no effect
upon self. In a survey performed by Lopata (1973), approximately 50 percent
of widows interviewed felt no close attachment or tie to any grandchild.

Myth Six: Children responsible for care

Although most children feel that responsibility for aged parents lies with
them, the majority of elderly individuals do not assign such responsibility to
their offspring (Shanas, 1962). In the opinion of most older people, responsibility during retirement and later maturity should be shouldered by aged
people themselves rather than by their children. Self-reliance, independence,
and autonomy are highly valued by members of the elderly population. In
part, feelings of self-reliance are exhibited in the reluctance of most older

people to assume a guest or subordinate role within their children's house-holds. In most instances children's responsibility for aged parents entails providing information, for example, regarding investments, pensions, and purchases, and mediation between various social agencies and institutions, as handling social security, taxes, insurance claims, and banking. Children frequently act as advisers, mediators, and facilitators without assuming significant responsibility for the care and well-being of their parents.

How Does Retirement Affect Our Adjustment?

Retirement, the withdrawal from formal and remunerative employment, is generally considered to be a benchmark in most people's lives. Retirement usually signals passage from middle age into old age and, more than any other social event, designates newly acquired membership within the aged population. Accompanying retirement are changes in daily activities and changes in the status of the individual. Whereas work had previously occupied a major part of the person's day, **leisure**—free or spare time—now predominates. Whereas a person may have identified himself or herself as a gainfully employed member of society, self-identity must now be sought elsewhere. Without exception, retirement imposes adjustment demands upon all retirees. The degree of success with which each person adjusts to retirement is related to a number of factors. Among such factors are health, freedom from financial worries (adequate income), participation in leisure activities, interpersonal relationships, and personality. In addition, adjustment to retirement is influenced by whether withdrawal from the work force was voluntary or involuntary. Of these factors, health and income appear to be most highly related to positive adjustment and happiness during the retirement years.

Personality characteristics of retired people

Reichard, Livson, and Petersen (1962) investigated the relationship between personality characteristics and successful retirement. In the course of their study, three personality types associated with good adjustment to retirement and two personality types associated with bad adjustment were identified.

> The largest group identified among the well adjusted we called the "mature." These men moved easily into old age. Relatively free of neurotic conflict, they were able to accept themselves realistically and to find genuine satisfaction in activities and personal relationships. Feeling their lives had been rewarding, they were able to grow old without regret for the past or loss in the present. They took old age for granted and made the best of it. A second group, whom we labeled the "rocking-chair men" because of their general passivity, welcomed the opportunity to be free of responsibility and to indulge their passive needs in old age. For these men, old age brought satisfactions that compensated for its disadvantages. A third well-adjusted group consisted of persons who maintained a highly developed but smoothly functioning system of defenses against anxiety. Unable to face passivity or helpless-

ness in old age, they warded off their dread of physical decline by keeping active. Their strong defenses protected them from their fear of growing old. We called them the "armored."

Among those who were poorly adjusted to aging, the largest group of individuals we called the "angry men." Bitter over having failed to achieve their goals earlier in life, they blamed others for their disappointments and were unable to reconcile themselves to growing old. A second group of maladjusted men also looked back on their past lives with a sense of disappointment and failure, but unlike the angry men they turned their resentment inward, blaming themselves for their misfortunes. These men tended to be depressed as they approached old age. Growing old underscored their feelings of inadequacy and worthlessness. We called this group the "self-haters."

With the exception of the mature group, many of whom had had difficulties in personal adjustment when they were younger, these personality types appeared to have been relatively stable throughout life. Poor adjustment to aging among the angry men and the self-haters seemed to stem from lifelong personality problems. Similarly, the histories of the armored and rocking-chair groups suggest that their personalities had changed very little throughout their lives. (Reichard, Livson, and Petersen, 1962, pp. 170–171)

The findings reached by Reichard and Associates are very similar to those reported by Neugarten and Associates, 1964 (see Chapter 6). Such data are important to our conceptualization of retirement as an event and process that draws upon established coping techniques and adjustment strategies. If people have adjusted successfully throughout earlier years, there is a good probability that they will adjust successfully to retirement. Likewise, if poor or marginal adjustment has characterized functioning at an earlier age, poor or marginal adjustment to retirement will probably be exhibited. Such data are also important because attention is drawn to different behavioral patterns associated with a satisfying retirement. For some people, happiness in retirement may involve sitting and rocking. For others, happiness is associated with various activities and interpersonal relationships. Although both types of individuals may be happy or satisfied, neither would be happy if forced to assume the role of the other. Recognition of the relationship between personality and adjustment to retirement would preclude attempts to force all retirees into a common behavioral mold. Likewise, recognition of individual differences should promote caution among those who make judgments concerning adjustment on the basis of various behavioral manifestations. The particular role assumed by the retiree will, to a large degree, be influenced by personality. The extent to which retirement will be experienced as rewarding or satisfying will depend greatly upon the psychological characteristics—needs, interests, anxieties, and motivations—of the individual.

Preretirement attitudes and expectations

Retirement adjustment is related to preretirement attitudes and expectations. If a person looks forward to retirement, anticipates it with pleasure, and makes plans accordingly, the odds are in favor of positive adjustment. However, if the prospect of retirement is feared, dreaded, or denied, successful retirement adjustment becomes less probable. According to Streib and

Schneider (1971), a great many people are pleasantly surprised when retirement turns out to be a more satisfying experience than expected. For such individuals, retirement adjustment may be initially difficult during the period in which negative attitudes and expectations predominate. As the positive aspects of retirement become increasingly apparent, a more satisfying adjustment will be achieved. Four to six years after leaving the work force, one third of retirees report that retirement has been a more positive experience than anticipated. Retirement was perceived as worse than anticipated by only 4 to 5 percent of those sampled (Streib and Schneider, 1971).

Occupational level and retirement

In addition to preretirement attitudes and expectations, retirement adjustment appears to be related to the occupational level of the individual. In research conducted by Ingraham (1974), it was found that persons who have worked in professional positions, such as doctors, lawyers, teachers, and scientists, were likely to experience retirement as highly satisfying and to adjust quite successfully. Satisfaction is probably high because such individuals do not totally relinquish their work or completely lose the status associated with formal employment. Many professional persons continue to participate in activities (as researching, studying, traveling, and writing) related to their work long after withdrawal from the structured work situation. For such persons, retirement provides the opportunity to pursue work-related subjects in an unrestricted manner. Studying the relationship between occupational level and retirement adjustment, Simpson and McKinny (1972), observed that retirement was more likely to be welcomed and enjoyed by white-collar and skilled blue-collar workers than by unskilled blue-collar workers. Likewise, individuals drawn from higher level occupational categories were more likely to adjust successfully to retirement than were those drawn from lower-level categories. However, the relationship between occupational level and retirement adjustment is far from clear. It is possible that income rather than specific occupational level is the critical factor affecting adjustment. Because middle-level employees or workers are more likely than lower-level ones to possess adequate income during retirement, they would be more likely to operate free from financial stress, to have the opportunity and ability to pursue various interests and activities, and to enjoy options presented by increased leisure time. In the absence of adequate finances, the probability of successful retirement adjustment diminishes for all people.

Retirement and longevity

Although it is widely believed that retirement hastens death or adversely affects health, research does not support this notion. Contrary to popular belief, longevity is not cut short by withdrawal from the working force. Although it cannot be denied that many people die shortly after retiring, it must be recognized that many people opt to leave their jobs because of poor health and are already ill before actual retirement. Rather than retirement precipitating poor health, poor health precipitates retirement. However, if retirement is characterized by elevated stress, anxiety, and low morale, there is little doubt that health will be negatively affected. The strong relationship between physical health and psychological well-being is widely recognized and accepted. Still, no direct relationship has been established between continued formal employment and increased longevity. Conversely, no relationship between retirement and decreased life expectancy has been observed.

Summing up

Many factors affect adjustment in retirement. To a great extent, such factors are not particularly different from those affecting adjustment in earlier years. If a person is in good health, possesses adequate financial resources, is able to maintain a positive self-image and self-identity, and is capable of pursuing activities that are personally gratifying, good adjustment may be predicted. Likewise, if our personality is such that successful adjustment and coping strategies have been developed and refined over the years, retirement is not likely to present insurmountable obstacles to satisfactory functioning. Retirement, like all major milestones in life, requires adjustment. However, whether adjustment is positive or negative depends upon social variables and the individual.

Do Leisure Activities Change As We Age?

Studying the relationship between life-cycle stage and leisure activity, Gordon, Gaitz, and Scott (1976) identified 17 specific activities and organized these activities into 5 categories. The categories were differentiated on the basis of expressive involvement intensity. The activities and their involvement intensity are enumerated in Table 10.2 (p. 216).

As part of the same study, subjects were divided into 5 age groups, each corresponding to a particular life-cycle stage. In order to obtain information concerning age-related differences in leisure participation, 1441 subjects were interviewed belonging to various age groups (see Table 10.3, p. 217).

Popular activities among young and old

When the 17 leisure categories were examined in terms of frequency of participation with increasing age, it was found that lower frequency of participation with increasing age was exhibited by 8 categories; 7 categories showed equal frequency throughout the life span; and higher frequency of participation with increased age was noted in 2 categories. Lower frequency activities were dancing and drinking, attending movies, participating in sports or physical exercise, using guns, outdoor activities, traveling, reading, and cultural production. Activities that exhibited equal frequency across the life span were television viewing, discussion, spectator sports, cultural consumption, entertaining, participating in organizations, and home embellishment.

Table 10.2:   Seventeen Specific Leisure Activities Arrayed According to Increasing Expressive Involvement Intensity

I. Relaxation

    1. Solitude: Having time to be alone to think, daydream, plan, or just do nothing.

II. Diversion

    2. Television viewing: Hours of TV watched on an average day.

    3. Cultural consumption: Looking at paintings or listening to music.

    4. Reading: Reading and finishing any book within the last year.

    5. Movies: Going to the movies.

    6. Spectator Sports: Watching sporting events either at the game or on television.

    7. Entertaining: Visiting with friends in one's home or going to someone else's house.

III. Developmental

    8. Outdoor activities: Going to the country, the beach, camping, fishing, walking in the woods, etc.

    9. Travel: Taking trips to other cities for reasons other than business.

    10. Organizations: Belonging to social or civic clubs or organizations.

IV. Creativity

    11. Cooking: Cooking, baking, barbecuing—fixing food for oneself, one's family or one's friends.

    12. Home embellishment: Sewing, mending, decorating, fixing, building, or working in the yard.

    13. Discussion: Talking about local or national problems and issues.

    14. Cultural production: Singing, drawing or painting, playing a musical instrument.

V. Sensual Transcendence

    15. Guns: Using firearms in sports like hunting or target practice.

    16. Participation in sports or exercise: Vigorous physical activity either inside the home or out.

    17. Dancing and drinking: Going out for an evening to a place where you can dance or drink.

Source: From *Handbook of Aging and the Social Sciences,* edited by Robert H. Binstock and Ethel Shanas, p. 325. © 1976 by Litton Educational Publishing, Inc. Reprinted by permission of Van Nostrand Reinhold Company.

Activities that increased in frequency among older people were relaxation and solitude, and cooking (mainly for the male subjects).

When data incorporating all categories were analyzed, it was found that high participation (above the median, or most frequent score for the entire sample) in leisure activities declined as individuals were drawn from succes-

Table 10.3: Subjects Interviewed for Leisure Participation Study

Age Group	Life-Cycle Stage	N
20–29	Young adult	248
30–44	Early maturity	308
45–64	Full maturity	425
65–74	Old age	242
75–94	Very old age	218
		1,441

sively older age groups. ". . . the older the respondent, the lower the level of general leisure activity." (p. 326)

As may be observed in Figure 10.1 below, approximately 80 percent of young adults reported above median levels of leisure participation, but this figure drops to only 24 percent among the very old. It is interesting to note that the negative relationship between increased age and high-level participation in leisure activities does not vary across the entire life span and that significant differences between males and females are not exhibited.

Figure 10.1: Percentage of persons showing high leisure participation by age group and sex.

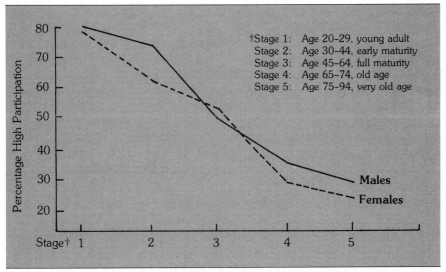

Conclusions

On the basis of their findings, the researchers conclude the following:

> . . . the older the respondent, the lower the level of general leisure activity, the narrower its breadth, the less "intense" the forms, and the less likely a person to engage in the forms of leisure activity that can be characterized as highly active, external to the home, and physically demanding. Other leisure activities, the moderate intensity and home-centered forms of sociability and media-based symbolic interactions, continued into the oldest age group, and there was no evidence that individuals "disengage" from immediate relatives and friends.
>
> We also found that active and external leisure forms are negatively associated with age, much more so than the passive and the internal leisure forms. Social leisure participations also are negatively associated with age. . . . Reports of relaxation and solitude are positively correlated with age. Development and creativity do not vary with age, but diversion and sensual transcendence are negatively associated with age-position in the life span. (pp. 333–334)

In later maturity, greater amounts of time are devoted to leisure. However, with increased age, the types or range of leisure activities participated in by the individual becomes increasingly restricted or narrow (Robinson, 1969). Likewise, with increased age, leisure activities tend to become increasingly sedentary and restricted to the home (Campbell, 1969). Because patterns of leisure activity and participation encountered in old age have evolved across the entire life span, there is little reason to believe that factors such as retirement, children leaving home, or various role changes occurring in later maturity will significantly affect normative leisure behavior among members of the aged population. Pertinent factors may include decreasing physical strength, energy declines, changes in interests and values, age-related social norms, personality variables, and psychological well-being.

How Do Economic Conditions Affect the Elderly?

If you're old, you're more than twice as likely to be poor (Brotman, 1971). As we have already pointed out, the older population fares less well economically than other age segments within our society. In the early 1970s it was estimated that one elderly couple in five had incomes of $3,000 or less and that approximately one half of all aged couples lived on incomes of less than $5,000. In recent years it has been estimated that the median income of families whose head is 65 or over is about one half the median income of all families within the United States.

Shift in economic control

Not only are elderly families less well-off than other families, the chances of improving their economic condition through personal initiative or effort are severely limited. Although all older persons are certainly not poor, most older people are dependent upon economic resources that lie outside their sphere of control. In most cases our economic status in old age is largely dependent upon a **fixed income** as pension or retirement payments, social security, and supplemental assistance grants from the state. Although many older people may receive private income from employment, investments, and property, such sources of revenue are usually supplemental and do not generally meet day-to-day living expenses.

Since many older individuals live on fixed incomes, they are particularly vulnerable to the effects of inflation, which has been extremely high in recent years. As a result, many older people are experiencing poverty for the first time in their lives.

When people plan for their retirement or old age, estimates of their economic need are usually based upon current functioning and demands. For example, if a person needed $500 a month income in 1960, steps might have been taken to assure $500 a month retirement income in 1970 or 1975. By taking such steps, people may have believed that their accustomed standard of living would be maintained throughout old age. Anticipating reduced family responsibilities, people may have hoped that their economic circumstances would improve in later maturity as a result of careful financial planning. Unfortunately for much of the present elderly generation, economic expectations regarding the "golden years" have not coincided with economic realities. A person who lived comfortably on $500 in 1960 could be poverty-stricken in 1980. At the present time, the earlier persons retire upon a fixed income, the more economic difficulty they are likely to face. In essence, many elderly individuals who are on fixed incomes are fighting a losing and increasingly desperate battle.

Decline in opportunities for earned income

When consideration is given to financial resources in old age, many economic principles that pervade our society are no longer applicable. Basic to our economic system is the idea that "time is money" or that our time can be exchanged for income. In old age opportunities to exchange time for earned income are restricted. Although job discrimination on the basis of age has been outlawed by the government, older individuals are less likely than younger individuals to possess training and skills necessary to function in many present-day positions. Likewise, many jobs that are readily accessible may be beyond the physical capabilities of the elderly person to perform, for example, jobs requiring physical strength and endurance. Finally, opportunities afforded many elderly individuals to exchange time for income are restricted by the fact that large numbers of older people frequently congregate within a relatively small geographic area, as in Florida. As the elderly population grows in a particular location, opportunities for employment among older people diminish proportionately. In such situations relatively few older people will be able to secure jobs.

Diminished choices

The economic issue is critical in old age because it can overshadow all aspects of the individual's life. In the absence of sufficient income, behavioral options are drastically reduced.

Where a person lives, where a person goes, what a person eats, how a person travels, who a person sees, and what a person does depends, to a large extent, upon economic considerations. Our income will frequently determine the amount of freedom and control we have in solving problems, making personal choices, and directing affairs. Without adequate income, personal options and freedom usually shrink drastically. Moreover, in the absence of adequate income, feelings of autonomy, self-esteem, and personal worth are likely to suffer.

A final word

At the present time three rather broad observations can be made concerning the economic condition of the elderly. These observations are based upon normative data and do not apply to all elderly persons.

1. As a group, the aged population is worse off economically than any other age segment of the population and is worse off than the population as a whole.

2. In old age, economic inequality tends to become increasingly pronounced. Greater economic differences exist among older people than among younger people.

3. Basic economic needs of all elderly individuals are not met within our society. For many older people, poverty is a fact of life.

How Does Increased Age Affect Choice of Housing?

Precise information concerning the types of dwellings occupied by all members of the aged population is not available at the present time. However, on the basis of census data, various estimates regarding dominant patterns of housing among the elderly have been formulated.

General housing patterns

It is presently believed that approximately 90 percent of all persons 65 and over live within their own home. In this context, *own home* may refer to a single-family dwelling (private house), apartment, mobile home or trailer, retirement community, condominium, room, boarding house, or hotel. Approximately 70 percent (7 in every 10 persons) actually own the home they reside in. It is estimated that 60 percent of the elderly population live within metropolitan areas. Within this group, about 61 percent live within the central or inner city and about 39 percent live in the suburbs. Seventeen percent of aged individuals live in rural nonfarm areas and 5 percent live on farms.

It is further estimated that one in every twenty (5 percent) elderly persons resides within institutional settings. Most older people who do not live within their own home reside within institutions or have moved in with relatives. Finally, about 3 percent of the elderly live in government-sponsored low-rent units (Housing and Urban Development programs). Drawing upon available statistical data, it would appear that "typical" elderly persons own their home, live within their own home, and dwell within a metropolitan area.

The strain of home ownership

For many elderly people, home ownership becomes difficult. There are a number of reasons for this. As property values increase and taxes go up, home ownership may become an economic strain for persons on fixed incomes. It is not unusual for older persons to be forced to sell their home because it has become too valuable. Although many states, counties, and cities give the elderly certain property tax breaks, ability to pay may still be exceeded by tax demands. Likewise, many taxing authorities will not evict an older person for failure to pay taxes. However, in such situations, taxes must be paid by heirs or property will be turned over to the taxing authority upon the death of the owner. For many individuals, both options are unacceptable.

The strain of home ownership may also be intensified by the fact that decaying neighborhoods frequently impinge upon and ultimately envelop the dwellings of the elderly. In such situations continued home ownership may relegate the elderly to living environments that are undesirable, intolerable, and potentially harmful. As neighborhoods decay, public services are curtailed, crime increases, and recreational and shopping facilities relocate. As the social, safety, and recreation needs of elderly persons are decreasingly met within such neighborhoods, pressures to relinquish ownership of their home may increase. In such circumstances social forces rather than personal inclination will motivate individuals to sell their house and relocate.

Problems involving home maintenance become more critical with advanced age. The younger person may have little difficulty performing routine maintenance chores around the home, but age-related reductions in physical strength and energy may make the older person incapable of such undertakings. It may become necessary to find others who will shovel the snow, mow the lawn, paint the house, and clean the garage. If family members or friends are not available to perform such functions, the elderly person may be forced to tolerate deteriorating conditions, to hire someone for maintenance purposes, or to move. Of these three options, all impose hardships and may be perceived as personally undesirable by the elderly individual. At the present time increased recognition of the fact that elderly people prefer to stay within their own homes has prompted various governmental agencies and social groups to provide needed home maintenance assistance to the aged. Whether an older person lives in acceptable or substandard housing may depend upon the availability of maintenance assistance. Likewise, availability of maintenance assistance may determine whether older people continue to live within their own home or are forced by necessity to move.

A decent living environment

Consideration of housing and the aged cannot be restricted to the physical structures in which they dwell. Where persons live is usually more important than the specific residential unit in which they reside. Adjustment and psychological well-being are dependent upon the entire **living environment** or the total atmosphere in which the individual functions or dwells. When attention is given to the subject of housing for the elderly, the following factors or elements relating to living environment are significant (Havighurst, 1969):

1. Physical condition and availability of maintenance funds.

2. Age of residence and who owns it.

3. Location of needed services in relation to residence.

4. Nearness to stores and recreational activities.

5. Nearness to relatives and similar aged individuals.

6. Accessibility and availability of transportation.

7. Relative safety of the surrounding environment.

Although the relative impact of each element may vary from individual to individual, there is a high probability that each of these elements will directly or indirectly affect the behavior and adjustment of most individuals during later maturity.

For many elderly people within our society, housing—dwelling and living environment—constitutes a major problem. Although a great deal of research, discussion, and planning has been devoted to the subject of housing in later maturity, little of a definitive or consequential nature has been done to actually improve the living situations of most elderly people.

It is currently estimated that slightly less than 50 percent of the elderly live in substandard housing and that "hundreds of thousands of aged persons are today on waiting lists to get into public or other subsidized housing" (Special Committee on Aging, 1975, p. 79). At this time many elderly persons must pay disproportionate amounts of their incomes for rent. Some older people are forced to live in neighborhoods that are extremely dangerous. Others live within environments that effectively isolate them from needed facilities, social services, and meaningful interpersonal contacts.

Although the housing needs of the elderly have, to a large degree, been identified, strategies designed to meet such needs have yet to be specifically formulated and implemented. Fortunately, it is becoming increasingly recognized that diversity within the older population must be reflected in diverse housing. Because older individuals are more heterogeneous than younger individuals, it is logical to assume that one type of housing or living environment cannot suit all older people. Without giving consideration to unique characteristics within the aged population, attempts to design optimal housing or living environments for the elderly are likely to be less than successful.

Summary

Each person's behavior and adjustment is influenced by the society in which he or she lives. Societies establish norms for acceptable behavior and impose pressures designed to assure compliance or conformity to such norms. Social expectations often guide behavior. If personal needs clash with social norms and expectations, problems are likely to result. In old age changes in social roles and statuses are common. Role restriction and status reduction rather than role expansion and status elevation is usually characteristic in later maturity. When consideration is given to various social aspects of aging, emphasis is upon normative or average behavior. However, within the aged population, great diversity exists and deviations from the norm are not uncommon.

A number of stereotypes or myths concerning old age and the family are accepted by many people within our society. The most common myths are the following: (1) If elderly persons are not institutionalized, they will ultimately end up moving in with family members, usually their children. (2) In most instances elderly people are neglected or abandoned by their children. (3) Most elderly people are a source of financial drain and are dependent upon the resources of various family members. (4) Grandparents spoil their grandchildren. (5) Grandparenting is universally enjoyed. (6) Most elderly people feel that it is their children's responsibility to care for them in old age.

Retirement is a milestone in most people's lives. All individuals who retire must make some adjustments. The extent to which a person adjusts successfully to retirement depends upon personality factors, established coping techniques, preretirement attitudes and expectations, occupational level, health, income, retirement activities, interpersonal relationships, and whether retirement was voluntary or involuntary. The belief that retirement hastens death is erroneous.

In later maturity greater amounts of time are devoted to leisure. However, with increased age, the types or range of leisure activities become restricted or narrow. Leisure participation, intensity, and frequency all decline with increased age. Relaxation and solitude increase with age. Factors related to age-related changes in leisure activities may be reduced physical strength and energy, changes in interests and values, age-related social norms, personality variables, and psychological well-being.

The elderly are twice as likely to be poor within our society. In old age chances of improving ourselves financially tend to be quite limited. Economic resources usually lie outside the elderly person's sphere of control. For many older people, the necessity of living upon a fixed income imposes great economic strain. During times of inflation, it is likely that aged individuals will experience poverty for the first time in their lives. Opportunities for elderly people to earn an income are quite restricted. The possibility of exchanging time for money may not exist for many aged individuals. Without adequate income, personal options and freedom shrink dramatically. In the absence of adequate income, feelings of autonomy, self-esteem, and personal worth are likely to suffer. As a group, the elderly are worse off than any other age segment of the population and are worse off than the total population. Economic inequality increases in later maturity. In our society the basic economic needs of all aged individuals are not met.

The average elderly person owns his or her home, lives in his or her own home, and dwells within a metropolitan area. For many elderly people, home ownership becomes a strain for a number of social reasons. As property taxes rise and neighborhoods decay, elderly individuals may be forced to leave their homes. Likewise, if elderly individuals are unable or unwilling to obtain maintenance assistance, home ownership may become difficult or impossible. Considerations of housing and the aged should encompass both physical structure and the living environment. For many older people, housing constitutes a major problem. If attempts to deal with this problem are to be successful, diversity within the aged population must be acknowledged and taken into account.

Progress Check

1. What are some ways in which society might affect our behavior? (pp. 206–208)

2. What is the common pattern of social role and status change in later maturity?   (pp. 207–208)

3. What is the difference between social role and status? How are they related to each other?   (pp. 207–208)

4. What are three common myths concerning old age and the family? (pp. 208–212)

5. What three factors are likely to influence our adjustment to retirement? (pp. 212–215)

6. What are some quantitative and qualitative changes in leisure activities that are noted in conjunction with increased age?   (pp. 215–218)

7. What factors might operate against economic well-being in old age? (pp. 218–220)

8. Why is economic power or control frequently not in the hands of elderly persons?   (pp. 219–220)

9. Why is poverty often the economic condition of many elderly persons? (pp. 219–220)

10. What is the relationship between economic condition and adjustment in old age?   (p. 220)

11. Based upon statistics, what are the housing characteristics of the "typical" elderly person?   (pp. 220–221)

12. What factors operate against home ownership in old age? (pp. 221–222)

13. What are some important elements within each person's living environment?   (pp. 222–223)

14. What do you think are the most important age-related social considerations?

Recommended Readings

Neugarten, B. L. & K. K. Weinstein. The changing American grandparent. *Journal of Marriage and the Family,* 1964, 26, 266–273.
A presentation of research findings concerning different patterns of interaction assumed by grandparents with their grandchildren. Factors influencing enactment of the grandparent role are discussed and typical behaviors defined.

Simpson, I. H. & J. C. McKinny. *Social Aspects of Aging.* Durham, N.C.: Duke University Press, 1966.
A comprehensive review of social factors that affect and determine aging within our society. Consideration is given to individual response to social variables in old age.

Streib, G. F. & C. J. Schneider. *Retirement in American Society: Impact and Process.* Ithaca, N.Y.: Cornell University Press, 1971.
This work examines the influence of retirement upon adjustment and successful functioning. Adjustment to retirement is viewed as a gradual process following a specific change event.

11

Death and Dying

Preview ∞ *In this chapter we will consider ambiguities surrounding the definition of death. A distinction will be drawn between death as an event and dying as a process, and the relationship between age and death will be discussed. We will also examine a number of attitudes commonly held in reference to death and dying. Frequently encountered reactions of persons who are dying and reactions of persons who interact with dying individuals will be presented. Finally, we will give consideration to a number of normal reactions following the death of someone who is valued or loved.*

Life is finite and death is inevitable. Death is an event that marks the end of life. It is a natural occurrence and a predictable stage in the developmental process of every human being. The fact that death may be feared, welcomed, dreaded, or denied has no effect upon its eventuality. Although it may be difficult for many people to accept, nothing in life is more certain than death.

How Can We Define Death and Dying?

Death is a biological event resulting from the cessation of various physical activities. Until recently, heart activity and breathing were used to distinguish between life and death. However, with the development of more sophisticated medical equipment, bodily functions that were formerly unobservable can easily be monitored. Machines capable of maintaining organ functions for indefinite periods of time are now available. As a result, conflicts concerning specific definitions of life and death have arisen. Do changes in the brain and nervous system indicate death or do changes in heart activity and respiration? Can individuals be considered dead if their heart activity and respiration are dependent upon some mechanical device and other vital signs are absent? This question, of course, has not been resolved to the satisfaction of all. Because organs of the human body cease functioning at different rates, the point at which clinical death actually occurs is open to debate and interpretation. Living organisms do not die at one specific point in time.

In an attempt to establish specific criteria for death, the following determinants were presented in the *Journal of the American Medical Association:* (1) unreceptivity and unresponsivity, (2) absence of movements or breathing, (3) no reflexes confirmed by (4) a flat electroencephalogram (Cassell, Kass, and Associates, 1972). Although this definition of death is widely accepted by many states and physicians, it fails to give attention to individuals who have lost brain functioning (intellectual, sensory, and perceptual abilities) and must be kept alive artificially without hope of recovery. Is such a person alive? Should such a person be maintained mechanically? Violent differences of opinion are evoked by these questions, and the probability of reaching consensus in the coming years is quite low.

Whereas death is an event, **dying** is a process. It can be maintained that dying begins at the moment of conception. Life initiates an uninterrupted progression toward death. Although such an orientation toward dying may seem rather bizarre, it cannot be denied that every moment a person lives brings him or her one moment closer to death.

A more generally accepted view is that dying is a process that occurs within restricted parameters, which begins by change—as by organ malfunction, accident, or disease—and culminates in death. For some people the process of dying may be brief and apparently painless. For others dying may be prolonged and involve a great degree of suffering. When dying occurs over an extended period of time, psychological stresses upon dying individuals and those with whom they interact are likely to be great. Likewise, ability to cope may become severely strained as attempts are made to adjust to the immediate reality of death. When death occurs suddenly, psychological attention is focused solely upon coping strategies and patterns of adjustment exhibited by involved survivors. In either situation, ability to cope successfully is likely to be more strongly tested than at any other time.

Does Death Become a More Potent Force As We Age?

Although people die at all ages, the positive relationship between increased age and mortality makes death and dying the appropriate concern of gerontology. Most people who die within our society are old. No one ever died of "old age"; yet, the probability and proximity of death increases with advanced age.

Relationship between old age and death

The relationship between age and death is universal and is alluded to by Bromley in his definition of aging:

> Aging can be regarded simply as an accumulation of pathological processes, which eventually kill off the individual by interfering with a vital function of the body. (1974, p. 115)

In the United States the five major causes of death are, first, diseases of the heart; second, cancer and other malignant neoplasms; third, cerebral hemorrhage and other vascular lesions (strokes); fourth, accidents; and fifth, influenza and pneumonia (U.S. Public Health Service, 1974). The median age of individuals dying from heart diseases and cerebral hemorrhage is 75.6 years. The median age at which persons die from malignant neoplasms (cancer) is 67.5, and 74.5 is the the median age at death from influenza and pneumonia. The median age of people dying from accidents is 39.9 (U.S. Public Health Service, 1974). In essence, we can look at four of the five major causes of death in the United States and see that median age at death exceeds the official chronological designation of old age (65 years). In the mid 1970s 70 percent of those dying in the United States were 65 years and over.

Awareness of death and its effect on behavior

In old age recognition of the proximity of death may influence behavior in a number of ways. Individuals may become acutely conscious of the limited time remaining. As a result, they may feel reluctant to undertake projects or commitments that offer little promise of completion before death. People may become increasingly concerned with spending their remaining time in ways that they perceive as fulfilling and personally meaningful. A pronounced reluctance to waste time on unwanted relationships or activities may develop. When time is perceived as limited, many people will strive to make the most of it.

For some individuals, the perception of limited time and the proximity of death will prompt a turning inward and gradual withdrawal from the external world. Former attachments will become less important as attention is progressively focused inward. Only those attachments that are most important to the individual will persist. From a social perspective, adjustment is characterized by disengagement.

For other persons, awareness of limited time may provoke feelings of anxiety, depression, or despair. In such cases feelings of guilt and regret concerning past activities or how one's life has been spent are common. Such feelings are often accompanied by the acute realization that the past can't be changed and that there will be no opportunities to make amends or correct past mistakes.

Finally, the perception of limited remaining time will motivate some to engage in a number of activities designed to "tie up loose ends" or satisfactorily settle personal and business affairs. Because people respond in vastly different ways, there is no way to predict exactly how an individual will react to increased awareness of the proximity of death. None of the previously cited responses are typical of the entire aged population. However, it should be recognized that consciousness of impending death increases with advanced age, affects adjustment, and influences behavior. Regardless of health status, many elderly persons engage in behaviors that are similar to those engaged in by younger persons who are actually in the process of dying. Anticipation of the inevitable becomes an increasingly potent force in later maturity.

Old age and exposure to death and dying

Whereas a correlation exists between age and death, a correlation also exists between age and exposure to death and dying. With increased age, a person becomes more likely to confront the deaths of family members, acquaintances, and age peers.

In advanced age it is not unusual for the individual to be exposed to a number of deaths that occur in relatively rapid succession. Before recovering from the effects of one loss, an elderly person may have to cope with another. In some cases cumulative stress resulting from death-related losses may far exceed our ability to cope successfully. As a person's ability to adjust becomes overtaxed, physical and psychological problems are likely to occur.

In later life Noel Coward, the English writer and entertainer, remarked that one of the hardest things about growing old was the loss of friends his age. Undoubtedly, this sentiment is shared by a great many elderly persons.

What Are Our Attitudes Toward Death?

Attitudes are predispositions to respond to persons, objects, situations, or values in a particular manner. Such predispositions are expressive of personal opinions and are fundamentally affective (emotional) and evaluative.

Attitudes may or may not have any rational bases. Attitudes are learned, and many become firmly established early in life.

Fear and denial

Within western society, two of the most common attitudes toward death are fear and denial. Although these two orientations are discussed separately, there is a close relationship between fear and denial. It is well known that if people fear someone or something, they may cope by denying the existence of that which is feared. As long as denial operates effectively as a defense mechanism, threats and fears will be kept under control and anxiety relegated to the unconscious. The relationship between fear and denial has been noted by many physicians who, after informing a patient regarding the presence of serious illness, find that the information has not been consciously grasped or seemed unheard by the individual. The news of illness was so frightening that it was immediately denied.

Evidence of death-related fear and denial pervades our society and reflects dominant attitudes regarding death.

> American culture has attempted to cope with death by disguising it and pretending that it is not a basic condition of all life. We tend to take refuge in euphemistic language; we pass on, join our forefathers, exit, become defunct, or demised . . . but very rarely do we die. We establish an industry which has a major interest in the creation of lifelike qualities in the dead. The military makes death impersonal. Prevalent entertainment treats death not as tragedy but as dramatic illusion. (Feifel, 1973, p. 1)

The evidence

A number of realities support the contention that death is denied and feared within our society. Among such realities are the following: (1) Very few people have ever seen a dead person before treatment by an undertaker. (2) Every effort is made to impart lifelike qualities (asleep) upon the dead. (3) In reference to a specific death, euphemisms are commonly used. (4) The subject of death is rarely broached. (5) Children are shielded from the reality of death. (6) Great anxiety is often associated with attending funerals or other death-related functions. (7) Some people have difficulty interacting socially with persons whose profession it is to care for the dead—morticians, undertakers, embalmers. (8) Many people refuse to arrange for their own funerals even if death is a relatively immediate prospect. (9) Some people refuse to purchase or even discuss life insurance because of death-related fear and denial. (10) When interacting with a dying person, many people will act as though nothing has changed and the subject of death will be avoided. (11) Many people refuse to live near a cemetery, enter a cemetery alone, or venture in or by a cemetery after dark. (12) The focus of many horror stories and movies is the dead and their manifestations—ghosts, zombies, vampires, and mummies. (13) External signs of mourning are minimized.

Are Our Attitudes Toward Death Age-Related?

Death-related fear and denial are pervasive within our society. Yet, great variations in attitudes are noted among different people and within the same person over a period of time.

Contrasts between older and younger people's attitudes

To some extent, differences in attitudes toward death appear to be age-related. According to Simone de Beauvoir (1972), death may become less feared in old age because life has become less meaningful.

> Even if the old person is struck by no particular misfortune, he has usually either lost his reasons for living or he has discovered their absence. The reason why death fills us with anxiety is that it is the inescapable reverse of our projects: when a man is no longer active in any way, when he has ceased all undertakings, all plans, then there remains nothing that death can destroy. It is usual to put forward wearing-out and fatigue as an explanation for the way some old people resign themselves to death; but if all a man needed was to vegetate he could put up with this life in slow motion. But for man living means self-transcendence. A consequence of biological decay is the impossibility of surpassing oneself and of becoming passionately concerned with anything; it kills all projects, and it is by this expedient that it renders death acceptable. (de Beauvoir, 1972, p. 443)

Several research studies have supported the notion that elderly individuals tend to fear death less than younger individuals (Kalish & Johnson, 1972; Kogan & Wallach, 1961; Kalish & Reynolds, 1976). Yet, whereas death-related fear tends to decline with advanced age, preoccupation with death tends to increase (Kalish & Reynolds, 1976; Butler, 1963). Old people spend more time thinking and talking about death than do young people. Although it seems reasonable that both death-related fear and preoccupation would increase with its proximity, such is not the case. It is possible that reduced death-related fear noted in old age may result from intensified denial; older people are less likely than younger people to feel deprived or "short-changed" by the prospect of death. Just as the rich man has more reason than the poor man to fear thieves, the young person has more reason than the old person to fear death. Elderly people have lived an expected number of years, have had a vast number of experiences, and have passed through childhood, adolescence, and adulthood. Death cannot deprive the aged individual of such experiences, development, and time. However, in youth such things are vulnerable to death.

Finally, it may be assumed that death-related fear decreases for people in later maturity because society and elderly individuals themselves place less value upon their lives. According to Glaser (1966), the value placed upon the elderly person's life by society is less than the value placed upon the life of the younger person. Results obtained by Sudnow (1967) also indicate that as a person grows old, society places diminished value upon his or her life.

When the treatment of older and younger people in hospitals and emergency rooms was compared, it was found that older people who appeared to be dead were less likely to receive thorough medical examinations or extraordinary attention. Older people were more likely to be judged dead or without hope of recovery than were younger persons. In addition to the elderly, the following persons were also more likely to be perceived as hopeless:

> The suicide victim, the dope addict, the known prostitute, the assailant in a crime of violence, the vagrant, the known wife-beater, and generally, those persons whose moral characters are considered reproachable. (Sudnow, 1967, p. 105)

In old age the value placed by individuals upon their own lives also diminishes (Glaser, 1966). This devaluation may be related to changes in physical attractiveness and ability, poor health, economic problems, loss of significant roles and statuses, and so forth. However, regardless of cause, as life becomes less satisfying, less enjoyable, or less valued, fear of death will probably subside.

Death-related losses.   A relationship may exist between fear of death and value attached to death-related losses, that is, the more people are concerned with specific losses resulting from death, the greater their fear of death will be. Investigating the relative concerns of individuals in reference to death, Diggory and Rothman (1961) identified seven death-related losses: (1) loss of ability to experience, (2) loss of ability to predict future events, (3) loss of body, (4) loss experienced by friends and family, (5) loss of ability to care for dependents, (6) loss of opportunity to continue plans and projects, (7) loss of being in a relatively painful state. When the relative concerns of young adults and middle-aged persons were ascertained, it was found that the greatest concern of young adults centered upon causing grief to others whereas inability to care for dependents was most important in middle-age. Investigating concerns pertaining to death-related losses among elderly persons, Kalish and Reynolds (1976) noted that causing grief to friends and family and inability to care for dependents became less important in old age. In general, less value was attached to death-related losses by elderly persons. It should, of course, be stated that as people reach advanced age, the probability increases that fewer family members and friends still survive and that dependents will no longer be present. It is possible that value attached to death-related losses by older people may be related to various social factors rather than to age. For example, if a 70-year-old person has three dependent children, his or her concern regarding inability to care for dependents might not be significantly different from that exhibited by someone middle-aged.

Factors other than age that influence attitudes

In reality very little is known about the direct relationship between attitudes toward death and age. It is extremely difficult to segregate age from other variables that may influence death-related attitudes. Attitudes toward death may be affected by religious orientation, socioeconomic status, state of health, race, education, and marital status. Unless age can be isolated from such potentially influential factors, it cannot be assumed that attitudes toward death change as a function of increased age. Differences between age groups may be noted, but cause-and-effect relationships cannot be established.

Religious orientation, for example, does appear to exert a strong influence upon attitudes toward death. People who are more religious tend to have less fear and anxiety concerning death than do those who are less religious (Templer, 1972; Williams & Cole, 1968; Kalish & Reynolds, 1976). Although people do not usually "get religion" as they approach and enter later maturity, those people who are currently old within our society tend to be more religious than their younger counterparts. They have been more religious throughout their lives. When the relationship between death-related fear and religious orientation is combined with the observation that the elderly tend to be more religious than the young, it might be predicted that older people would have less fear of death than younger people. However, this difference between age groups is a function of religiosity rather than increased age.

Riley (1963) found that attitudes toward death were more highly related to educational level than to age. When subjects were asked to respond to two negative statements regarding death: (1) "Death always comes too soon"; (2)"To die is to suffer"; people from higher educational levels were more likely than people from lower educational levels to reject such negative statements (see Table 11.1).

Upon examination of Table 11.1, it may be noted that attitudinal differences among age groups were significantly smaller than attitudinal differences among educational levels. On the basis of this study, we might assume a negative correlation between educational level and agreement with negative attitudes toward death, that is, lower educational level is related to higher agreement with negative views, and higher educational level is related to lower agreement with negative views. If such is the case, differences in attitudes toward death again cannot be attributed to age.

Attitudes may change over time

Five potential attitudes toward death have been identified by Shneidman and Farberow (1957):

1. Death is welcomed and perceived as an end to problems, pains, and stress.

2. Death is viewed as a fact of life to which the individual must be resigned.

3. Regardless of cost, death must be postponed.

4. Death is to be scorned and met bravely.

5. Death is a terrifying experience to be met with great fear and agitation.

Table 11.1: Percent Who Agree With Two Negative Views of Death by Age and Education

Age	Education			
	Junior High School or less	High School	College	"Effect" of Higher Education
(a) Death always comes too soon				
30 and under	65	53	40	− 25
31–40	58	50	24	− 34
41–50	75	64	49	− 26
51–60	70	50	53	− 17
61 +	58	59	29	− 29
"Effect" of older age	− 7	+ 6	− 11	
(b) To die is to suffer				
30 and under	31	13	5	− 26
31–40	23	5	7	− 16
41–50	18	11	10	− 8
51–60	28	8	9	− 19
61 +	24	13	8	− 16
"Effect" of older age	− 7		+ 3	

Source: From *Aging and Society,* vol. 1, Exhibit 14–17, J. Riley, © 1969 The Russell Sage Foundation, New York.

Factors such as early childhood experiences and learning, experiences with death during the course of life, present state of health, perceived proximity of death, satisfaction with life, and general philosophical orientation will strongly affect individual attitudes toward death. It should not be assumed that one particular attitude toward death becomes established at an early age and continues more or less unchanged throughout maturity. Depending upon external and internal circumstances, significant variation in death-related attitudes may be exhibited by individuals over the entire course of their life. Attitudes toward death, like all attitudes, are subject to modification. Death-related attitudes, like most attitudes, exert significant influence upon daily behavior, adjustment, and ability to cope.

How Does the Dying Person React?

As a result of work with dying patients, Elisabeth Kübler-Ross, a psychiatrist, has identified five stages through which individuals may pass between awareness of terminal illness and death. These stages represent normative reactions to dying. All dying individuals do not pass through these five stages, do not progress through a specific predetermined sequence of reactions, and do not, during a specified time interval, manifest one particular reaction to the exclusion of all others. A person may become fixated at one stage, may move from one stage to another in an unpredictable manner, or may exhibit relatively few common psychological reactions associated with the process of dying. According to Kübler-Ross (1974), stages do not always occur in the same order and some patients may manifest characteristics of two or more stages simultaneously. The five stages through which individuals may pass between awareness of terminal illness and death are (1) *denial,* (2) *anger,* (3) *bargaining,* (4) *depression,* and (5) *acceptance.*

Denial

The first stage is **denial.** When people are told that they have a serious illness, the most common reaction is shock and denial. The individual may refuse to believe that the diagnosis is correct, may feel that some mistake has been made, and, in an attempt to rectify the error, may seek other opinions and help. Denial is, of course, a commonly employed defense mechanism in times of acute stress. If something can be denied for a relatively short period of time, psychological resources can be rallied and strategies designed for long-term coping can develop. Because denial provides a person with time to adjust and adapt, it is considered a positive or healthy way to cope with shocking experiences.

Although the denial stage may persist for minutes, weeks, or months, it is usually relinquished by the individual prior to death. Of those interviewed by Kübler-Ross, less than 1 percent maintained denial or continued to reject the reality of impending death until the very end. For most people, objective realities such as bodily degeneration, reactions of family and friends, and confirmed diagnoses operate against successful maintenance of denial for indefinite or prolonged periods of time. However, if individuals do continue to deny death, this choice should be respected. Ill-advised attempts to divest the person of denial may prove devastating to personal adjustment and ability to cope.

Anger

The second stage is **anger.** When objective realities impinge upon the individual and denial can no longer be maintained, angry feelings and behaviors become increasingly characteristic. According to Kübler-Ross, the individual is likely to become critical, demanding, nasty, and difficult. Underlying feelings of anger is the question, "Why me?"

During the anger stage, hostility may be directed toward anyone. Anger may be directed toward God for letting such a thing happen, toward health care professionals for their inability to change the situation, and toward friends and relatives because they are healthy, independent, and continuing to pursue their own lives.

If such hostility is perceived by those around the dying person as a personal attack rather than a manifestation of frustration and rage, their response is likely to involve avoidance, anger, and withdrawal. Those who interact with the dying individual may begin to visit less frequently, engage in hostile interchanges, or severely restrict verbal interactions and physical contact. During the anger stage, their patience, understanding, and ability to cope may be severely strained. However, recognition of the fact that the dying person's anger about impending death is being displaced upon self and others may do much to promote patience and understanding. According to Kübler-Ross, if patients are encouraged to openly vent feelings of anger and rage concerning their impending death and are permitted such expressions in an atmosphere of acceptance and understanding, anger and bitterness are likely to subside. When anger is directed toward the actual source of frustration, death itself, hostile behaviors tend to cease and interpersonal relationships become more positive.

Bargaining

The **bargaining stage** usually evolves as anger subsides. During this stage, the individual attempts to trade something for good health, prolonged life, and cessation of pain. It is not unusual for such bargaining to be directed toward God. The dying person may promise to attend religious services, to lead a good life, to make amends for past wrongs, or to do good things for other people. In some instances bargains may be struck with caregivers or members of the hospital staff. Kübler-Ross writes:

> We had a woman who asked to be relieved of some of her tremendous pain for one day so that she would not be dependent on injections around the clock. She said she would just love to go home one more day and the reason for this was that her favorite son was getting married. We tried everything, and finally we were able to teach her self-hypnosis to relieve her pain. She left the hospital and looked like a million dollars. She attended her son's wedding. I was curious about patients who only ask for one single day; how do they react when their bargaining time is up? It must be extremely difficult. I waited for her, she saw me in the hallway and she was not happy to see me at all. Before I could ask her a question, she said, "Dr. Ross, don't forget, I have another son." This is the most typical part of bargaining. Promises are never kept; patients say, "If I could live just long enough for my children to go through high school," and then they add college, and then they add I just want a son-in-law, and then they would like to have a grandchild, and it goes on and on. (Kübler-Ross, 1977, p. 373)

As a coping strategy, bargaining tends to be successful for relatively short periods of time. As illness progresses, awareness of the fact that no bargain exists becomes increasingly apparent. As the futility of bargaining is recognized, the reality and proximity of death is forced upon the individual.

Depression

When the unconditional reality of death is faced by dying persons, they usually move into the fourth stage, **depression.** During this stage, two types of depression may be exhibited by the dying person. The first type is reactive depression. The second type is preparatory depression.

During **reactive depression** the individual mourns losses that have already been experienced, for example, the loss of physical strength, power, health, and attractive appearance. When the individual mourns future losses—friendships, loves, and pleasures relinquished with death—preparatory depression or grief is experienced. During **preparatory depression,** dying persons are beginning to separate themselves from the people, things, and experiences that will be lost with death. Preparation is for the final separation from everything that is known. According to Kübler-Ross, attempts to "cheer up" the individual who is experiencing preparatory depression are counterproductive and may retard movement toward peaceful acceptance of one's own death.

> The patient is in the process of losing everything and everybody he loves. If he is allowed to express his sorrow he will find a final acceptance much easier, and he will be grateful to those who can sit with him during this stage of depression without constantly telling him not to be sad. (Kübler-Ross, 1969, p. 77)

In essence, preparatory depression is a necessary and positive experience that promotes acceptance and peace in the person who is about to die. As such, its expression should be facilitated, accepted, and allowed to progress in an unimpeded manner.

Acceptance

The final stage between awareness of serious illness and death is **acceptance.** During this stage, separation from others continues and feelings of anxiety and fear are replaced with feelings of peace and quiet expectation. Regarding the stage of acceptance, Kübler-Ross writes:

> . . . the patients will ask once more to see the relatives, then the children, and at the very end, only one beloved person, who is usually husband or wife and, in the case of children, naturally, the parents. This is what we call . . . **decathexis,** when the patient begins to separate; when he begins to feel no longer like talking; when he has finished all his unfinished business; when he just wants the companionship of a person who is comfortable, who can sit and hold his hand. It is much more important than words in this final stage. (Kübler-Ross, 1977, p. 374)

The stage of acceptance is not highly emotional. In fact, during this stage, the individual appears to be almost beyond emotion or affect. This fifth stage is described as "almost void of feelings" (Kübler-Ross, 1969, p. 113). During the final stage of acceptance, individuals appear ready for death, no longer fear the prospect of death, and cease to perceive death as something to be avoided at all costs. Although they may not want to die, they are emotionally prepared for this contingency. This orientation during the stage of acceptance is described in an example cited by Kübler-Ross:

> A woman who was always hoping for a miracle drug that would cure her suddenly looked with an almost beaming face and said, "You know, Dr. Ross, a miracle has happened." I said, "What miracle?" and she replied, "The miracle that I am ready to go now and it is not any longer frightening." (Kübler-Ross, 1977, p. 374)

How Do Others React to the Dying Person?

In our society there are no guidelines concerning how a person should behave when confronted with the dying of another human being. How a person should react to the dying individual, how grief should be expressed, and how the subject of death should be broached remain undefined.

Personal variance

In the absence of definite behavioral guidelines, reactions to the dying of another person tend to be a personal matter, influenced by factors such as personality, ethnic background, and socioeconomic status. In many instances, reactions are quite unpredictable. When faced with someone who is dying, one individual may increase contact with that person while another may avoid all contact. How one responds to the dying person is left more or less to the discretion of each individual. Because little is available to help guide behavior in situations involving dying, most of us feel awkward and ill at ease when interacting with a person who we know is dying. We may not know what to say, may feel embarrassed about discussing our activities and life, and may fervently hope that the subject of death or dying will not enter the conversation. In some instances we may be so uncomfortable that interactions with the dying person become impossible.

Mutual pretense

According to Glaser and Strauss (1977), interactions between the dying individual and other persons frequently involve mutually agreed upon pretense. Although never verbalized, such pretense operates upon the basis of certain rules that function to guide interactions. Among such rules are: (1) Dangerous topics are to be avoided by the dying individual and those who are interacting with that person. Examples of dangerous topics are the patient's declining health, the patient's death, and the events and procedures that will follow the patient's death. (2) When discussions focus upon the distant future, everyone will pretend that the dying person will share in that future. (3) Conversation should focus upon safe topics or remain as ordinary as possible. Small talk is quite acceptable. (4) When anything is said or done to reveal the true nature of the situation, everyone will pretend that the interaction or event has passed unnoticed. For example, if a small child says something about Grandpa dying, everyone in the room will either ignore the remark or quickly discount its importance. (5) Each person must assume responsibility for keeping the situation as "normal" as possible. No one should look or behave as though a person were dying.

> Patients dress for the part of not-dying patient, including careful attention to grooming, and to hair and makeup by female patients. The terminal patient may also fix up his room so that it looks and feels "just like home," an activity that supports his enactment of normalcy. (Glaser & Strauss, 1977, p. 273)

Although the pretense between dying persons and those with whom they interact is initiated and persists through mutual consent, withdrawal of consent by one party will not assure collapse of the previously struck agreement. Thus, if one person attempts to bring the subject of death and dying into the open, others may insist that the pretense be continued. In order to maintain pretense, those who interact with the dying person may argue against the probability of death ("Don't be silly! You're going to get well."), may change the topic of conversation whenever death or dying are mentioned, or may act as though references to dying are not heard. If both parties to an interaction are not willing to acknowledge the proximity and reality of death, mutual pretense is frequently reinstated.

> She was going to live, while he, of her own age, was going to die. She knew he wanted to talk to her, but she always turned the talk into a little joke or into some evasive reassurance, which had to fail. The patient knew and she knew because he saw her desperate attempts to escape; he took pity on her and kept to himself what he wanted to share with another human being. So he died and did not bother her. (Kübler-Ross, 1977, p. 372)

In some instances those who are interacting with the dying person may be coping with the situation by employing denial as a defense mechanism. When others try to abolish pretense associated with this stress-provoking situation, ability to guard against anxiety may be threatened and attempts to preserve the denial/pretense facade may become intensified. The more others try to bring the reality of the situation into open awareness, the more we will deny and reject that reality. As resistance to acknowledging reality becomes more pronounced, efforts to bring the subject of death and dying into open awareness may be abandoned.

Preparatory or anticipatory grief

Just as the dying person may experience preparatory depression or grief, the process of preparatory or **anticipatory grief** is common among those who will survive the dying individual. Beginning with awareness of serious illness, anticipatory grieving will progress throughout the dying process.

Many behaviors and emotions characteristic of bereavement may be exhibited by the individual before the actual death loss. As part of such grieving, emotions and attitudes associated with the actual death may be experienced during the time before death actually occurs. When dying progresses over an extended period of time, it is not unusual for the intensity and duration of grief preceding death to exceed that which is experienced following death. When the actual death does finally occur, many emotions and feelings focusing upon the death have already been worked through and resolved.

According to Fulton and Fulton (1971), because anticipatory grief can be so painful, it is not uncommon for an individual to experience a feeling of relief when death finally becomes an accomplished fact. For some people who are close to a dying person, psychological support and aid may be more critical during the period preceding death than during the period following death. Without adequate emotional support during this period of high stress, successful postdeath adjustment may be severely hampered.

How Do We React to the Death-Related Loss?

Bereavement is the state or condition of being deprived of something valued or loved. The term is most commonly used to denote deprivation resulting from death. Psychological and behavioral reactions associated with bereavement are mourning and grief. **Mourning** is a process involving both overt and covert manifestations of bereavement, for example, wearing black, abstaining from social activities, and expressing feelings of sorrow. **Grief** is a completely personal and subjective experience associated with a major loss or death. Grief involves suffering, pain, and distress. Subjective feelings or experiences frequently associated with grief are guilt, anger, helplessness, despair, anxiety, and restlessness. Long after all external signs of mourning have disappeared, feelings of grief may continue unabated.

Bereavement

No one can predict how long bereavement will affect the psychological and behavioral responses of any individual. Factors such as personality, intensity of the relationship with the deceased, availability of emotional support, circumstances surrounding death, and the day-to-day environment of the bereaved will influence the duration of mourning and grief. Although some people will never completely get over the death of a loved one, significant loss-related effects upon behaviors and emotions often tend to persist for one or two years. Following this period of time, most people who have experienced the death of someone close will return to normal functioning. With the passage of time, emotions associated with bereavement tend to be worked out and successful adjustment is usually achieved. Grief and mourning without end is not normal.

General emotions.   Interviewing more than 100 recently widowed individuals, Clayton, Halikes, and Maurice (1971) identified various symptoms associated with bereavement. During the first month of bereavement, the most common symptoms were crying, depression, sleep disturbance, difficulty concentrating or poor memory, lack of appetite or weight loss, use of medicines for sleep or nerves, fatigue, and loss of interest in friends and activities. Approximately one in every five bereaved individuals reported various somatic symptoms, for example, headaches, pains in different parts of the body, blurred vision, stomach pains, and constipation. Approximately one in every four bereaved individuals reported feelings of guilt or self-condemnation in relation to the deceased. During their first month of bereavement, only a very small percentage of those interviewed indicated feelings of anger. Although it is known that anger is a definite symptom of bereavement, it would appear that this reaction is not manifested soon after the actual loss is experienced. In addition, a very small percentage of those interviewed had experienced symptoms of severe psychiatric disturbance (for example, hallucinations) during the first month of bereavement.

Although there is no way to predict the intensity and duration of grief reactions, certain responses in association with the death of a loved one have a high probability of occurrence (Parkes, 1972; Kalish & Reynolds, 1976; Kübler-Ross, 1969; Caine, 1974). Over an extended period of time, we might expect to react to the death of a loved one with feelings of guilt, anger, depression, restlessness and tension, and preoccupation. It should be emphasized these reactions are all defined as normal.

Feelings of guilt. In many instances feelings of **guilt** are experienced in association with loss. Such feelings often have no objective bases, that is, the survivor imagines or fantasizes situations or interactions for which responsibility is unjustifiably assumed. Guilt often focuses upon what the survivor might have done for the deceased, upon imagined or real interpersonal problems or disagreements, and upon failure to make amends with the deceased before death. Thoughts such as, "If I had only invited Mother to live with me," "If I had only been there when he died," and "If I had only been more understanding and loving," may preoccupy the survivor. As feelings of guilt predominate, positive aspects of the relationship with the deceased may be ignored or relegated to a position of no importance. That which was bad (real or imagined) will overshadow that which was good. In some instances guilt may arise from attitudes held toward the individual before death. For example, if a son or daughter felt resentful or hostile toward a parent, acute feelings of guilt concerning such attitudes may be experienced following the death of the mother or father. In retrospect, children may wonder how they could have ever felt that way about the parent and may believe that everything would be different if only the parent were again alive. Parental behaviors that may have provoked feelings of resentment and hostility are frequently discounted or repressed. Perceptions of the deceased are often characterized by a strong positive bias, that is, after a person has died, we tend to focus upon and magnify that which was good in the individual. This operates against a realistic assessment of interpersonal relationships with the person who has died. Guilt may intensify as the survivor fixates upon negative qualities in self and positive qualities in the deceased.

Feelings of anger. Following the death of someone close, it is not uncommon for expressions of anger to be directed toward those who worked with the dying person, most often nurses and physicians, and toward friends and family members. Anger toward health care professionals may focus upon treatment which has been perceived as inadequate or inappropriate and upon a perceived lack of concern or commitment on the part of caretakers. A physician, nurse, or hospital is often angrily blamed for an individual's death even when everything conceivable has been done to save or prolong his or her life.

Many people who have attended funerals have observed bereaved persons directing feelings of anger toward friends or family members. Friends and relatives may be berated for past behaviors toward the deceased, for failure to visit and provide care and support, or for failure to take responsibility for the deceased. Anger may be expressed by the bereaved in statements such as "You had time to come to the funeral but never had time to visit when he was alive," or "His life would have been happy if you hadn't caused so many problems," or "You have some nerve showing your face here after the way you treated him!" When anger is expressed toward family and friends, bereaved persons may act as though they are speaking for the deceased, for example, "John wouldn't have wanted you to come to his funeral," or "Sarah knew you'd pretend to be sorry when she died." By assuming the position of spokesperson for the deceased, the individual is able to express feelings of anger and hostility while assuming no personal or direct responsibility for such statements. In some instances, anger expressed by the bereaved has been pent up for years and is permitted expression only during times of acute stress. Death often occasions verbal interactions that may be regretted later but will never be completely forgotten.

In addition to feeling angry toward health care professionals, family, and friends, it has been recognized during recent years that bereaved persons experience feelings of anger toward the person who was loved and has died. Bereaved people may feel angry toward the deceased for having abandoned them. The deceased may be perceived as having deprived the survivor of feelings of constancy and security. Likewise, bereaved persons may feel that the deceased has left them to face the problems, conflicts, and demands of daily living without the needed support of the loved one. Although anger toward the person who has died may appear to be irrational, such anger is normal and must be confronted by many individuals during the process of working through and resolving feelings of grief.

Episodes of depression.   During bereavement, we are likely to experience periodic and severe episodes of depression. Acute depression that persists over prolonged periods of time is not a normal aspect of bereavement. Episodes of depression may occur in conjunction with some event or occasion that reminds us of the person who has died or may occur in the absence of any discernible precipitating factor. Susceptibility to depression may increase at nighttime or when we are tired. Feelings of hopelessness, pronounced sorrow, and defeat are likely to be experienced by depressed persons. They may feel that life has no meaning, that no reason for living exists, and that the future holds nothing but unhappiness. Suicidal thoughts are frequent accompaniments of depression. During acute episodes of depression, the individual may feel physically exhausted, may lack energy to perform even the most simple task, and may be confused and unable to make rational decisions.

Emotional support during periods of depression is critical for a person in bereavement. Such emotional support may be provided by the person who is willing to listen to the thoughts, feelings, and apprehensions of the bereaved individual. In many instances the person who has suffered a significant loss will desperately need a sympathetic and empathic ear. Without giving advice or directing behavior, we can help another by simply listening. During periods of depression, the bereaved person may be helped by those who are willing to assume short-term responsibility for the performance of daily tasks and duties. Such duties and tasks may require tremendous effort on the part of the bereaved person whose energy and powers of concentration may be severely reduced. For the person who is experiencing depression, minor functions may demand inordinate effort. Finally the depressed person may receive much emotional support from the knowledge that others are readily available in times of perceived need. It is important that bereaved persons know that they are not alone and that others may be called upon if circumstances demand.

Tension and restlessness.　　A major reaction to the death of a loved one is tension and restlessness. Such tension and restlessness may be manifested in a number of ways.

Although bereaved persons may feel physically exhausted when going to bed, they may find it impossible to relax and go to sleep. Likewise, bereaved persons may find it difficult to remain sedentary for extended periods of time or to maintain prolonged involvement in one activity. Although individuals may experience subjective feelings of exhaustion, they may be physically and mentally unable to rest and unwind. In repose, feelings of anxiety, tension, and restlessness may intensify.

For many bereaved people, ability to relax is related to willingness to participate in activities that are physically exhausting, for example, strenuous exercise. When tension is discharged through physical exercise, restlessness and anxiety are likely to decrease. However, persons who already feel tired and rundown may look upon physical exercise as an additional drain upon remaining energy. At a time when exercise might be highly beneficial, the individual may feel unwilling or unable to participate. Instead of dissipating stress-related energy (tension) through physical exertion as walking, swimming, dancing, or mowing the lawn, relaxation and tension reduction is often sought in the medicine cabinet. Failing to recognize that positive measures may be taken to cope with feelings of restlessness and tension, the individual may become dependent upon sleeping aids and tranquilizers.

In addition, while failing to recognize that restlessness and tension are normal aspects of bereavement, the individual may perceive such feelings as pathological and demanding medical attention. Although feelings of restlessness and tension may be extremely difficult to tolerate, they are normal accompaniments of bereavement that will diminish as mourning progresses and time passes. In the long run, measures taken to repress or artificially eliminate such feelings may prove harmful to the successful adjustment of the bereaved individual. Although painful, such feelings must be worked through.

Preoccupation with the deceased. Finally, preoccupation with thoughts of the deceased is a normal grief-related reaction. It is not uncommon for bereaved individuals to "converse" with the lost loved one, to feel they have met or seen the dead person, or to experience feelings of physical closeness with the deceased. However, in the midst of such preoccupation, the bereaved person will recognize that physical contact with the deceased is an impossibility. In most cases preoccupation with the person who has died will not overshadow our reality or rational orientation toward life and death. Fixation upon the image of the deceased is likely to persist regardless of activities engaged in by the bereaved. Whether alone or in a group, whether working or relaxing, whether awake or asleep, most thoughts are likely to focus upon the person who has died. Preoccupation with the deceased tends to be most pronounced and vivid during the period immediately following death. With the passage of time, images of the deceased begin to become less "real" and the amount of time occupied with thoughts of the loved one gradually diminishes. In most instances, reduced preoccupation with the dead person occurs naturally as one works through feelings of grief and bereavement.

Grief

Colin Parkes (1970), a consulting psychiatrist to St. Christopher's **Hospice** (a facility for individuals who appear beyond hope of medical cure), has identified a predictable pattern of reactions following a loss or death. According to Parkes, there are four phases of grief: (1) *numbness*, (2) *pining*, (3) *dejection*, and (4) *recovery*.

Numbness. The **numbness phase** is characterized by a lack of emotionality. The bereaved may appear dazed, removed from the immediate environment, and withdrawn. Overt emotional responses may not be exhibited at all. The phase of numbness may last for several hours or a few days. When the bereaved moves from the phase of numbness or shock, the painful sensations associated with grief are experienced as the individual begins to pine or yearn for the lost person.

Pining. During the **pining phase,** preoccupation with the deceased is most pronounced. Situations, objects, and people who remind the bereaved of the deceased may precipitate acute episodes of painful yearning or grief. In an attempt to avoid painful feelings of grief, some individuals may try to dispose of all items associated with the dead person. However, such behavior usually operates to postpone rather than prevent grief. Others attempt to avoid the pain of grief by engaging in a number of activities that will serve as distractions and prevent painful thoughts from entering the mind. Again, such behavior tends to be futile in that grief is, at best, temporarily postponed. According to Parkes, when grief is postponed, its ultimate expression is likely to be more disruptive and painful than grief that has been completely expressed at the time of death.

Dejection. With the passage of time, acute pain associated with grief tends to diminish in frequency and intensity. Feelings of intense pain are replaced by feelings of apathy, hopelessness, and dejection. During the **dejection phase,** the extent and nature of the loss achieves full awareness. As the bereaved relinquishes hope of regaining the loved object, life is increasingly perceived as devoid of meaning and interest. As the permanence of the loss is gradually accepted, feelings of depression grow.

Recovery. When all unrealistic hopes of recovering the loved object are finally relinquished, recovery has begun. Recovery is a process. During this **recovery phase,** the individual may very gradually begin to rediscover and experience the world. A person may find that a television show is entertaining and brings a smile. A growing interest in personal appearance may be experienced. A desire for some particular food might exhibit itself. As the phase of recovery begins, the bereaved person embarks upon the road to normal functioning. Psychologically the bereaved individual begins to move back into the world.

Variability of phases. Although phases of normal grieving have been fairly well defined, it should not be assumed that such phases constitute discrete entities. Pangs of grief may be experienced by the individual long after recovery has been achieved. Likewise, feelings of hopelessness, dejection, and depression may periodically arise.

However, the quality of such grief-related feelings will differ from those originally experienced in association with the loss. Subsequent feelings of grief will lack the intensity and pain initially experienced. With the passage of time, memories of the person who has died often assume a pleasurable or nostalgic quality. In reference to grief, time appears to be the most important curative agent.

Summary

Whereas death is an event, dying is a process. At the present time, no universally agreed-upon criteria for death has been established. However, dying is generally viewed as a process that occurs within restricted parameters, beginning by physical change and eventuating in death. Psychological concerns relating to death and dying are influenced by whether dying occurs over an extended period of time or occurs suddenly.

Death and dying is the appropriate concern of gerontology because the probability and proximity of death increases with advanced age. In the mid-

1970s 70 percent of those dying in the United States were 65 years and over. In later maturity, individuals may exhibit behaviors similar to those manifested by younger persons who are actually dying. The elderly person may be reluctant to undertake commitments that offer little promise of completion prior to death, may become increasingly reluctant to waste time, may turn inward and gradually withdraw from the external world, may experience feelings of anxiety, depression, or despair, and may attempt to settle personal and business affairs. A correlation exists between age and death and between age and exposure to death and dying.

Fear and denial are the two most common attitudes toward death within our society. The manner in which we perceive death and react to the dead and dying reflects pervasive attitudes of fear and denial. To some extent, attitudes toward death appear to be age-related. With increased age, death-related fear tends to decrease as preoccupation with death tends to increase. Diminished fear of death with increased age may be related to decreased value placed upon the elderly individual by self and society, changes in value placed upon death-related losses, and feelings that death deprives the individual of little during old age. Age-related attitudes toward death may also reflect intensified denial. Studies indicate that attitudes toward death are also influenced by factors other than age, for example, education and religion.

Elisabeth Kübler-Ross has identified five stages through which individuals may pass between awareness of serious illness and death. The five stages are (1) denial, (2) anger, (3) bargaining, (4) depression, and (5) acceptance. All individuals who are dying do not pass through these five stages, do not progress through a specific predetermined sequence of reactions, and do not, during a specified time interval, exhibit one particular reaction to the exclusion of all others.

Our society does not teach a person how to behave when confronted with the dying of another human being. Such behavior tends to be personal and influenced by factors such as personality, religion, and ethnic background. Many interactions between the dying individual and other persons involve mutually agreed-upon pretense. Such pretense operates upon the basis of certain rules and may persist even when the consent of one party is withdrawn. For those interacting with the dying person, denial is a frequently used defense mechanism. Beginning with awareness of serious illness, those close to a dying person may begin to experience anticipatory grief. Many behaviors and emotions characteristic of bereavement may be exhibited by the individual before the actual death loss.

Following the death of someone who is loved or close, the bereaved person may react with feelings of guilt, anger, depression, restlessness and tension, and preoccupation. Such grief-related reactions are normal. A predictable pattern of reactions following a loss by death has been identified. There appear to be four major phases of grief: (1) numbness, (2) pining, (3) dejection, and (4) recovery. It is normal and healthy for the bereaved individual to progress through all stages as feelings of grief are worked through and resolved.

Progress Check

1. How might we define clinical death?   (p. 228)

2. What is the difference between death and dying?   (p. 228)

3. Why is death and dying of particular concern to gerontologists?
    (pp. 229–230)

4. What are three reasons why attitudes toward death might be age-related?
    (pp. 232–233)

5. Why might the elderly have less fear of death than do the young?
    (pp. 232–233)

6. What factors might influence our attitudes toward death?
    (pp. 234–235)

7. What five stages might a person pass through during the process of
    dying?   (pp. 235–238)

8. What is the difference between reactive and preparatory depression?
    (pp. 237–238)

9. Why might we not know how to behave in the company of a dying
    person?   (pp. 239–240)

10. What is mutual pretense and what rules govern this interaction pattern
    between the dying person and others?   (pp. 239–240)

11. What are four common and normal grief-related reactions?
    (pp. 242–245)

12. What are the four frequently recognized phases of grief?
    (pp. 245–246)

13. How might we help the person who is experiencing grief?

Recommended Readings

Caine, L. *Widow.* New York: William Morrow & Co., Inc., 1974.
    This engrossing book presents a woman's own experiences following the
    death of her husband. Of particular interest are her grief reactions and her
    struggle to survive and continue functioning following her significant loss.

Kübler-Ross, E. *On Death and Dying.* New York: Macmillan, 1969.
    This book is a basic reference in the study of death and dying. It is a
    pioneering effort that investigates the various reactions of persons who are
    actually in the process of dying. Although scientific, this work evokes
    feelings of empathy and strong concern in the reader.

Parkes, C. M. *Bereavement.* New York: International Universities Press, 1972.
    An excellent discussion of reactions to the death of someone loved. The
    author examines the sequential stages of grief and provides a detailed
    account of behaviors and emotions typically associated with bereavement.

12

Well-Being in Old Age

Preview ～ *This chapter differs from the previous ones in that its orientation is prescriptive rather than descriptive. Little research has been done in the area of well-being in old age. Yet its interest to all of us is self-evident. How do we promote our psychological and physical well-being in old age? In dealing with this topic, we will consider certain behaviors, orientations, and attitudes that are conducive to both physical and mental health in later maturity. Our emphasis will be upon the interrelationship between optimal psychological functioning and optimal physical functioning. The concept of longevity will be introduced and various factors related to long life will be presented. The importance of assuming responsibility for our own well-being will be reinforced throughout this chapter.*

If you are young, now is the time to lay the foundation for well-being in old age. If you are old, now is the time to adopt behaviors and practices that will promote continued well-being throughout later maturity.

What Is Well-Being in Old Age?

Well-being in old age is the product of social, psychological, and physical factors. Such factors interact with each other in a variety of ways to produce positive or negative adjustment and health during later maturity. Overall well-being is dependent upon our ability to reasonably maintain good physical health, to function within a social structure that is conducive to positive adjustment, and to sustain psychological equilibrium as we interact with the environment and relate to self. Physical and psychological well-being are not natural factors of life. They are both achieved by persons who expend time and energy in their pursuit. Although there is no way to guarantee good physical or mental health in old age, the probability of their occurrence can be greatly increased by adherence to certain rules, practices, and principles. For some people, rules, practices, and principles conducive to overall well-being in old age are nothing more than common-sense behaviors and precautions that have been exercised throughout the previous course of their life. For other persons, such "common-sense" rules, practices, and principles have been ignored or have never exerted a significant influence upon their actions or life-style. Of course, the person with a history of health-oriented behaviors has a head start upon well-being in old age. However, it is never too late to start. Regardless of whether behaviors and precautions conducive to well-being in old age have been practiced or ignored during earlier years, feelings of physical and psychological health are highly dependent upon their conscientious exercise in later maturity.

Is Physical Activity Necessary in Old Age?

For optimal maintenance of psychological and physical well-being in later maturity, physical activity is mandatory. Regular physical exercise increases oxygen intake, can bring about significant improvements in the cardiovascular and respiratory systems, increases muscle tone, operates to prevent obesity, and helps the body rid itself of poisons. As a person exercises, increased oxygen becomes available to the brain, lungs and heart work at an accelerated pace, and blood vessels are kept open. As a result, a person who exercises is likely to feel physically and mentally better.

The link between physical activity and mental health

The link between physical activity and mental health is very real. Without adequate oxygen to the brain, a person may have difficulty thinking clearly, may experience increased susceptibility to episodes of depression and listlessness, and be unable to intellectually and emotionally adapt in a flexible and composed manner. Regular physical exercise enables a person to handle physical and psychological stress in a more effective manner. Such activity is a "natural" tranquilizer. DeVries and Adams (1972) compared the tranquilizing effects of exercise with the tranquilizing effects of meprobamate ("Miltown" or "Equanil"). In this study it was observed that the tranquilizer effect of exercise was significantly greater than the tranquilizer effect of meprobamate. This significant difference was noted under conditions of only moderate activity—a 15-minute walking exercise at a moderate rate. The tranquilizer effect derived from exercise was, of course, enjoyed without the negative side effects commonly associated with medicinal tranquilizers. In essence, physical exercise may be the key to increased relaxation, reduced susceptibility to the negative effects of stress, and improved mental health. When anxious, tense, or pressured, a person might, instead of walking to the medicine cabinet, be better off walking around the block.

A lifetime exercise program

Regardless of chronological age, physical immobility accelerates the aging process. Conversely, physical activity or exercise slows the aging process. Physical activity is desirable and beneficial throughout the life span of the individual.

In old age exercises designed to maximize rhythmic activity of large muscles and minimize high activity of small muscles are deemed most beneficial (Lind & McNicol, 1968; deVries, 1971). Exercises that maximize the rhythmic action of large muscles are swimming, walking, running, and jogging. Such activities may be engaged in with various degrees of intensity. The extent to which each elderly person can engage in such activities will depend upon factors such as physical health, history of exercise, and present level of conditioning. It is recommended that a physician be consulted before starting any exercise program, that increases in activity levels occur gradually, and that exercise be perceived as a way of life rather than a short-term commitment to improvement. In old age it is important that the relationship between physical conditioning and well-being is recognized and used to the advantage of the individual.

Are Eating Habits Important in Old Age?

Good nutrition is important at any age. Although most older people know the meaning of good nutrition and have successfully fed themselves and their families for a number of years, adequate attention may not be given to good food and good eating habits in later maturity.

Why good nutrition might be neglected

There are a number of reasons why good nutrition might be neglected in old age. If people live alone, they may feel little motivation to prepare and eat well-balanced meals. Cooking for one may be perceived as too much trouble or not worth the effort. The elderly man who lives alone may have never cooked for himself and may be unable or unwilling to undertake this task in old age. The elderly woman who has been accustomed to cooking for a family may find it difficult to modify long-standing habits in order to accommodate the needs of a single person.

Because eating is viewed as a social activity by many people, older people who are forced to eat alone may abandon established meals in favor of snacks or "picking." Without the company of others, much pleasure associated with eating is lost.

For some other people, changes in the senses of taste and smell may precipitate negative changes in eating habits (see Chapter 5). Previously enjoyed nutritious foods may become less attractive as sensitivity to taste and smell diminish. In such cases the individual may become increasingly prone to abstain from eating or to choose foods that provide intensified sensory stimulation but are not nutritionally sound, for example, very sweet foods. Whereas failure to eat adequate amounts of nutritious food may adversely affect the well-being of some elderly persons, ingestion of too much food and too many calories may harm others. When caloric intake does not diminish in conjunction with diminished participation in physical activities, the individual will gain weight. Likewise, when food is turned to in times of loneliness, frustration, or depression, obesity may result.

Surprisingly, ingestion of too much food does not guarantee that the individual is being well fed. Malnutrition is common among the obese. Overeating, eating nutritionally unsound foods, and eating inadequate amounts of proper food must be avoided in old age if physical and psychological well-being are to be maintained. Unfortunately, following the national trend, many older people are turning away from planning and preparing wholesome meals to foods that are fast, convenient, fattening, and devoid of nutritional value.

Daily requirements

According to the Food and Nutrition Board of the United States Academy of Sciences–National Research Council, males age 55 and over require 2400 calories with 65 grams of protein daily. Females age 55 and over require 1700 calories with 55 grams of protein. Adequate protein is essential to good health. Optimal physical and psychological well-being cannot be maintained on a diet of fats and carbohydrates. Research suggests that certain protein foods are more healthful than others. Protein sources that are low in animal fat, low in cholesterol, and low in calories are more conducive to health than are sources that contain high animal fat, cholesterol, and caloric levels. For this reason, it is recommended that protein of animal origin not constitute a person's entire daily consumption of protein. Animal protein—eggs, dairy products, meats—should be reduced and vegetable protein—grains, nuts, and beans—increased. When animal protein is eaten, sources having relatively low fat content, such as chicken, turkey, and fish, can be chosen over sources containing relatively high levels of fat, such as beef, ham, and duck. As an added benefit, it should be noted that low fat and vegetable sources of protein are not only more healthful but usually less expensive and within the economic means of most people.

In later maturity many people have restrictions placed upon their diets. The most common restriction is salt intake. In most cases the possible relationship between **sodium chloride** (table salt) and **hypertension** (high blood pressure) underlies efforts to significantly reduce salt intake. Dahl (1972) has done much to establish the causal relationship between sodium chloride and vascular hypertension. On the basis of clinical observations, it has been determined that the blood pressure of hypertensive patients will fall when a low sodium diet is followed. Nevertheless, it is not clear whether a high salt diet is detrimental to the normal person. There is little clinical evidence to support the notion that high salt intake will cause the blood pressure of a normal person to rise. However, studies failing to establish a relationship between high blood pressure and salt intake are of short duration and may not accurately reflect possible long-term detrimental effects of high sodium intake. It is known that the proportion of hypertensive persons in a population grows as salt intake increases, that is, hypertension and strokes are more common in populations eating high sodium diets. Many dieticians believe that salt naturally present in foods is sufficient to meet dietary needs. For most people, there is no reason for extra salt to be added to food during cooking or at the table.

Promoting proper nutrition

Although certain basic ideas concerning nutrition have been mentioned, it should be remembered that most elderly people have lived long lives, in part, because proper nutritional habits have been followed. Lack of knowledge concerning nutrition is generally not the cause of malnutrition or poor eating habits in later maturity. Although most elderly persons know *how* to eat, factors such as social interactions, diminished activity levels, physical or mental discomfort, loneliness and isolation, and changing patterns of motivation may promote poor nutrition in old age. For this reason, when attempts are made to improve the nutrition of elderly persons, close attention must be given to environmental and psychological factors influencing eating behavior. If people lack the will or motivation to eat well, they will probably not follow a nutritionally sound diet.

Finally, it is recommended that great care be exercised when attempting to modify the eating habits of any healthy elderly person. In terms of nutrition, it should be recognized that the healthy elderly individual must be doing something right. During her last visit to the doctor, my healthy 95-year-old great-grandmother was told to stop eating eggs because they weren't good for her. Although this advice was ignored, it seemed incredible that any doctor would attempt to change an eating pattern that had proven its worth for almost a century. The fact that this elderly woman was in "perfect" physical condition, made the recommendation even more ludicrous.

Proper nutrition among the elderly may be promoted in a number of ways.

Opportunities to eat within pleasant social settings may be provided. For some persons, social interactions are requisite to enjoyment of food. Stores could offer small packages of nutritionally sound food. The elderly person who must cook for one may balk at the prospect of buying a whole turkey or 10 pounds of potatoes. Unfortunately, most stores are geared toward the consumer who is shopping for a family. A consumer who is shopping for one is often penalized by having to pay higher prices for smaller portions or is unable to find portions suited to his or her needs. In many stores the needs of the single consumer are catered to only by fast, convenient, or frozen foods, such as TV dinners. These foods tend to be expensive and do not provide a person with needed nutrients.

Good nutrition in old age may also depend on the availability of transportation to and from a good grocery store. Without convenient transportation, the elderly person may be forced to shop at a small neighborhood grocery which offers only a limited selection of food at prices higher than those found in large supermarkets. An elderly person may also be limited in the choice of food by what can be physically carried if transportation is a problem.

For elderly individuals who cannot leave the home or are unable to prepare their own meals, proper nutrition may depend upon the provision of meals by others. In such circumstances meals may be brought to the home or someone may go to the person's home in order to prepare meals. In either case, the elderly person may benefit from both good-quality food and incidental social interactions.

Finally, if the elderly individual turns to food in an attempt to stave off boredom or to occupy time, participation in various activities and interests may do much to promote proper nutrition. If people are happily occupied or involved, they will be less likely to turn to food as a source of gratification, diversion, or entertainment.

Why Is Safety in the Home Important?

Most accidents in old age occur in the home. This is because with increased age more time is spent in the home and because certain situations within the home become more dangerous as our reflexes slow and sensory acuity diminishes. If we hope to increase the probability of living a safe, accident-free life in old age, potential hazards within the home should be identified and steps should be taken to guard against possible sources of danger. Recognition of the fact that the home is full of potential hazards is the first step toward creating a safe living environment.

In an attempt to promote safety in old age, the elderly person's home should be carefully examined for potential hazards. Most accidents can be prevented. During examination of the elderly person's home, attention should focus upon the list of safety factors found in Table 12.1.

Table 12.1: Safety in the Home

1. Are areas within and outside the home properly lighted?
2. Is the home properly ventilated?
3. Is furniture placed in such a way that a person might trip over it?
4. Is adequate attention called to potentially hazardous areas (as stairs, hanging light fixtures, appliance controls) within the house?
5. In case of fire, are exit paths open from all parts of the house?
6. Are scatter rugs and floor coverings safe and secure?
7. Are appliances (as electric blankets, heaters, blenders) properly used by the elderly person?
8. Is electrical wiring safe and adequate?
9. Are potentially hazardous substances (as insecticides, paints, oils, cleansers) stored and used safely?
10. Are needed objects stored in places that are easily accessible without reaching or climbing?
11. Is there a possibility that the elderly person might come in contact with electricity when wet? Bathrooms, kitchens, and laundry rooms should be carefully checked.
12. Are bathroom surfaces slippery?
13. Are handles available for support in the bathtub?
14. Are bathtubs or showers enclosed with shatterproof plastic or safety glass?
15. Are hot and cold water faucets secure and clearly labeled?
16. Are medicines and poisons kept in a lockable cabinet?
17. Are floors in poor repair (such as broken tiles, warped wood, loose boards)?
18. Is heating equipment within the home safe—properly vented, guarded to protect against burns, away from flammable objects?
19. Are old papers, magazines, ribbons, boxes, and so forth accumulated and stored in places that may be hazardous—as in unventilated areas where the probability of internal combustion is great?
20. Are electrical appliances properly grounded?
21. Are potentially hazardous instruments (as knives, scissors, and razors) stored in an uncluttered area?
22. Are flame-retardant fabrics used in home furnishings? (Substances are now available that can be applied to fabrics in order to make them flame-retardant.)
23. Are polishes or cleansers used that leave the floor slippery?
24. Are drawers secured to prevent them from falling out when opened?
25. Is the kitchen range placed away from flammable materials (such as kitchen curtains, aprons, cleansers)?
26. Are traffic paths kept clear and uncluttered?
27. Are potentially harmful substances stored with food?
28. Are windows and doors easily opened—not painted or nailed shut?
29. Do stairs have handrails?
30. Are all medicines clearly labeled for internal or external use?
31. In case of emergency, can the elderly person get help quickly and easily?

The consequences of accidents

Although it is important that a safe living environment be assured at all ages, the provision of such an environment becomes more important as we grow older. As people age, they may fail to perceive the presence of dangers—the footstool left in the way may not be seen, or a burning substance may not be smelled. When a person doesn't perceive the presence of danger, the probability of incurring injury increases.

Also, with advanced age, our ability to react quickly to avoid accidents or injury is reduced. The younger person may be able to quickly recover from tripping and thus avoid a fall, but the older person may lack the ability to make such a recovery. Moreover, such mishaps are likely to have far graver consequences than those occurring during earlier years. If young people trip on a rug and fall, they may arise with little more than a bruise and some embarrassment. However, when elderly people trip and fall, the probability is higher that they will incur serious injury. Bones that become increasingly brittle as a person ages will break easily upon impact. As a result of a "minor" mishap, a hip may be broken, an arm may be shattered, or a skull may be fractured. Because older persons recover and heal more slowly than younger persons, injuries occurring in later maturity may incapacitate the individual for very long periods of time. They may also negatively affect the injured person for the remainder of his or her life and may entail a great deal of physical and psychological sacrifice and suffering.

As a person ages, it becomes increasingly critical that potential sources of danger be eliminated from the home. When consideration is given to safety in old age, prevention is the key word. By expending a small amount of time and energy, injury and death may be prevented through the elimination of hazards possessing catastrophic potential.

Can We Achieve Protection Against Crime?

As with safety, the key word concerning crime in later maturity is prevention. In most cases a person can avoid being the victim of a crime by taking certain precautions or by not providing others with the opportunity to commit criminal acts. The person who is an "easy target" is more likely to be victimized than the person who is not.

Because the elderly person is more likely than a young person to be perceived as an easy target, specific precautions designed to protect against crime become more important with advanced age. By following certain rules and taking basic precautionary measures, elderly people can greatly decrease their chances of falling prey to a criminal. With the objective of preventing crimes directed toward our person or property, it is recommended that the rules and behaviors listed in Table 12.2 be adopted.

Common crimes against the elderly

Contrary to popular belief, the probability is relatively low that the elderly person will be the victim of crimes of violence. It is far more likely that he or she will be the target of the pickpocket, the purse snatcher, the mugger, the burglar, the car thief, the con artist, and other perpetrators of fraud.

Many crimes directed toward the older population are occasioned by behaviors and circumstances that provide the criminal with ready opportunities

Table 12.2: Precautions Against Crime

---

1. Never prominently display or flash large amounts of money or valuables.
2. Never tell strangers or discuss in public the amount of money you have or what valuables you own.
3. Carry money in places other than purses or hip pockets.
4. When possible, travel in the company of others.
5. When walking or traveling in a car, choose busy and well-lit streets.
6. Avoid walking close to buildings, shrubs, alleys, or anything that may provide an assailant a hiding place.
7. Avoid traveling, shopping, or visiting in high-crime areas.
8. Never open the door without knowing who is there. If a stranger is unable to produce proper credentials, the door should not be opened.
9. Keep all doors locked when in the home.
10. When in the yard or garden, lock the doors to the house.
11. Never leave the house without locking it up.
12. When buying something or dealing with money, do not be distracted from the business at hand.
13. Carry your purse close to the body to discourage purse snatchers.
14. Keep car doors locked when driving. Keep windows rolled up enough to prevent others from reaching inside.
15. When at stop signs, keep the car in gear.
16. Always lock the car when leaving it.
17. Never pick up a hitchhiker.
18. When carrying valuables such as jewelry or money, avoid deserted areas (as public restrooms, laundry rooms).
19. Be cautious about entering isolated areas (as elevators, parking areas) when alone.
20. Do not converse with, or provide information to, unknown telephone callers.
21. Make sure that effective locks are on all doors and windows.
22. Keep the area surrounding your home well-lit.
23. Take special care of your house and car keys.
24. Attach no type of identification to your house or car keys.
25. Have locks reset when moving into a new residence.
26. Women living alone should use last name and initials in telephone directories or on mail boxes.
27. When leaving home for extended periods of time, plan to maintain your home's "lived-in" appearance.
28. Mark valuable possessions with an electric etching tool.
29. Be wary of financial or business opportunities that are "too good to be true." They usually *are.*
30. Sign no contract until it has been checked by a knowledgeable person as a lawyer or banker.
31. Give no advance money to persons who come to the door and offer to perform home or yard services. Business transactions with traveling repairpersons should be avoided.
32. Avoid hiding house or car keys. Criminals know most of the hiding places.
33. Before entering a car, check to see if anyone is hiding in it.
34. When returning home, have your keys ready to open the door immediately.
35. Try not to keep a large amount of money or valuable items in the home.
36. Report any and all crimes or attempted crimes to the police.

---

to strike. Very often, if basic anticrime precautions are taken, the chances that we will be criminally victimized in old age become extremely remote. At the present time, whether or not elderly persons will be the victim of crime is highly dependent upon their own behavior. Precautionary behaviors and prudent habits are the elderly person's greatest protection against crime.

How Can Friendships Contribute to Well-Being?

Friendships or positive interpersonal relationships are important contributors to mental health and feelings of well-being in later maturity. Relationships with other human beings are significantly more important than specific activities as a person grows older. This is not to suggest that a person cannot successfully adjust to old age without friendships. However, if optimal levels of well-being are to be achieved and maintained, friendships or close interpersonal relationships are a necessity.

Feelings of self-worth

From social relationships, feelings of self-worth or self-esteem are derived. A person's feelings of personal worth are often reflected in the eyes of friends. When elderly persons are loved, respected, needed, and enjoyed by others, the probability increases that they will hold positive attitudes toward themselves.

Such positive attitudes will do much to promote generalized feelings of psychological and physical well-being in old age. Feelings of self-worth are likely to suffer if the elderly individual becomes cut off from friends and no longer has opportunities to engage in meaningful interpersonal relationships.

Recreation, emotional support, and intellectual stimulation

In addition to contributing to feelings of self-worth, friends are important sources of recreation, emotional support, and intellectual stimulation in old age. When interacting with friends, ideas may be exchanged, experiences may be shared, gripes may be aired, guards may be let down, and mutually gratifying behaviors may be exhibited. In times of need, the individual may be sustained solely on the basis of available friendships or interpersonal relationships. Without the emotional (and sometimes physical) support of a friend, the elderly person may face periods in which successful coping may prove to be a physical or mental impossibility. A friend may provide emotional support by merely listening to the thoughts, aspirations, or fears of another human being, by encouraging another individual upon a chosen course of action, or by providing company when feelings of isolation or loneliness arise. Although such emotionally supportive behaviors may appear insignificant and may require little time or effort, they can critically influence our ability to successfully cope and to function happily and effectively. Friendships are important contributors to well-being in old age because they provide opportunities for giving and accepting help, for entertaining and being entertained, for giving and receiving affection, for talking and listening, and for empathizing and sympathizing. In many instances one friend can do more for the well-being of an elderly person than a carload of professional helpers.

Expanding friendships

It is a mistake to assume that only "old" friends are worthwhile in later maturity. Although friends of long-standing may be extremely important to the elderly person, as a person ages, it is only natural that the circle of friends will change. Old friends should be cherished and valued, but new friends should be sought and cultivated. If people hope to make new friends and keep old friends, they should recognize that this objective must be actively pursued. A person who sits at home waiting for others to call, who makes no move to become socially involved, or who consistently fails to reciprocate socially is not likely to have many friends. If friendships are desired, a concerted effort toward achieving this goal must be made.

In an attempt to make friends, elderly people might invite others to their home, attend recreational activities alone in order to meet others, and join various social, civic, or educational groups. In most cases, friendships are more likely to develop among people sharing common interests and activities. However, strong friendships occasionally develop between individuals who apparently have little in common. If people hope to make friends, the most important thing they should remember is that contact with other people is necessary to acquiring friends. When a person opts to stay alone or does not actively seek interpersonal contact, friends will not be made. Without friendships or close interpersonal relationships, the probability is high that the individual will not experience optimal levels of well-being and satisfaction in later maturity.

How Do Activities Contribute to Our Well-Being?

Activities that are personally enjoyable, intellectually stimulating, or emotionally satisfying contribute greatly to feelings of well-being. The extent to which any particular activity is experienced as enjoyable, stimulating, or satisfying is, of course, dependent upon the person engaged in the activity rather than upon the activity itself. For example, although some people may derive great personal benefits from doing volunteer work, others may find such work tedious and boring. It is impossible to isolate one specific activity and suggest that it would promote feelings of well-being among all persons. For this reason, attempts to impose a single activity pattern upon all individuals should be avoided and recognized as counterproductive and potentially harmful. Regardless of age, all people don't want or like to do the same things.

Choosing how time will be spent

Increased leisure time is a reality of old age. In later maturity people usually have more free time, have more freedom to choose how time will be spent, and have more flexible time schedules and commitments. Regardless of who the elderly person is, increased leisure time accompanying old age will be filled with some activity. Some people may fill their hours watching television or pacing about the house, others may eat or sleep, others may delve into various hobbies and recreational pursuits, and still others may pursue some vocation or intellectual undertaking. We all fill in our time by doing something. When consideration is given to well-being in later maturity, the critical factor is not "finding something to do" or discovering a means of filling in time. Rather, it is important that attention be focused upon finding and involving ourselves in activities that are personally stimulating or gratifying. Likewise, it is important that activities experienced as personally boring, unrewarding, or debilitating be avoided. In essence, what we do with our time is not nearly so important as how we feel about what we're doing.

With the provision of increased leisure time in old age, feelings of well-being may become more dependent upon the individual's willingness to investigate the unknown, to be open to new experiences, and to discover activities that are personally fulfilling. Unless a flexible and open attitude toward new activities can be maintained, opportunities to become involved in exciting pursuits may be missed and potentially rewarding activities may remain unexplored. By rigidly adhering to accustomed, and perhaps unsatisfying, patterns of behavior, individuals may unnecessarily restrict the amount of pleasure and satisfaction that could be derived from their lives. During our entire lives, it is important that we remain open to new experiences.

Broadening our range

If people hope to discover and become involved in personally rewarding activities, it is important that they experience a variety of activities before rejecting any out of hand. Because each of us has various preconceptions concerning the personal desirability of certain activities, we may be reluctant to undertake or try anything that we don't anticipate liking. For example, although you may have never painted a picture, fixed a car, knitted a sweater, or raced a boat, you may not "like" these activities and refuse to give them a try. By assuming such an attitude, many potentially enjoyable pursuits may never be experienced. Without trying something, there is no way to be sure that you will or will not like it. It is important to remember that if a new activity is tried and found enjoyable, the individual profits. Likewise, if a new activity is not enjoyed, it can always be abandoned in favor of something else. New activities should be given a fair chance.

A major criteria governing our choice of activities in later maturity should be personal enjoyment. We should not abstain from personally enjoyable activities because society may deem them inappropriate to old age—for example, flying a kite, sun bathing, or frequenting the local discos. As we grow older, there is no reason to commit or restrict ourselves to those activities that conform to established social expectations concerning old age, such as cooking, gardening, taking walks, or caring for grandchildren. Whenever possible, activities should be chosen on the basis of what the elderly person *wants* to do rather than on the basis of what others say *should* be done.

What Are Some General Do's and Don't's in Old Age?

In later maturity certain behaviors and orientations might be adopted and others avoided in the pursuit of psychological and physical well-being. By adhering to certain prescriptions for physical and mental health in old age, we may greatly increase the probability that we will live satisfying, stimulating, and vital existences throughout later maturity. Again, well-being in old age can never be guaranteed. However, the likelihood of our achieving and maintaining well-being is greatly increased as a function to commitment and effort on the part of the elderly person. The following "do's and don't's" concerning behaviors and orientations in old age are suggested as general guidelines for successful functioning in later maturity.

Reject myths

Don't accept negative myths concerning aging and old age. If a person accepts the notion that old age will result in intellectual decline, sexual inadequacy, and inability to learn, such beliefs will negatively influence feelings of personal worth and self-esteem. Also, behavior and adjustment will be affected by such stereotypic misconceptions.

Old age should be viewed as a normal developmental stage that offers unique possibilities as an integral part of the ongoing life process. A person should not expect to feel or act like a different person when old age is attained. Needs, desires, values, and interests are likely to change little in old age and established patterns of adjustment and behavior will tend to persist throughout later maturity.

Individuals should expect to continue to grow, to contribute, to lead useful, fulfilling lives, and to preserve their unique style and demeanor throughout old age. Individuality persists throughout later maturity and the idea that elderly people should or must behave in a particular way should not be accepted.

Expect some stress

Don't expect old age to be a period devoid of psychological and physical stress. During this period of life, increased levels of stress resulting from frustration and loss are likely to be encountered and intensified demands upon the individual's ability to cope should be anticipated.

It is important that coping strategies that are basically constructive, growth-oriented, and healthy be developed and used during old age. Actions designed to reduce or remove stress rather than deaden awareness of its effects should be adopted. Attempts to cope with problems by turning to drugs, alcohol, or food are fundamentally destructive and should be avoided. Likewise, one should avoid keeping stress-related emotions bottled up inside. Repressed emotions are not conducive to physical or psychological well-being. Energy resulting from frustration or loss should be expressed without feelings of embarrassment or regret. Finally, when faced with increased stress, the elderly person should expect to assume major responsibility for successful coping. Although others may help in times of crises, positive adjustment is ultimately dependent upon the efforts and involvement of the stressed individual. Others cannot be expected to solve our problems during old age. Successful coping within problem or stress-provoking situations demands the active participation of the elderly person involved.

Expect good health

Do expect to feel physically well in old age. Aging is not a disease. Aches, pains, and illnesses occurring in old age should not be perceived as "normal." Physical and psychological problems should not be ignored and attributed to advanced chronological age. Unless identified and faced, such problems are not likely to go away. Likewise, diminished sensory acuity should not be ignored or tolerated in later maturity. Aids designed to compensate for some sensory declines are readily available and should be obtained when needed. There is no reason why most people should not continue to see and hear well throughout old age. Although declines in physical stamina and strength may be expected in later maturity, claims upon health and effective sensory functioning should not be relinquished in the name of age.

Continue activities

Don't abandon pleasurable or accustomed activities because they are perceived as inappropriate to old age. In later maturity a person should continue to choose and engage in activities and social interactions on the basis of personal preference and desire rather than age-related norms and expectations. For example, the elderly person should not abstain from sexual activities and physical intimacies because such behaviors are deemed inappropriate to old age. Elderly individuals should continue to enjoy and cultivate interpersonal relationships, to seek satisfaction in the present, to be open to new ideas, sensations, and adventures, and to remain involved in activities or behaviors that are personally gratifying or pleasurable. In essence, elderly persons should decide what is "right" for them and behave accordingly.

Make a commitment to well-being

Do make a total commitment to physical and mental health in old age. Responsibility for physical and psychological well-being in old age lies mainly with the elderly individual. With the goal of maintaining well-being, attention should be given to nutritional requirements, safety hazards, physical activity, intellectual stimulation, and so forth. The elderly person should recognize that optimal functioning in later maturity demands an attitude of total commitment to health. Also, it should be recognized that feelings of health and well-being are maintained, for the most part, by self-initiated and self-motivated behaviors. Total responsibility for physical and mental well-being in old age cannot be assumed by other than the elderly person.

A final word

The preceding suggestions are not presented as definitive injunctions and prescriptions for all elderly persons. Great differences exist within the aged population, and it would be presumptuous to suggest that any set of guidelines apply equally to all older persons. However, for most elderly people, following the previously cited do's and don't's may add greatly to feelings of physical health and psychological well-being.

Living a Long Life: What Are Our Chances?

At the present time, no one really knows why some people live to be old or very old and other people do not survive through an average life span. Unfortunately—for researchers—some people do all the "wrong" things and live to be very old while others do all the "right" things and die young. No prescription for long life exists. However, although no prescription for long life is presently available, a number of factors related to **longevity** (length of life) and survival have been identified by researchers. When consideration is given to such factors, it should be remembered that observed relationships with longevity are not causal. That is, although certain factors may occur in conjunction with longevity, it cannot be assumed that such factors cause long life.

Environmental and health factors

Hardin Jones (1956) investigated a number of environmental and health factors related to length of life. At the time of his study, it was noted that factors such as marital status, smoking, survival age of parents and grandparents, and presence or absence of various diseases could be used to predict the longevity of the individual. By observing Table 12.3, it may be seen that living in the country as opposed to living in the city would result in a predicted average five-year addition to length of life. If a person had a mother and father who both lived to age 90 years, predicted longevity would increase 7.4 years. The relationship between parent and grandparent longevity and predicted life span focuses upon the contribution of heredity to long life. Of course, it is generally accepted that heredity and genetic composition influence longevity. People who are genetically identical (one-egg twins) tend to live for very similar lengths of time (Kallmann and Jarvik, 1959).

It may also be noted in Table 12.3 that longevity is related to marital status. Persons who are married may expect to live five years longer than those who are not. However, this is not to suggest that marriage extends life. Rather, it is possible that people who are healthy and active are more likely to

Table 12.3: Physiological Age and Life-Span Differences

Reversible		Permanent	
Comparison	Years	Comparison	Years
Country versus city dwelling ... + 5		Female versus male sex .... + 3	
Married status versus single, widowed, divorced .... + 5		Familial constitutions 2 grandparents lived to 80 yr. .... + 2	
Overweight 25 percent overweight group − 3.6 35 percent overweight group − 4.3 45 percent overweight group − 6.6 55 percent overweight group − 11.4 67 percent overweight group − 15.1 *Or:* an average effect of 1 percent overweight .... − 0.17		4 grandparents lived to 80 yr. .... + 4 Mother lived to age 90 yr.... + 3 Father lived to age 90 yr..... + 4.4 Both mother and father lived to age 90 yr............. + 7.4 Mother lived to age 80 yr.... + 1.5 Father lived to age 80 yr..... + 2.2	
Smoking 1 package cigarettes per day − 7 2 packages cigarettes per day .... − 12		Both mother and father lived to age 80 yr............. + 3.7 Mother died at 60 yr. .... − 0.7 Father died at 60 yr......... − 1.1 Both mother and father died at age 60 yr............. − 1.8	
Atherosclerosis Fat metabolism In 25th percentile of population having "ideal" lipoprotein concentrations .... + 10 Having average lipoprotein concentrations .... 0 In 25th percentile of population having elevated lipoproteins.... − 7 In 5th percentile of population having highest elevation of lipoproteins........... − 15		Recession of childhood and infectious disease over past century in Western countries. + 15 Life Insurance *Impairment Study* Rheumatic heart disease, evidenced by: Heart murmur .... − 11 Heart murmur + tonsillitis . − 18 Heart murmur + streptococcal infection.. − 13 Rapid pulse................ − 3.5 Phlebitis................... − 3.5 Varicose veins .... − 0.2 Epilepsy................... − 20.0 Skull fracture .... − 2.9	
Diabetes Uncontrolled, before insulin, 1900................... − 35 Controlled with insulin 1920 Joslin Clinic record.. − 20 1940 Joslin Clinic record.. − 15 1950 Joslin Clinic record.. − 10		Tuberculosis .... − 1.8 Nephrectomy .... − 2.0 Trace of albumin in urine ... − 5.0 Moderate albumin in urine .. − 13.5	

be married than those who are not. Again, one must be cautious about establishing cause-and-effect relationships.

Palmore (1969; 1971) identified three factors significantly related to length of life. Obesity and smoking were negatively related to long life. People who smoked or were overweight or both tended to die earlier than those who avoided smoking and maintained proper body weight. In addition, it was found that activity and exercise were significantly related to longevity. On the basis of available data, it would appear that above-average life expectancy is not related to a sedentary life-style.

Social factors

People who derive satisfaction from their work (Palmore, 1969), who possess higher levels of education, occupational status, and intelligence (Pfeiffer, 1970), and who enjoy higher socioeconomic status (Rose, 1964) are more likely to live longer than those who don't. Of course, differences in socioeconomic status, education, and occupational status will influence factors such as housing, nutrition, medical care, and health. There is little doubt that these factors do influence longevity.

Taking charge

In essence, if you want to improve your chances of living a long life, you should be very careful in your choice of parents. However, if your parents did not live long lives, your chances of attaining a long life can improve if care is given to physical well-being—don't smoke; don't get fat; don't sit around all day; don't neglect your body. Likewise, work that is personally rewarding and gratifying should be found. The manner in which you behave throughout your life will significantly influence your longevity. According to Jewett (1973), if a person hopes to live a long life, energy should be expended in the pursuit and maintenance of good health, feelings of physical and psychological well-being, creative leisure activities, and enjoyment of life. Most researchers agree that longevity and feelings of health and well-being are related to the behaviors and attitudes of the individual. Psychological and physical well-being and long life do not just happen. They must be earned.

Summary

Well-being in old age is the result of social, psychological, and physical factors. Psychological and physical well-being are not natural accompaniments of life. Their achievement requires expenditures of time and energy. By adhering to certain rules, practices, and principles, we can greatly increase the probability that good physical and mental health will be enjoyed in old age. It is generally believed that physical activity, proper nutrition, precautions against accidents and crime, interpersonal relationships, and enjoyable activities are important determinants of well-being in later maturity. In the pursuit of psychological and physical well-being, certain behaviors and orientations should be adopted by the elderly person. If the older person adheres to a number of basic "do's and don't's," feelings of physical and mental well-being are likely to increase.

Although no one knows what causes long life, certain factors are related to longevity. A relationship has been established between longevity and heredity, marital status, smoking, disease, living environment, activity and exercise, obesity, job satisfaction, socioeconomic status, educational level, and intelligence. Certain factors may be related to longevity, but the relationship is probably not causal. However, it is generally agreed that behaviors and attitudes do influence length of life.

Progress Check

1. Why is it important that we each assume responsibility for our own well-being? (p. 252)

2. What are two arguments in favor of physical exercise in later maturity? (pp. 252–253)

3. What type of exercise appears to be most desirable in old age? (p. 253)

4. What are three reasons why a person might fail to eat properly in old age? (pp. 253–254)

5. What are three things that might be done to promote proper nutrition in old age? (pp. 255–256)

6. Why does safety within our home become more important as we grow older? (p. 256)

7. What are five things that might be done to promote home safety? (Table 12.1, p. 257)

8. What are four things that might be done in old age to avoid being an easy target for criminals? (Table 12.2, p. 259)

9. What are some advantages of keeping old friendships and making new ones in later maturity? (pp. 260–261)

10. Discuss three "do's and don't's" concerning behaviors and orientations in old age. (pp. 263–265)

11. What are five factors positively related to length of life? (pp. 265–267)

12. What can you do to increase your chances of living a long life?

Recommended Readings

deVries, H. A. Physiology of exercise and aging. In D. Woodruff & J. Birren, eds., *Aging: Scientific Perspectives and Social Issues.* New York: D. Van Nostrand Co., 1975.
Various effects of aging are perceived as the result of physical conditioning. When older people engage in different types of exercise, improvement is noted in several psychological and physical areas.

Jones, H. A special consideration of the aging process, disease, and life expectancy. In J. H. Lawrence & C. A. Tobias, eds., *Advances in Biological and Medical Physics,* Vol. 4. New York: Academic Press, 1956.
Various factors that statistically influence life expectancy probability are presented. Relationships between heredity and longevity are examined. Also, relationships between long life and various environmental variables are considered.

Glossary

ACCEPTANCE STATE: (Kübler-Ross) The final stage through which persons may pass between awareness of terminal illness and their own death. (238)

ACCOMMODATION: The ability to see clearly those objects that are either near or far. (96)

ACQUISITION: Memory; The input of sensory impressions. (86)

ACUITY: The ability to perceive small objects or details clearly. (97)

ADAPTATION: The ability to make adjustments to dark and light. (97)

ADJUSTMENT: The process of adapting to internal or external change. (132)

AFFECTIVE PSYCHOSES: Mental disturbances characterized by pronounced swings or changes in moods or emotions. (165)

AGEISM: Systematic prejudicial attitudes and behaviors directed toward aging, old age, or the elderly. (16)

AGING: The process of growing older; see pathological, normal, chronological, functional, social, biological, and psychological aging. (3)

ALARM REACTION: The first phase of Selye's General Adaptation Syndrome. (148)

ALCOHOLISM: Chronic and excessive use of alcohol; addiction to the drug. (178)

ANGER STAGE: (Kübler-Ross) The second stage through which persons may pass between awareness of terminal illness and their own death. (236)

ANTICIPATION INTERVAL: Time between presentations of stimuli. (75)

ANTICIPATORY GRIEF: Behaviors and emotions characteristic of bereavement occurring prior to actual loss or death. (240)

ANTISOCIAL BEHAVIOR: Actions that are contrary to established social standards of permitted behavior. See character disorder. (178)

ANXIETY: A persistent fear arising from sources that may or may not be known to the individual; characteristic of neurosis and arising in association with conflict, threat, or frustration. (171)

ANXIETY REACTION: Subjective experiencing of severe and disabling levels of anxiety or fear. (172)

ARTERIOSCLEROSIS: A chronic disease of the arteries characterized by abnormal thickening and hardening of the vessel walls; results in reduction of blood and oxygen to the brain. (66)

ATTITUDE: Predisposition to respond to persons, objects, situations, or values in a particular manner. (230)

ATTRITION: "Drop-out"; failure to continue to participate. (49)

AUDITION: Hearing; the sense of hearing. (99)

AUTOIMMUNITY THEORY: A biological theory proposing a relationship between aging and the body's rejection of its own tissues. (34)

BARGAINING STAGE: (Kübler-Ross) The third stage through which persons may pass between awareness of terminal illness and their own death. (237)

BEHAVIOR DISORDER: See Character Disorder. (178)

BEREAVEMENT: The stage or condition of being deprived of something or someone valued or loved. (241)

BIOLOGICAL AGING: Anatomical and physiological age-related changes that occur over time. (28)

CHARACTER DISORDER (behavior disorder): Abnormal patterns of adjustment characterized by actions contrary to established and accepted social values, morals, and norms. (178)

CHRONOLOGICAL AGING: Growing older in terms of temporal units such as days, months, and years. (30)

COGNITIVE: Related to intellectual and mental experiences and processes. (73)

COHORT: Individuals who are members of the same generation. (48)

COITUS: Sexual intercourse. (196)

COLLAGEN THEORY: Based upon established relationships between collagen—the fibrous protein found in muscles, joints, bones, cartilage, ligaments, and vessels—and age-related change. (35)

COLOR DISCRIMINATION: The ability to accurately identify, differentiate between, and match colors. (97)

COMMISSION ERRORS: Incorrect responses or behaviors. (74)

CONFORMITY: Behavior that is in accordance with established social norms. (206)

COPING: Dealing with problems and difficulties by adopting specific behaviors and orientations. (144)

CORE PERSONALITY: The underlying or "true" personality structure. (118)

CROSS-SECTIONAL RESEARCH METHOD: Strategy used to study the relationship between variables using two or more groups simultaneously. (47)

CRYSTALLIZED INTELLIGENCE: Cattell's term for the mental acquisitions gained as a product of acculturation; general knowledge, skills, and information acquired through education and experience. (52)

DEATH: A biological event resulting from the cessation of various physical activities. (228)

DECATHEXIS: To let go; to withdraw emotions and energies previously invested in another person. (238)

DEFENSE MECHANISM: Unconscious strategy for resolving inner conflicts and for repressing anxiety. (175)

DEJECTION PHASE: (Parkes) The third phase of the grief reaction. (246)

DELIRIUM TREMENS (DT's): A severe brain disturbance associated with alcohol addiction and withdrawal; may involve hallucinations, delusions, and disorientation. (179)

DELUSIONS: Thoughts or beliefs that are false or contrary to reality. (167)

DEMOGRAPHIC: Related to statistical aspects of the human population. (6)

DENIAL: Defense mechanism; refusal to admit or accept the existence of material that is anxiety-provoking. (175)

DENIAL STAGE: (Kübler-Ross) The first stage through which persons may pass between awareness of terminal illness and their own death. (236)

DEPRESSION (psychotic): An affective disturbance involving pronounced feelings of hopelessness, sadness, despair, and apathy. (165)

DEPRESSION STAGE: (Kübler-Ross) The fourth stage through which persons may pass between awareness of terminal illness and their own death. (237)

DEVELOPMENT: An orderly sequence of changes in behavior or physical attributes. (3)

DEVELOPMENTAL TASKS: Behavioral requirements commonly associated with chronological age. (130)

DISENGAGEMENT THEORY: Proposes a relationship between chronological age and a natural tendency to withdraw psychologically and socially from the environment. (36)

DYING: A biological process resulting in the cessation of various physical activities. (228)

EGO: Self; the concept of self. (38)

EGO DEVELOPMENT THEORY: (Erikson) Poses a progression through sequential stages with accompanying crises. (38)

EJACULATION: To expel semen in orgasm. (198)

ESTROGEN: A female sex hormone associated with development of secondary sex characteristics and reproductive functions. (195)

EXHAUSTION: The third phase of Selye's General Adaptation Syndrome. (149)

EXTROVERSION: Carl Jung's term for an orientation that is mainly directed toward the external or objective world. (39)

FAMILY: Pairs or groups of persons who are related by blood or marriage. (208)

FIXED INCOME: Monetary benefits not liable to variation. (219)

FLUID INTELLIGENCE: Cattell's term for neurologically determined aspects of intelligence; ability to shift thinking, to use novel approaches, to have insight, and to adjust problem-solving behavior. (52)

FREQUENCY: A physical property of sound. Pitch is the psychological correlate of frequency. (100)

FRUSTRATION: The condition resulting from the blocking of the individual's goals. (150)

FRUSTRATION-AGGRESSION HYPOTHESIS: Aggression is proposed as the most common human reaction to frustration. (150)

FUNCTIONAL AGING: Changes in behaviors and abilities associated with the passage of time. (30)

FUNCTIONAL DISORDERS: Psychological disturbances occurring in the absence of any detectable physiological or organic cause. (164)

FUNCTIONAL PSYCHOSIS: An *acute* psychological disturbance for which there is no identifiable organic basis; characterized by possible loss of contact with reality, disturbed thought processes, pronounced swings of mood, and severely impaired interpersonal relationships. (165)

GENERAL ADAPTATION SYNDROME: Selye's term for sequential psychological and physical reaction to stress; the three phases are alarm, resistance, and exhaustion. (148)

GERONTOLOGY: The systematic study of old age and the aging process. (2)

GEROPSYCHOLOGY: The scientific study of behavior as a correlate of aging and age. (30)

GESTALT: Psychological term which refers to wholeness or whole. (132)

GRIEF: A completely personal and subjective experience associated with a major loss or death. (241)

GUILT: Feelings produced when behaviors are contrary to moral dictates or standards. (242)

GUSTATION: Tasting; the sense of taste. (102)

HALLUCINATIONS: Mental images that are mistaken for reality. (170)

HALO EFFECT: Loss of rater objectivity in evaluation situations. (122)

HOSPICE: A facility for individuals who appear beyond hope of medical cure; a place to die with dignity. (245)

HYPERTENSION: High blood pressure. (255)

HYPERTENSIVE TYPE: Personality type subject to high blood pressure and coronary disease. (153)

HYPOCHONDRIASIS: Excessive preoccupation with health or bodily functions. (172)

HYSTERECTOMY: Surgical removal of the uterus. (187)

ILLUSION: Special type of perception that is inconsistent with the physical stimulus from which it arises. (111)

IMPOTENCE: Inability to attain erection; can have physical or psychological cause. (193)

INCENTIVE: An external inducement to act or behave in a particular manner. (136)

INFERENCE: A guess, grounded in probability; an "educated" guess. (44)

INFLEXIBILITY: A psychological orientation characterized by rigid resistance to change and the inability to adapt to new situations and circumstances. (12)

INSPECTION INTERVAL: Pacing; time permitted to examine or view stimuli. (75)

INTELLIGENCE: A complex hypothetical mental ability defined in terms of performance. (45)

INTERFERENCE: Any intervening event or factor that hinders learning or memory. (87)

INTROVERSION: Carl Jung's term for an orientation that is mainly introspective or directed toward the inner, subjective world. (39)

IQ (intelligence quotient): A numeric representation of intelligence based upon measures of selected behavioral samples; mental age/chronological age × 100 = IQ. (46)

LATER MATURITY: Term used interchangeably with old age; 65 years and over. (6)

LEARNING: A relatively permanent change in behavior resulting from experience. (13)

LEISURE: Free or spare time; a period of unemployment or retirement. (212)

LIFE CHANGE UNITS: Numerical stress ratings assigned various stress-provoking situations to which individuals may be subject. (145)

LIFE EXPECTANCY: An expected number of years of life based upon statistical probability. (7)

LIPOFUSCIN: Age pigment. A metabolic waste product that accumulates in the body in conjunction with increased age; "liver spots." (34)

LIVER SPOTS: Accumulations of lipofuscin or age pigment in the skin. (34)

LIVING ENVIRONMENT: The total atmosphere in which the person functions and dwells. (222)

LONGEVITY: Length of life. (265)

LONGITUDINAL METHOD: Strategy used to study the relationship between variables using the same group over time. (48)

LONG-TERM MEMORY (LTM): Retention of information for prolonged periods of time, perhaps permanently. (86)

MANIA: An affective disturbance involving feelings of marked enthusiasm, euphoria, and optimism. (167)

MASTECTOMY: Surgical removal of the breast. (187)

MASTURBATION: Autoeroticism or sexual self-stimulation. (192)

MATCHED SAMPLING: Subjects equated on the basis of one or more variables. (50)

MEMORY: A cognitive process involving the ability to acquire, retain, and retrieve material. (86)

MENOPAUSE (change of life): Cessation of menstruation occurring usually between ages 45 and 50. (193)

METABOLIC WASTE THEORY: Proposes a relationship between aging and the accumulation of injurious metabolic waste products in the human body. (34)

MNEMONICS: Techniques used to aid memory. (80)

MOTIVATION: The intensity of an individual's drive directed toward a specific reward, goal, or incentive. (136)

MOURNING: The process involving both overt and covert manifestations of bereavement. (241)

MUTATION THEORY (somatic mutation): Poses a relationship between aging and the abnormal or atypical dividing of body cells. (35)

NEUROSES: Emotional or behavioral disturbances involving excessive and potentially disruptive amounts of anxiety. (171)

NOCTURNAL EMISSION: Ejaculation of semen during sleep. (197)

NONCOGNITIVE: Not related to intrinsic intellectual and mental experiences and processes. (73)

NORMAL AGING: Changes that occur as natural results of the passage of time. (31)

NORMS: Guidelines for acceptable or normal behavior. (206)

NUMBNESS PHASE: (Parkes) The first phase of the grief reaction. (245)

OBSESSIVE REACTIONS: Unconscious attempts to control anxiety with the intrusion of persistent ideas, thoughts, or images. (173)

OLD AGE: Defined operationally as 65 years and over. (6)

OLFACTION: Smelling; the sense of smell. (102)

OMISSION ERRORS: Mistakes resulting when no response or behavior is exhibited. (74)

OMNIBUS INTELLIGENCE: A combination of crystallized and fluid intelligence. (52)

ORGANIC BRAIN SYNDROME (OBS): Specific types of mental disorders resulting from neural impairment or brain damage; acute and chronic. (168)

ORGANIC DISORDERS: Psychological disturbances resulting from physiological change. (164)

ORGASM: The climax of sexual excitement. (194)

OVERCOMPENSATION: Defense mechanism; overreactions to potential sources of threatened anxiety. (176)

PACING: A noncognitive factor affecting behavior within the performance situation; involves rate and speed. (74)

PAIRED-ASSOCIATE LEARNING: Acquiring associations or relationships between cues, usually verbal. (74)

PARANOIA: A psychological disturbance characterized by delusional systems, often related to persecution or grandeur. (167)

PATHOLOGICAL AGING: Age-related changes resulting from pathology or disease. (31)

PERCEPTION: The processing, mental organization, or interpretation of sensory stimuli. (108)

PERFORMANCE: External acts or behaviors. (72)

PERSONALITY: The psychological composition and characteristic behaviors of the individual as a whole. (117)

PHOBIAS: Intense, irrational fears occurring in association with stimuli that hold little potential of actual danger or harm. (174)

PINING PHASE: (Parkes) The second phase of the grief reaction. (245)

PITCH: The psychological correlate of frequency, related to sound. (100)

PLACEBO (sugar pill): A treatment or medication having no inherent treatment or medicinal effect. (78)

PREPARATORY DEPRESSION: Emotional reaction associated with the mourning of future losses. (238)

PRESBYCUSIS: Age-related losses in hearing. (99)

PRESBYOPIA ("old" sightedness or far-sightedness): A visual deficiency involving loss of accommodation. (97)

PROJECTION: Defense mechanism; involves the attributing of our own characteristics or behaviors to another. (175)

PROJECTIVE TECHNIQUES: Assessment strategy in which personality characteristics are imposed upon neutral stimuli. (119)

PSYCHOLOGICAL AGING: Age-related changes in behavior and mental processes. (29)

PSYCHOLOGY: The scientific study of behavior. (30)

PSYCHOPATHOLOGY: A broad term used to denote mental and emotional disturbances and disorders. (163)

PSYCHOSES: Major psychological disturbances involving personality disorganization. (165)

PSYCHOSOMATIC DISORDER: Identifiable disease, illness, or physiological damage resulting from psychological rather than physiological causes. (177)

QUESTIONNAIRE: Personality assessment technique requiring the provision of self-descriptions through responses to specific statements. (119)

RANDOM SAMPLING: Subjects drawn from a population in a manner that assures each individual an equal opportunity to participate. (50)

RATING SCALE: Instrument used to provide outside evaluations of an individual based upon prior knowledge or direct observations of behavior. (119)

RATIONALIZATION: Defense mechanism; based on the use of logical and acceptable explanations of behavior to conceal actual motives. (176)

REACTIVE DEPRESSION: Emotional reaction associated with the mourning of losses that have already been experienced. (237)

RECALL: A means of memory retrieval involving extraction of information without the aid of contextual cues. (86)

RECOGNITION: A means of memory retrieval involving identifying previously experienced stimuli. (86)

RECOVERY PHASE: (Parkes) The final phase of the grief reaction. (246)

RESISTANCE: The second phase of Selye's General Adaptation Syndrome. (149)

RETENTION: The recording and storage of sensory impressions in memory. (86)

RETIREMENT: Withdrawal from formal and remunerative employment, mandatory or voluntary. (212)

RETRIEVAL: The extraction of information from memory; recognition and recall. (86)

ROLE ACTIVITY THEORY: Poses a relationship between aging and maintenance of social roles. (37)

SECONDARY IMPOTENCE: Inability to copulate resulting from psychological causes. (198)

SELF-ACTUALIZATION: Abraham Maslow's term for the realization of an individual's full potential. (131)

SELF-CONCEPT (self-identity): How a person views, values, and appraises self in relation to others and the environment. (207)

SELF-ESTEEM: Feelings of worth, value, and regard in reference to self. (207)

SENILITY: Not an accepted clinical term. Loosely used to describe certain pathological brain dysfunctions and abnormal behaviors noted in old age. (10)

SENSATION: The input or experiencing of physical stimuli. (108)

SENSES: The five modalities through which physical stimuli are received; sight, hearing, taste, smell, and touch. (95)

SEX DRIVE: The motive that leads the individual to become more sexually receptive and to engage in the pursuit of sex-related goals. (196)

SEX RATIO: The proportion of males to females. (7)

SEXUAL BEHAVIOR: Specific actions designed to obtain sexual gratification. (186)

SEXUALITY: A dimension of personality structure that forms a basis for self-identity; gender; masculinity/femininity. (186)

SHORT-TERM MEMORY (STM): Retention in which information is kept for a short period of time. (86)

SOCIAL AGING: Age-related changes resulting from social forces and the individual's or group's responses to socially imposed factors. (29)

SOCIAL NORMS: Social standards of appropriate or normal behavior. (206)

SOCIAL ROLES: Patterns of activity and customary functions intrinsic to a particular position; as student, mother, boss. (207)

SOCIAL STATUS: Relative position within the social structure entailing certain rights, privileges, duties, and responsibilities. (207)

SOCIETY: A defined organization of people and institutions. (206)

SODIUM CHLORIDE: Table salt. (255)

STEREOTYPE: A standardized picture or rigid perception of groups, persons, events, or things. Often an oversimplification and prejudicial misconception. (9)

STRESS: A state of psychological or physical strain resulting from the actual or perceived presence of threat. (142)

TACTILE: Touching; the sense of touch. (105)

TRANQUILIZERS: Drugs taken to calm and relax; often psychologically and physically addictive. (149)

TRANSFER: The effect of previous acquisitions upon present learning; may be either negative or positive. (84)

TRAUMA: Physical or psychological injury. (164)

TYPE A PERSONALITY: (Friedman and Rosenman) Stressful personality type related to incidence of coronary heart disease. (152)

WAIS (Wechsler Adult Intelligence Scale): An individual intelligence instrument for adults. (56)

WEAR AND TEAR THEORY: Views human aging as analogous to the aging and deterioration of a machine as a result of use. (34)

WELL-BEING: Feelings of good physical and mental health. (252)

References

Allport, G. W. *Becoming: Basic considerations for a psychology of personality.* New Haven: Yale University Press, 1955.

Anderson, W. F., & Davidson, R. Concomitant physical states. In J. G. Howells (Ed.), *Modern perspectives in the psychiatry of old age.* New York: Brunner-Mazel, 1975, pp. 84–106.

Arenberg, D. Anticipation interval and age differences in verbal learning. *Journal of Abnormal Psychology,* 1965, *70,* 419–425.

Aronoff, C. Old age in prime time. *Journal of Communication,* 1974, *24,* 86–87.

Baltes, P. B., & Labouvie, G. V. Adult development of intellectual performance: Description, explanation, and modification. In C. Eisdorfer & M. P. Lawton (Eds.), *The psychology of adult development and aging.* Washington, D.C.: American Psychological Association, 1973.

Baltes, P. B., & Schaie, K. W. Aging and IQ: The myth of the twilight years. *Psychology Today,* 1974, *7,* 35–40.

Baltes, P. B., Schaie, K. W., & Nardi, A. H. Age and experimental mortality in a seven-year longitudinal study of cognitive behavior. *Developmental Psychology,* 1971, *5,* 18–26.

Balzar, D., & Palmore, E. Religion and aging in a longitudinal panel. *Gerontologist,* 1976, *16,* 82–85.

Beck, A. T. *Depression: Causes and treatment.* Philadelphia: University of Pennsylvania Press, 1972.

Bengtson, V. L., & Haber, D. A. Sociological approaches to aging. In D. S. Woodruff & J. E. Birren (Eds.), *Aging: Scientific perspectives and social issues.* New York: D. Van Nostrand, 1975.

Binstock, R., & Shanas, E. (Eds.). *Handbook of aging and the social sciences.* New York: Van Nostrand, 1976.

Birren, J. E. *The psychology of aging.* Englewood Cliffs, N.J.: Prentice-Hall Inc., 1964.

Birren, J. E., Butler, R. N., Greenhouse, S. W., Sokoloff, L., & Yarrow, M. (Eds.). *Human aging: A biological and behavioral study.* Washington, D.C.: U.S. Government Printing Office, 1963.

Birren, J. E., & Morrison, D. F. Analysis of the WAIS subtests in relation to age and education. *Journal of Gerontology,* 1961, *16,* 363–369.

Bischof, L. J. *Adult psychology* (2nd Ed.). New York: Harper & Row, Publishers, 1976.

Blessed, G., Tomlinson, B. F., & Roth, N. The association between quantitative measures of dementia and of senile change in the cerebral grey matter of elderly subjects. *British Journal of Psychiatry,* 1968, *114,* 797–811.

Botwinick, J. Learning in children and in older adults. In L. R. Goulet & P. B. Baltes (Eds.), *Life span developmental psychology.* New York: Academic Press, 1970.

Botwinick, J. *Aging and behavior.* New York: Springer Publishing Co., Inc., 1973.

Botwinick, J. Intellectual abilities. In J. E. Birren & K. W. Schaie (Eds.), *Handbook of the psychology of aging.* New York: Van Nostrand Reinhold, 1977.

Bourlière, F., Cendron, H., & Rapaport, A. Modification avec l'âge des secils gustatifs de perception et de reconaissance aux saveurs salée et sucrée chez l'homme. *Gerontologia*, 1958, *2*, 104–111.

Broadbent, D. E., & Heron, A. Effects of a subsidiary task on performance involving immediate memory in younger and older men. *British Journal of Psychology*, 1962, *53*, 189–198.

Brod, J. The influence of higher nervous processes induced by psychosocial environment on the development of essential hypertension. In L. Levi (Ed.), *Society, stress, and disease.* New York: Oxford University Press, 1971, pp. 312–323.

Bromley, D. B. *The psychology of human ageing* (rev. ed.). New York: Penguin Books, 1974.

Brotman, H. B. One in ten: A statistical portrait. *Medical World News, Geriatrics*, 1972.

Brückner, R. Longitudinal research on the eye. *Gerontology Clinician*, 1967, *9*, 87–95.

Busse, E. W. The mental health of the elderly. *International Mental Health Research Newsletter*, 1968, *10*, 13–16.

Busse, E. W., Barnes, R. H., Silverman, A. J., Thaler, M., & Frost, L. L. Studies of the process of aging (X): The strength and weakness of psychic function in the aged. *American Journal of Psychiatry*, 1955, *111*, 896–903.

Busse, E. W., & Pfeiffer, E. *Mental illness in later life.* Washington, D.C.: American Psychiatric Association, 1973.

Busse, E. W., & Pfeiffer, E. (Eds.). *Behavior and adaptation in late life.* Boston: Little, Brown & Co., 1977.

Butler, R. N. Intensive psychotherapy for the hospitalized aged. *Geriatrics*, 1960, *15*, 644–653.

Butler, R. N. The life review: An interpretation of reminiscence in the aged. *Psychiatry*, 1963, *26*, 65–76.

Butler, R. N. Research and clinical observations on the psychologic reactions to physical changes with age. *Mayo Clinic Proceedings*, 1967, *42*, 596–619.

Butler, R. N. Age-ism: Another form of bigotry. *Gerontologist*, 1969, *14*, 243–249.

Butler, R. N., & Lewis, M. I. *Aging and mental health* (2nd Ed.). St. Louis: Mosby, 1977.

Caine, L. *Widow.* New York: William Morrow & Co., Inc., 1974.

Cameron, P., & Biber, N. Sexual thought throughout the life-span. *Gerontologist*, 1973, *13*, 144–147.

Campbell, D. E. Analysis of leisure time profiles of four age groups of adult males. *The Research Quarterly*, 1969, *40*, 266–273.

Campbell, D. T., & Stanley, J. C. Experimental and quasi-experimental designs for research on teaching. In N. L. Gage (Ed.), *Handbook of research on teaching.* Chicago: Rand McNally, 1963.

Canestrari, R. E., Jr. Paced and self-paced learning in young and elderly adults. *Journal of Gerontology*, 1963, *18*, 165–168.

Canestrari, R. E., Jr. The effects of commonality on paired-associate learning in two age groups. *Journal of Genetic Psychology*, 1966, *108*, 3–7.

Canestrari, R. E., Jr. Age changes in acquisition. In G. A. Talland (Ed.), *Human aging and behavior.* New York: Academic Press, 1968.

Cassell, E., Kass, L. R., & Associates. Refinements in criteria for the determination of death: An appraisal. *Journal of the American Medical Association*, 1972, *221*, 48–54.

Survey of religions in the U.S. *Catholic Digest* 1966, *7*, 27.

Cattell, R. B. Theory of fluid and crystallized intelligence: A critical experiment. *Journal of Educational Psychology*, 1963, *54*, 1–22.

Chown, S. M. Personality and aging. In K. W. Schaie (Ed.), *Theory and methods of research on aging.* Morgantown, W.

Va.: West Virginia University Press, 1968.

Christenson, C. V., & Gagnon, J. H. Sexual behavior in a group of older women. *Journal of Gerontology,* 1965, *20,* 351–356.

Claman, A. D. Introduction to panel discussion: Sexual difficulties after 50. *Canadian Medical Association Journal,* 1966, *94,* 207.

Clayton, P. J., Halikes, J., & Maurice, W. L. The bereavement of the widowed. *Diseases of the Nervous System,* 1971, *32* (9), 597–604.

Cooper, R. M., Bilash, I., & Zubek, J. P. The effect of age on taste sensitivity. *Journal of Gerontology,* 1959, *14,* 56–58.

Coppinger, N. W. The relationship between critical flicker frequency and chronological age for varying levels of stimulus brightness. *Journal of Gerontology,* 1955, *10,* 48–52.

Corso, J. F. Sensory processes and age effects in normal adults. *Journal of Gerontology,* 1971, *26,* 90–105.

Cumming, E., & Henry, W. *Growing old: The process of disengagement.* New York: Basic Books, 1961.

Curtin, S. Aging in the land of the young. In S. H. Zarit (Ed.), *Readings in aging and death: Contemporary perspectives.* New York: Harper & Row, Publishers, 1977.

Cutler, S., & Kaufman, R. Cohort changes in political attitudes. *Public Opinion Quarterly,* 1975, *39,* 69–81.

Dahl, L. K. Salt and hypertension. *American Journal of Clinical Nutrition,* 1972, *25,* 231–244.

Dalderup, L. M., & Fredericks, M. L. C. Colour sensitivity in old age. *Journal of the American Geriatric Society,* 1969, *17,* 388–390.

Dean, L. Aging and decline of affect. *Journal of Gerontology,* 1962, *17,* 440–446.

de Beauvoir, Simone. *The coming of age.* New York: G. P. Putnam's Sons, 1972.

deVries, H. A. Exercise intensity threshold for improvement of cardiovascular respiratory function in older men. *Geriatrics,* 1971, *26,* 94–101.

deVries, H. A. Physiology of exercise and aging. In D. Woodruff & J. Birren (Eds.), *Aging: Scientific perspectives and social issues.* New York: D. Van Nostrand, 1975.

deVries, H. A., & Adams, G. M. Electromyographic comparison of single doses of exercise and meprobamate as to effects on muscular relaxation. *American Journal of Physical Medicine,* 1972, *51,* 130–141.

Diggory, J. C., & Rothman, D. Z. Values destroyed by death. *Journal of Abnormal and Social Psychology,* 1961, *30,* 11–17.

Dollard, J., Doob, L. W., Miller, N. E., Mowrer, O. H., & Sears, R. R. *Frustration and aggression.* New Haven, Conn.: Yale University Press, 1939.

Domey, R. G., McFarland, R. A., & Chadwick, E. Threshold and rate of dark adaptation as functions of age and time. *Human Factors,* 1960, *2,* 109–119.

Doppelt, J. E., & Wallace, W. L. Standardization of the Wechsler Adult Intelligence scale for older persons. *Journal of Abnormal and Social Psychology,* 1955, *51,* 312–330.

Earley, L. W., & von Mering, O. Growing old the outpatient way. *American Journal of Psychiatry,* 1969, *125,* 963–967.

Eisdorfer, C. Developmental level and sensory impairment in the aged. *Journal of Projective Techniques,* 1960, *24,* 129–132.

Eisdorfer, C. The WAIS performance of the aged: A retest evaluation. *Journal of Gerontology,* 1963, *18,* 169–172.

Eisdorfer, C. Verbal learning and response time in the aged. *Journal of Genetic Psychology,* 1965, *107,* 15–22.

Eisdorfer, C. Arousal and performance: Experiments in verbal learning and a tentative theory. In G. A. Talland (Ed.), *Human aging and behavior.* New York: Academic Press, 1968.

Eisdorfer, C., Axelrod, S., & Wilkie, F. Stimulus exposure time as a factor in serial learning in an aged sample. *Journal of Abnormal and Social Psychology,* 1963, *67,* 594–600.

Eisdorfer, C., Busse, E. W., & Cohen, L. D. The WAIS performance of an aged sample: The relationship between verbal and performance IQs. *Journal of Gerontology,* 1959, *14,* 197–201.

Eisdorfer, C., Nowlin, J., & Wilkie, F. Improvement of learning in the aged by modification of autonomic nervous system activity. *Science,* 1970, *170,* 1327–1329.

Eisdorfer, C., & Wilkie, F. Intellectual changes with advancing age. In L. F. Jarvik, C. Eisdorfer, & J. E. Blum (Eds.), *Intellectual functioning in adults.* New York: Springer, 1973.

Eisner, D. A., & Schaie, K. W. Age change in response to visual illusions from middle to old age. *Journal of Gerontology,* 1971, *26,* 146–150.

Engel, G. L., & Romano, J. Delirium, a syndrome of cerebral insufficiency. *Journal of Chronic Diseases,* 1959, *9,* 260–277.

Erikson, E. H. *Childhood and society* (2nd Ed.). New York: Norton, 1963.

Farquhar, M., & Leibowitz, H. W. The magnitude of the Ponzo illusion as a function of age for large and small stimulus configurations. *Psychological Science,* 1971, *25,* 97–99.

Feifel, H. The meaning of dying in American society. In Richard H. Davis (Ed.), *Dealing with death.* Los Angeles: University of Southern California Press, 1973.

Friedman, M., and Rosenman, R. H. *Type A behavior and your heart.* New York: Alfred A. Knopf, 1974.

Fulton, R., & Fulton, J. A psychosocial aspect of terminal care: Anticipatory grief. *Omega,* 1971, *2,* 91–100.

Gajo, F. D. *Visual illusions.* Unpublished doctoral dissertation, Washington University, St. Louis, Missouri, 1966.

Gardner, E., Bahn, A. K., & Mach, M. Suicide and psychiatric care in the aging. *Archives of General Psychiatry,* 1963, *10,* 547–553.

Gerber, I., Rusalem, R., Hannon, N., Battin, D., & Arkin, A. Anticipatory grief and aged widows and widowers. *Journal of Gerontology,* 1975, *30,* 225–229.

Gilbert, J. G. Memory loss in senescence. *Journal of Abnormal and Social Psychology,* 1941, *36,* 73–86.

Gilbert, J. G. Age changes in color matching. *Journal of Gerontology,* 1957, *12,* 210–215.

Glaser, B. G. The social loss of aged dying patients. *Gerontologist,* 1966, *6,* 77–80.

Glaser, B. G., & Strauss, A. L. The ritual drama of mutual pretense. In S. H. Zarit (Ed.), *Readings in aging and death: Contemporary perspectives.* New York: Harper & Row, Publishers, 1977, pp. 271–276.

Goldfarb, A. E., Hochstadt, N. J., Jacobson, J. H., & Weinstein, E. A. Hyperbaric oxygen treatment of organic mental syndromes in aged persons. *Journal of Gerontology,* 1972, *27,* 212–217.

Gordon, C., Gaitz, C. M., & Scott, J. Leisure and lives: Personal expressivity across the life span. In R. Binstock & E. Shanas (Eds.), *Handbook of aging and the social sciences.* New York: Van Nostrand Reinhold Co., 1976.

Green, R. F. Age-intelligence relationship between ages sixteen and sixty-four: A rising trend. *Developmental Psychology,* 1969, *1,* 618–627.

Gutman, G. M. A note on the MPI: Age and sex differences in extroversion and neuroticism in a Canadian sample. *Brit-*

ish Journal of Social and Clinical Psychology, 1966, 5, 128–129.

Harris, L. The myth and reality of aging in America. Washington, D.C.: National Council on the Aging, 1975.

Harris, R. E., & Singer, M. T. Interaction of personality and stress in the pathogenesis of essential hypertension. Hypertension, Proc. Council High Blood Pressure Research, 1967, 16, 104–115.

Harwood, E., & Naylor, G. F. K. Changes in the constitution of the WAIS intelligence pattern with advancing age. Australian Journal of Psychology, 1971, 23, 297–303.

Hausknecht, M. The joiners. New York: Bedminster Press, 1962.

Havighurst, R. J. Research and development goals in social gerontology: A report of a special committee of the Gerontological Society. Gerontologist, 1969, 9, 1–90.

Havighurst, R. J. Developmental tasks and education (3rd Ed.). New York: Mackay, 1972.

Havighurst, R. J., Neugarten, B. L., & Tobin, S. S. Disengagement and patterns of aging. In B. L. Neugarten (Ed.), Middle age and aging. Chicago: University of Chicago Press, 1968, 161–172.

Hendricks, J., & Hendricks, C. D. Aging in mass society: Myths and realities. Cambridge, Mass.: Winthrop Publishers, Inc., 1977.

Heron, A., & Chown, S. M. Age and function. London: Churchill, 1967.

Hilgard, E., & Bower, G. Theories of learning (4th Ed.). Englewood Cliffs, N.J.: Prentice-Hall, Inc., 1975.

Hill, R., Fotte, N., Aldous, J., Carlson, R., & MacDonald, P. Family development in three generations. Cambridge, Mass.: Schenkman, 1970.

Holmes, T. H., & Masuda, M. Life change and illness susceptibility. In J. P. Scott and E. C. Senay (Eds.), Symposium on separation and depression (Publication No. 94). Washington, D.C.:

American Association for the Advancement of Science, 1973, pp. 161–186.

Holmes, T. H., & Rahe, R. H. The social readjustment rating scale. Journal of Psychosomatic Research, 1967, 11, 213–218.

Horn, J. L. Psychometric studies of aging and intelligence. In S. Gershon & A. Raskin (Eds.), Aging (Vol. 2): Genesis and treatment of psychologic disorders in the elderly. New York: Raven, 1975.

Horn, J. L., & Cattell, R. B. Age differences in fluid and crystallized intelligence. Acta Psychologica, 1967, 26, 107–129.

Horn, J. L., & Donaldson, G. On the myth of intellectual decline in adulthood. American Psychologist, 1976, 31, 701–719.

Hulicka, I. M. Age differences in retention as a function of interference. Journal of Gerontology, 1967, 22, 180–184.

Hulicka, I. M., & Grossman, J. L. Age group comparisons for the use of mediators in paired-associate learning. Journal of Gerontology, 1967, 22, 46–51.

Ingraham, M. H. My purpose holds: Reactions and experiences in retirement of TIAA-CRFFF annuitants. Philadelphia: Teachers Insurance and Annuity Association, College Retirement Equities Fund, 1974.

Jewett, S. P. Longevity and the longevity syndrome. The Gerontologist, 1973, 13, 91–93.

Johnson, I. Memory loss with age: A storage or retrieval problem? Paper presented at the meeting of the Gerontological Society, San Juan, Puerto Rico, December 1972.

Jones, H. A special consideration of the aging process, disease, and life expectancy. In J. H. Lawrence and C. A. Tobias (Eds.), Advances in biological and medical physics (Vol. 4). New York: Academic Press, 1956.

Jung, C. Modern man in search of a soul. New York: Harcourt Brace Jovanovich, 1933.

Kahn, R. L. et al. Brief objective measures for the determination of mental status in the aged. *American Journal of Psychiatry*, 1960, *117*, 326–328.

Kahn, R. L., Pollack, M., & Goldfarb, A. I. Factors related to individual differences in mental status of institutionalized aged. In P. Hoch & J. Zubin (Eds.), *Psychopathology of aging*. New York: Grune & Stratton, 1961.

Kalish, R. A., & Johnson, A. I. Value similarities and differences in three generations of women. *Journal of Marriage and the Family*, 1972, *34*, 49–54.

Kalish, R. A., & Reynolds, D. K. *Death and ethnicity: A psychocultural study*. Los Angeles: University of Southern California Press, 1976.

Kallmann, F. J., & Jarvik, L. F. Individual differences in constitution and genetic background. In J. E. Birren (Ed.), *Handbook of aging and the individual*. Chicago: University of Chicago Press, 1959.

Kaplan, H. S. *The new sex therapy: Active treatment of sexual dysfunction*. New York: Brunner-Mazel, 1974.

Kelly, E. L. Consistency of the adult personality. *American Psychologist*, 1955, *10*, 659–681.

Kinsbourne, M., & Berryhill, J. The nature of the interaction between pacing and the age decrement in learning. *Journal of Gerontology*, 1972, *27*, 471–477.

Kinsey, A. C., Pomeroy, W. B., & Martin, C. I. *Sexual behavior in the human male*. Philadelphia: W. B. Saunders, 1947.

Kinsey, A. C., Pomeroy, W. B., Martin, C. I., & Gebhard, P. H. *Sexual behavior in the human female*. Philadelphia: W. B. Saunders, 1953.

Klodin, V. M. The relationship between scoring treatment and age in perceptual-integrative performance. *Experimental Aging Research*, 1976, *2*, 303.

Kogan, N., & Wallach, M. Age changes in values and attitudes. *Journal of Gerontology*, 1961, *16*, 272–280.

Kramer, M., Taube, C., & Redick, R. Patterns of use of psychiatric facilities by the aged: Past, present, and future. In C. Eisdorfer & M. P. Lawton (Eds.), *The Psychology of Adult Development and Aging*. Washington, D.C.: American Psychological Association, 1973.

Kübler-Ross, E. *On death and dying*. New York: Macmillan, 1969.

Kübler-Ross, E. *Questions and answers on death and dying*. New York: Macmillan, 1974.

Kübler-Ross, E. On death and dying. In L. Allman & D. Jaffe (Eds.), *Readings in adult psychology: Contemporary perspectives*. New York: Harper & Row, 1977, pp. 370–375.

Kuhlen, R. G. Personality change with age. In P. Worchel & D. Byrne (Eds.), *Personality change*. New York: John Wiley, 1964.

Leibowitz, H. W., & Judisch, J. M. The relation between age and the magnitude of the Ponzo illusion. *American Journal of Psychology*, 1967, *80*, 105–109.

Levi, L. (Ed.). *Society, stress, and disease*. New York: Oxford University Press, 1971.

Lieberman, M. A. Psychological correlates of impending death: Some preliminary observations. *Journal of Gerontology*, 1965, *20*, 181.

Lind, A. P., & McNicol, G. W. Cardiovascular responses to holding and carrying weights by hand and by shoulder harness. *Journal of Applied Physiology*, 1968, *25*, 261–267.

Liss, L., & Gomez, F. The nature of senile changes of the human olfactory bulb and tract. *Archives of Otolaryngology*, 1958, *67*, 167–170.

Lopata, H. *Widowhood in an American city*. Morristown, N.J.: General Learning Press, 1973.

Lowenthal, M. F., & Chiriboga, D. Transitions to the empty nest: Crisis, challenge, or relief? *Archives of General Psychiatry*, 1972, 8–14.

Maddox, G., & Douglas, E. Aging and individual differences. *Journal of Gerontology,* 1974, *29,* 555–563.

Maslow, A. H. *Motivation and personality.* New York: Harper & Row, Publishers, 1954.

Masters, W. H., & Johnson, V. E. *Human sexual response.* Boston: Little, Brown & Co., 1966.

Masters, W. H., & Johnson, V. E. *Human sexual inadequacy.* Boston: Little, Brown & Co., 1970.

McFarland, R. A. The sensory and perceptual processes in aging. In K. W. Schaie (Ed.), *Theory and methods of research on aging.* Morgantown, W. Va.: West Virginia University Press, 1968.

McFarland, R. A., Warren, A. B., & Karis, C. Alterations in critical flicker frequency as a function of age and light: dark ratio. *Journal of Experimental Psychology,* 1958, *56,* 529–538.

Melton, A. Implications of short-term memory for a general theory of memory. *Journal of Verbal Learning and Verbal Behavior,* 1963, *2,* 1–21.

Moberg, D. O. Religiosity in old age. *Gerontologist,* 1965, *5,* 78–87.

Moenster, P. A. Learning and memory in relation to age. *Journal of Gerontology,* 1972, *27,* 361–363.

Monge, R., & Hultsch, D. Paired-associated learning as a function of adult age and length of anticipation and inspection intervals. *Journal of Gerontology,* 1971, *26,* 157–162.

Nelson, P. D. Comment. In E. K. Gunderson & R. H. Rahe (Eds.), *Life stress and illness.* Springfield, Ill.: Charles C Thomas, 1974, pp. 79–89.

Nesselroade, J. R., Schaie, K. W., & Baltes, P. B. Ontogenetic and generational components of structural and quantitative change in adult cognitive behavior. *Journal of Gerontology,* 1972, *27,* 222–228.

Neugarten, B. L. Adaptation and the life cycle. *Journal of Geriatric Psychiatry,* 1970, *4,* 71–100.

Neugarten, B. L. Personality and the aging process. *The Gerontologist,* 1972, *12,* 9–15.

Neugarten, B. L. Personality change in late life: A developmental perspective. In C. Eisdorfer & M. P. Lawton (Eds.), *The psychology of adult development and aging.* Washington, D.C.: American Psychological Association, 1973, pp. 311–335.

Neugarten, B. L., & Associates. *Personality in middle and late life.* New York: Atherton Press, 1964.

Neugarten, B. L., Havighurst, R. J., & Tobin, S. S. The measurement of life satisfaction. *Journal of Gerontology,* 1961, *16,* 134–143.

Neugarten, B. L., Havighurst, R. J., & Tobin, S. S. Personality and patterns of aging. In B. L. Neugarten (Ed.), *Middle age and aging.* Chicago: University of Chicago Press, 1964, 173–177.

Neugarten, B. L., & Weinstein, K. K. The changing American grandparent. *Journal of Marriage and the Family,* 1964, *26,* 266–273.

Newman, G., & Nichols, C. R. Sexual activities and attitudes in older persons. *Journal of the American Medical Association,* 1960, *173,* 33–35.

Northcott, H. Too young, too old—age in the world of television. *Gerontologist,* 1975, *15,* 184–186.

Palmore, E. Physical, mental, and social factors in predicting longevity. *The Gerontologist,* 1969, *9,* 103–108.

Palmore, E. Health practices, illness, and longevity. In E. Palmore & F. C. Jeffers (Eds.), *Prediction of life span.* Lexington, Mass.: D. C. Heath & Co., 1971, pp. 71–77.

Palmore, E. *Normal aging* (II). Durham, N.C.: Duke University Press, 1974.

Parkes, C. M. "Seeking" and "finding" a lost object. *Social Science and Medicine,* 1970, *5,* 175–208.

Parkes, C. M. *Bereavement.* New York: International Universities Press, 1972.

Parkes, C. M., Benjamin, B., & Fritzgerald, R. G. Broken heart: A statistical study of increased mortality among widowers. *British Medical Journal,* 1969, *1,* 740–743.

Peak, D. T., Polansky, G., & Altholz, J. *Final report of the information and counseling service for older persons.* Durham, N.C.: Duke University, Center for the Study of Aging and Human Development, 1971.

Pfeiffer, E. *Disordered behavior.* New York: Oxford University Press, 1968.

Pfeiffer, E. Survival in old age: Physical, psychological, and social correlates of longevity. *Journal of the American Geriatrics Society,* 1970, *18,* 273–285.

Pfeiffer, E. *Multidimensional quantitative assessment of three populations of elderly.* Paper presented at Annual Meeting of the Gerontological Society, Miami Beach, Florida, 1973.

Pfeiffer, E. *Sexuality in the aging individual.* Paper presented at Symposium on Sexuality in the Aging Individual, 31st Annual Meeting of the American Geriatric Society, Toronto, Canada, 1974.

Pfeiffer, E. Psychopathology and social pathology. In J. E. Birren & K. W. Schaie (Eds.), *Handbook of the psychology of aging.* New York: Van Nostrand Reinhold, 1977, 650–671. (a)

Pfeiffer, E. Sexual behavior in old age. In E. W. Busse & E. Pfeiffer (Eds.), *Behavior and adaptation in late life* (2nd Ed.). Boston: Little, Brown & Co., 1977. (b)

Pfeiffer, E., & Davis, G. C. Determinants of sexual behavior in middle and old age. *Journal of the American Geriatrics Society,* 1972, *20,* 151–158.

Pollack, R. H. Some implications of ontogenetic changes in perception. In D. E. Elkind (Ed.), *Studies in cognitive development.* New York: Oxford University Press, 1969, 365–407.

Population Reference Bureau, Inc. The elderly in America. *Population Bulletin,* 1975, *30* (3).

Post, F. *The clinical psychiatry of late life.* Pergamon Press, 1965.

Powell, A. H., Eisdorfer, C., & Bogdonoff, M. Physiologic response patterns observed in a learning task. *Archives of General Psychiatry,* 1964, *10,* 192–195.

Powell, D., Buchanan, S., & Milligan, W. *Relationship between learning, performance, and arousal in aged versus younger VA patients.* Paper presented at the 28th Annual Meeting of the Gerontological Society, Louisville, October 1975.

Rahe, R. H. Multicultural correlations of life change scaling: America, Japan, Denmark, and Sweden. *Journal of Psychosomatic Research,* 1969, *13,* 191–195.

Rahe, R. H., & Arthur, R. J. Life changes surrounding illness experience. *Journal of Psychosomatic Research,* 1968, *11,* 341–345.

Redick, R. W., Kramer, M., & Taube, C. A. Epidemiology of mental illness and utilization of psychiatric facilities among older persons. In E. W. Busse & E. Pfeiffer (Eds.), *Mental illness in later life.* Washington, D.C.: American Psychiatric Association, 1973.

Reichard, S., Livson, F., & Petersen, P. *Aging and personality.* New York: Wiley, 1962.

Resnik, H. L. P., & Cantor, J. M. Suicide and aging. *Journal of the American Geriatrics Society,* 1970, *18,* 152–158.

Riegel, K. F., Riegel, R. M., & Meyer, M. A study of the dropout rate in longitudinal research on aging and the prediction of death. *Journal of Personality and Social Psychology,* 1967, *5,* 342–348.

Riley, J. W., Jr. Attitudes toward death (1963). Cited in M. W. Riley, A. Foner, & Associates, *Aging and society* (Vol. 1): *An inventory of research findings.* New York: Russell Sage Foundation, 1968.

Riley, M. W., Foner, A. et al. *Aging and society* (Vol. 1): *An inventory of research findings.* New York: Russell Sage Foundation, 1968.

Robins, E. et al. The communication of suicidal intent: A study of 134 consecutive cases of successful (completed) suicides. *American Journal of Psychiatry,* 1959, *115,* 724–733.

Robinson, J. P. Social changes as measured by time budgets. *Journal of Leisure Research,* 1969, *1,* 75–77.

Rose, C. L. Social factors in longevity. *Gerontologist,* 1964, *4,* 27–37.

Rosenman, R. H. The role of behavior patterns and neurogenic factors in the pathogenesis of coronary heart disease. In R. W. Eliot (Ed.), *Stress and the heart.* New York: Futura, 1974, pp. 123–141.

Rosenman, R. H. et al. Coronary heart disease in the western collaborative group study: A follow-up experience of 4-1/2 years. *Journal of Chronic Diseases,* 1970, *23,* 173–190.

Ross, E. Effects of challenging and supportive instructions in verbal learning in older persons. *Journal of Educational Psychology,* 1968, *59,* 261–266.

Rowe, E., & Schnore, M. Item concreteness and reported strategies in paired-associate learning as a function of age. *Journal of Gerontology,* 1971, *26,* 470–475.

Rubin, I. *Sexual life after sixty.* New York: Basic Books, 1976.

Sataloff, J., & Vassallo, L. Hard-of-hearing senior citizens and the physician. *Geriatrics,* 1966, *21,* 182–186.

Schaie, K. W. Rigidity-flexibility and intelligence: A cross-sectional study of the adult life span from 20 to 70 years. *Psychological Monographs,* 1958, *72,* (9, Whole No. 462).

Schaie, K. W. A general model for the study of developmental problems. *Psychological Bulletin,* 1965, *64,* 92–107.

Schaie, K. W. Age changes and age differences. *Gerontologist,* 1967, *7,* 128–132.

Schaie, K. W. A reinterpretation of age-related changes in cognitive structure and functioning. In L. R. Goulet & P. B. Baltes (Eds.), *Life-span developmental psychology: Research and theory.* New York: Academic Press, 1970.

Schaie, K. W. Quasi-experimental designs in the psychology of aging. In J. E. Birren & K. W. Schaie (Eds.), *Handbook of the psychology of aging.* New York: Van Nostrand Reinhold, 1977.

Schaie, K. W., Labouvie, G. V., & Buech, B. U. Generation and cohort specific differences in adult cognitive functioning: A fourteen-year study of independent samples. *Developmental Psychology,* 1973, *9,* 151–166.

Schaie, K. W., & Marquette, B. W. Personality in maturity and old age. In R. M. Dreger (Ed.), *Multivariate personality research: Contributions to the understanding of personality in honor of Raymond B. Cattell.* Baton Rouge, La.: Claitors Publishing Division, 1971.

Schaie, K. W., & Parham, I. A. Cohort-sequential analysis of adult intellectual development. *Developmental Psychology,* 1977, *13,* 649–653.

Schiffman, S. *Taste and smell changes of foods during the aging process.* Paper presented at the 28th Annual Meeting of the Gerontological Society, Louisville, 1975.

Schludermann, E., & Zubek, J. P. Effects of age on pain sensitivity. *Perceptual and Motor Skills,* 1962, *14,* 295–301.

Schonfield, E., & Robertson, B. Memory storage and aging. *Canadian Journal of Psychology,* 1966, *20,* 228–236.

Sealy, A. P., & Cattell, R. B. *Standard trends in personality development in men and women of 16 to 70 years, determined by 16 PF measurements.* Paper presented at British Psychological Society Conference, London, 1965.

Selye, H. *The stress of life* (rev. ed.). New York: McGraw-Hill, 1976.

Shanas, E. *The health of older people: A social survey.* Cambridge, Mass.: Harvard University Press, 1962.

Shanas, E. et al. *Old people in three industrial societies.* New York: Atherton Press, 1968.

Shneidman, E. S., & Farberow, N. L. (Eds.). *Clues to suicide.* New York: McGraw-Hill, 1957.

Simon, A. Psychological changes that influence patient care. In *The Psychosocial Needs of the Aged: Selected Papers.* Los Angeles: The Ethel Percy Andrus Gerontology Center, University of Southern California, 1973.

Simon, A. Aging: The psychiatrist's perspective. In R. H. Davis (Ed.), *Aging: Prospects and issues.* Los Angeles: The Ethel Percy Andrus Gerontology Center, University of Southern California, 1976.

Simon, A., Epstein, L. J., & Reynolds, L. Alcoholism in the geriatric mentally ill. *Geriatrics,* 1968, *23,* 125–131.

Simpson, I. H., & McKinny, J. C. *Social aspects of aging.* Durham, N.C.: Duke University Press, 1972.

Special Committee on Aging, U.S. Senate. *Developments in aging: 1974 and January–April 1975.* Washington, D.C.: U.S. Government Printing Office, 1975.

Srole, L., & Fisher, A. K. *Mental health in the metropolis: The midtown Manhattan study.* New York: New York University Press, 1978.

Streib, G. F., & Schneider, C. J. *Retirement in American society: Impact and process.* Ithaca, N.Y.: Cornell University Press, 1971.

Sudnow, D. *Passing on.* Englewood Cliffs, N.J.: Prentice-Hall, 1967.

Swartz, D. The urologist's view. Panel discussion: Sexual difficulties after 50. *Canadian Medical Association Journal,* 1966, *94,* 213–214.

Templer, D. I. Death anxiety in religiously very involved persons. *Psychological Reports.* 1972, *31,* 361–362.

Thomas, J. *Remembering the names of pictured objects.* Paper presented at the meeting of the Gerontological Society, San Juan, Puerto Rico, December 1972.

Thompson, L., Davis, G. C., Obrist, W. D., & Heyman, A. Effects of hyperbaric oxygen on behavioral and physiological measures in elderly demented patients. *Journal of Gerontology,* 1976, *31,* 176–183.

Thompson, L. W., Axelrod, S., & Cohen, L. D. Senescence and visual identification of tactual-kinesthetic forms. *Journal of Gerontology,* 1965, *20,* 244–249.

Timiras, P. S. *Developmental physiology and aging.* New York: Macmillan, 1972.

Tobin, J. D. Normal aging—The inevitability syndrome. In S. H. Zarit (Ed.), *Readings in aging and death: Contemporary perspectives.* New York: Harper & Row, 1977.

Tongas, P. N., & Gibson, R. W. *A study of older patients admitted to the Sheppard and Enoch Pratt Hospital, 1966–68.* Towson, Md.: Research Department, Sheppard and Enoch Pratt Hospital, 1969.

Torgersen, S., & Kringlen, E. Blood pressure and personality: A study of the relationship between intrapair differences in systolic blood pressure and personality in monozygotic twins. *Journal of Psychosomatic Research,* 1971, *15,* 183–191.

Townsend, C. *Old age: The last segregation.* New York: Grossman, 1971.

U.S. Bureau of the Census. *Statistical Abstract of the United States: 1978.* (99th ed.) Washington, D.C.: U.S. Government Printing Office, 1978, 41, 69.

U.S. Department of Housing and Urban Development. *Older Americans: Facts about incomes and housing.* Washington, D.C.: U.S. Government Printing Office, 1973.

U.S. Public Health Service, National Center for Health Statistics. *Vital statistics of the United States: 1970, mortality part A* (Vol. II). Washington, D.C.: U.S. Government Printing Office, 1974.

Verwoerdt, A., Pfeiffer, E., & Wang, H. S. Sexual behavior in senescence (I). Changes in sexual activity and interest of aging men and women. *Journal of Geriatric Psychiatry,* 1969, *2,* 163–180. (a)

Verwoerdt, A., Pfeiffer, E., & Wang, H. S. Sexual behavior in senescence (II). Patterns of sexual activity and interest. *Geriatrics,* 1969, *24,* 137–154. (b)

Wapner, S., Werner, H., & Comalli, P. E. Perception of part-whole relationships in middle and old age. *Journal of Gerontology,* 1960, *15,* 412–416.

Weale, R. A. On the eye. In A. T. Welford & J. E. Birren (Eds.), *Aging, behavior, and the nervous system.* Springfield, Ill.: Charles C Thomas, 1965, 307–325.

Wechsler, D. *The measurement and appraisal of adult intelligence* (4th Ed.). Baltimore: Williams & Wilkins, 1958.

Weg, R. Physiological changes that influence patient care. In E. Seymour (Ed.), *Psychosocial needs of the aged: A Health Care Perspective.* Los Angeles: The Ethel Percy Andrus Gerontology Center, University of Southern California, 1978.

Weiss, A. D. Auditory perception in aging. In J. E. Birren et al. (Eds.), *Human aging: A biological and behavioral study* (P.H.S. Publication No. 986). Washington, D.C.: U.S. Government Printing Office, 1963.

Welford, A. *Aging and human skill.* Westport, Conn.: Greenwood Press, 1958.

Whanger, A. D. *A study of institutionalized elderly of Durham County.* Paper presented at Annual Meeting, Gerontological Society, Miami Beach, Florida, 1973.

Williams, R. L., & Cole, S. Religiosity, generalized anxiety, and the apprehension concerning death. *Journal of Social Psychology,* 1968, *75,* 111–117.

Witte, K., & Freund, J. Paired-associate learning in young and old adults as related to stimulus concreteness and presentation method. *Journal of Gerontology,* 1976, *31,* 186–192.

Woodruff, D. S., & Birren, J. E. Age changes and cohort differences in personality. *Developmental Psychology,* 1972, *6,* 252–259.

Woodruff, D. S., & Walsh, D. Research in adult learning: The individual. *The Gerontologist,* 1977, 424–430.

Zaretsky, H., & Halberstam, J. Age differences in paired-associate learning. *Journal of Gerontology,* 1968, *23,* 165–168.

Zarit, S. H. Organic brain syndromes. In S. H. Zarit (Ed.), *Readings in aging and death: Contemporary perspectives.* New York: Harper & Row, 1977, pp. 225–227.

Zarit, S. H., & Kahn, R. L. Aging and adaptation to illness. *Journal of Gerontology,* 1975, *30,* 67–72.

Acknowledgments

Photo Credits

Cover: Rick Smolan; **Chapter 1:** John Rees/Black Star; **Chapter 2:** R. L. Stack/Black Star; **Chapter 3:** Wide World; **Chapter 4:** Charles Harbutt/Magnum; **Chapter 5:** Vito Palmisano; **Chapter 6:** Jean-Claude Lejeune; **Chapter 7:** Roy Zalesky/Black Star; **Chapter 8:** David Bookbinder/© Peter Arnold; **Chapter 9:** Rick Smolan; **Chapter 10:** Bruce Davidson/Magnum; **Chapter 11:** Michael Hayman/Black Star; **Chapter 12:** Ira Wyman/Sygma.

Literary Credits

From "Aging and IQ: The Myth of the Twlight Years" by Paul B. Baltes and K. Warner Schaie. Reprinted from *Psychology Today Magazine*. Copyright © 1974 Ziff-Davis Publishing Company.

Adapted from *On Death and Dying*, Chapters 3–7, by Elisabeth Kübler-Ross. Copyright © 1969 by Elisabeth Kübler-Ross. Reprinted by permission of the Macmillan Publishing Co., Inc.

From *On Death and Dying* by Elisabeth Kübler-Ross from *Journal of the American Medical Association*, 221: 174–179, 1972. Copyright © 1972 American Medical Association. Reprinted by permission of the American Medical Association and Dr. Elisabeth Kübler-Ross.

Adapted from *Human Sexual Response*, pp. 223–247, 248–270 by William H. Masters and Virginia E. Johnson. Copyright © 1966 by William H. Masters and Virginia E. Johnson. Reprinted by permission of Little, Brown and Company and the authors.

From *Aging and Personality*, by Suzanne Reichard, Florine Livson, and Paul G. Petersen. Copyright © 1962 by John Wiley & Sons, Inc. Reprinted by permission of John Wiley & Sons, Inc.

Edith Ross. "Effects of Challenging and Supportive Instructions on Verbal Learning in Older Persons." *Journal of Educational Psychology*, 1968, Vol. 59, No. 4, pp. 263, 265–266.

K. Warner Schaie, Gisela V. Labouvie, and Barbara U. Buech. "Generational and Cohort-Specific Differences in Adult Cognitive Functioning: A Fourteen-Year Study of Independent Samples." *Developmental Psychology*, 1973, Vol. 9, No. 2, pp. 161–162.

Adapted from "Personality Types in an Aged Population," from *Personality in Middle and Late Life: Empirical Studies* by Bernice L. Neugarten. Copyright © 1964 by Prentice-Hall, Inc. Reprinted by permission of the author.

Zarit, Steven H.: "Mental Status Questionnaire" (after Kahn, "Brief Objective Measures for the Determination of Mental Status in the Aged," *American Journal of Psychiatry)* in *Readings in Aging and Death* by Steven H. Zarit, Editor. Copyright © 1977 by Harper & Row, Publishers, Inc. By permission of the publisher.

From Jerome E. Doppelt and Wimburn L. Wallace, "Standardization of the Wechsler Adult Intelligence Scale for Older Persons," in *The Journal of Abnormal and Social Psychology, Vol. 51, No. 2,* p. 323. Copyright 1955 The American Psychological Association, Inc. Reprinted by permission.

Indexes

Name Index

Subject Index

Tactile sense. *See* Touch
Taste, changes in, 102–105, 113, 114, 254
Temperature sensitivity, 106, 107
Tension during bereavement, 244–45, 247
Tests
  of intelligence, 56–66
  of personality, 119–22
Thematic Apperception Test (TAT), 121
Theories
  of aging, 33–40
  of biological aging, 33–35, 40
  Erikson's, 38–39, 40, 129–30
  of frustration-aggression, 150–51
  Havighurst's, 130–31
  Jung's, 38, 39, 40
  Maslow's, 131–32
  of personality, 129–32, 133
  of psychological aging, 38–39, 40
  of social aging, 35–37, 40
  of stress, 148–50
Time
  and grief, 246
  and learning, 74–77, 82–83, 90–91
Titchener Circles illusion, 113
Touch, 105–107, 113, 114
Traits, 119, 121, 123, 136, 153
Tranquilizers, 149, 244, 252–53
Transfer, and learning, 84–85, 91
Transportation, 11, 19, 29, 222, 256
Trauma, 164, 179
Type A personalities, 152–53, 159
Types of aging, 25, 28–31, 39–40

Ulcers, 177, 181
Unintegrated personality, 124, 127–28, 137
Uniqueness, 8, 9–10. *See also* Individuality
U.S. Academy of Sciences, 254
U.S. Bureau of the Census, 7, 8
U.S. Public Health Service, 229
Universality of aging, 26, 28, 39

University of Chicago, 124, 130
Urban life, 100, 266

Vagina, 195, 196
Values
  and aging, 232–33, 247
  and attitudes, 17
  reordering of, 39
  of society, 178, 181
Verbal abilities, 55–56, 57–58, 62, 63
Violence, and the elderly, 258
Vision, changes in, 96–99, 109–10, 111–13
Visualization, 55, 56, 59, 61, 62, 63
Visuo-motor flexibility, 59, 61

Wear and tear theory, 33, 34, 40
Wechsler Adult Intelligence Scale (WAIS), 56–58, 62, 64, 65
Well-being in old age, 251–69
Widowers, 7–8
Widowhood, 7–8, 147–48, 191–92, 211
Withdrawal
  and aging, 36, 39, 229–30
  and grief, 245
  and personality, 127, 136–37
  and psychopathology, 165, 170, 173
  and sensory loss, 96, 107–108
  and stress, 157
Women
  and income, 8
  and life expectancy, 7, 266
  and nutrition, 254
  and physiological changes, 32–33, 195–96, 200
  and psychopathology, 173, 178
  ratio of, to males, 7–8, 20, 192
  and sexual activity, 189, 191–92, 195–97, 199, 200

Youth
  attitudes toward, 16–17, 20
  in disengagement theory, 36
  and dying, 232–33
  and religion, 234